Digital Culture & Society

Vol. 9, Issue 1/2023

Tim Hector, David Waldecker,
Niklas Strüver, Tanja Aal (eds.)
**Taming Digital Practices:
On the Domestication
of Data-Driven Technologies**

The journal is edited by
Mathias Fuchs and Ramón Reichert

Editorial Board
Maria Bakardjeva, David Berry, Jean Burgess, Mark Coté, Colin Cremin, Sean Cubitt, Mark Deuze, José van Dijck, Delia Dumitrica, Astrid Ensslin, Sonia Fizek, Federica Frabetti, Orit Halpern, Irina Kaldrack, Denisa Kera, Lev Manovich, Janet H. Murray, Jussi Parikka, Lisa Parks, Dominic Pettman, Rita Raley, Richard Rogers, Julian Rohrhuber, Marie-Laure Ryan, Mirko Tobias Schäfer, Jens Schröter, Trebor Scholz, Tamar Sharon, Roberto Simanowski, Nathaniel Takcz, Geoffrey Winthrop-Young, Sally Wyatt

[transcript]

The editorial work for this issue was funded by Deutsche Forschungsgemeinschaft (DFG, German Research Foundation) – Project-ID 262513311 – SFB 1187. | Die Herausgabe dieser Ausgabe wird gefördert durch die Deutsche Forschungsgemeinschaft (DFG) – Projektnummer 262513311 – SFB 1187.

Indexed in EBSCOhost databases

Bibliographic information published by the Deutsche Nationalbibliothek
The Deutsche Nationalbibliothek lists this publication in the Deutsche Nationalbibliografie; detailed bibliographic data are available on the Internet at http://dnb.d-nb.de

© 2023 transcript Verlag, Bielefeld

All rights reserved. No part of this book may be reprinted or reproduced or utilized in any form or by any electronic, mechanical, or other means, now known or hereafter invented, including photocopying and recording, or in any information storage or retrieval system, without permission in writing from the publisher.

Cover concept: Kordula Röckenhaus, Bielefeld
Typeset: Mark-Sebastian Schneider, Bielefeld

ISSN: 2364-2114
eISSN: 2364-2122
Print-ISBN 978-3-8376-6357-0
PDF-ISBN 978-3-8394-6357-4

Content

A Praxeological Approach Towards the Domestication of Connected Media Technologies
Introduction
David Waldecker and Tim Hector   5

I   Field Research and Case Studies

Rethinking Material Articulations of "Television" in Times After TV
Vera Klocke and Maren Hartmann   25

Cyborg Cooks: Mothers and the Anthropology of Smart Kitchens
Katharina Graf   49

Domesticating Motile Media
The Routes and Routines of Vacuum Robots
Max Kanderske   71

Frustration Free: How Alexa Orchestrates the Development of the Smart Home
Niklas Strüver   99

Reinventing Drones: From DIY Experimentation to Professionalization
Hendrik Bender and Marcus Burkhardt   125

Media Use of Older Adults in Bangladesh: Religion, Perceived Sinfulness and the Taming of Media
Tanja Aal, Dennis Kirschsieper, Md Rashidul Hasan, Claudia Müller   153

II Conceptual/Theoretical Reflection

Doing Home by Using Digital Assistive Technologies
On the Role of Meaning and Materiality in the Use of Digital Assistive Technologies at Older People's Domesticity
Cordula Endter, Florian Fischer and Tobias Wörle   179

III Entering the Field

Domestication of Smart Speakers by Older Users
Preliminary Findings From an Exploratory Qualitative Study
Alexander B. Kucharski and Sebastian Merkel   203

Crafting Home with E-Textiles: Accessing Concepts of the Home in a Socially and Culturally Diverse Setting
Anne Weibert, Konstantin Aal, Sarah Rüller, Markus Rohde and Volker Wulf   213

IV In Converstion with

The Questions Are Still Good
Domestication Theory and Digital Media Today
Leslie Haddon in Conversation with Niklas Strüver and David Waldecker   225

Biographical Notes   241

A Praxeological Approach Towards the Domestication of Connected Media Technologies
Introduction

David Waldecker and Tim Hector

In some way, getting a new media technology is like getting a new pet. When examining all the steps necessary to get, for example, a cat or a smartphone into your possession and to integrate them into your routines, we can see that this integration comes with certain, comparable challenges. The cat needs to get to know you, the food and feeding times you provide – and, most importantly, it needs to be trained to use a litter box. Similarly, you have to make the smartphone your own by copying your contacts, by installing certain apps and by deciding if you want to use a dark mode or the built-in voice assistant, for example. However, cats and smartphones, domestic animals and devices, both pose challenges that might lead to changes in your personal surroundings. The smartphone might lead to you staying up at night because a certain game now works a lot better; it might also force you to call others in your bathroom because its signal is worse than that of your previous phone; your cat in turn might force you to consider rearranging your living room because she keeps knocking that precious vase off the sideboard and because she keeps trying to jump off the bookshelf to reach the lamp.

So, what media and pets have in common is this: they both have to be domesticated. From La Mettrie (1996 [1748]) to Cybernetics and Behaviourism – analytic comparisons of animals and humans to automata abound. This strategy is also employed in a strand of media studies that looks at the way media technology is employed and used by individuals and in society at large. Domestication research (Berker et al. 2006) paints media as something that comes into the everyday life of users as foreign and wild, as something that has to be tamed and brought to relate to domestic routines. This adaption, of course, does not leave those routines untouched; instead, it leads to new constellations of individuals and devices, and to new media practices.

While the original domestication research of the late 20th century has focused on media such as the television, later work has focused, e.g., on the integration of the Internet into the home (Bakardjieva 2005; cf. Röser et al. 2019). As with the TV, the negotiations concerning the use of online devices and services in the home relate to questions about the location of the computer used to access the internet or the regulation of children's internet use. However, as Bakardjieva (2006) notes, the Internet is not only consumed in the way TV and radio shows are, but users interactively engage with it not only in leisure, but in homework, work, and overall research – this has become even more obvious with regards to the current growth of the "work from home" sector. In addition, online devices are not only used more interactively than a TV or radio set; they also reconfigure the public-private distinction through data flows. While earlier media such as the newspaper did already play on this distinction by bringing public concerns to the breakfast table and the living room, current media make the private space of the home – and the interactions within it – public to a number of mostly privately-owned online platforms, device manufacturers and service providers. That is, current media practices are embedded in and part of data practices.

As such, digital data have become a relevant factor in dealing with and analysing digital devices. These devices depend on data flows to deliver content, and they generate data that is analysed via machine learning off-site. In this way, data, as content, does not only arrive at the user's device, but data about and connected to device usage can be recorded and analysed by device manufacturers and service providers. As critics such as Joseph Turow and Nick Couldry (2018) have noted, this use and collection of data are not accidental but seem to be the primary motive in providing certain services: "media as data extraction" (ibid.). Terms used to describe this new phenomenon, such as "platform capitalism", "surveillance capitalism" or "data colonialism", all begin their discussion by positing data as a newly relevant resource that is being exploited (Srnicek 2016; Zuboff 2019; Couldry/Mejias 2019). For example, the production, collection, and analysis of big data sets via machine learning allow for data valuation due to the opportunity to glean and produce predictive statements about certain events; this valuation becomes relevant when placing advertisements online, as the success of Google continues to show. As Turow and Couldry argue, media studies in turn are tasked not only with analysing the way media are produced and used, but the ways in which their use is entangled with data – and how, accordingly, media and data practices are intertwined as well.

Against this backdrop, the relations between the domestic and the non-domestic seem to be questioned anew. Media are no longer restricted to local contexts in their use, nor are the changes sufficiently explained by their new "mobility", as the case of smart speakers and other smart home elements (smart bulbs, fridges, etc.) demonstrate: although their use is processed and enables processing that is far beyond the boundaries of a classical understanding of home, the speakers are stationary gadgets themselves. For instance, the necessary data queries to make Natural Language Processing possible via a smart speaker are carried out online and in exchange with cloud applications; today, even a connected coffee machine can request a cleaning from its users via their smartphones while they are not at home. As mobile and digital media become integral to home life, the domestic realm as a concept appears increasingly diffuse and malleable.

At the same time, it is not only local practices and circumstances that are tasked with handling datafication and algorithmisation. These developments can also be observed in business, administration, government, and other sectors. While some hail the benefits of big data and automation, others fear the loss of autonomy and other negative side effects. As such, digital and interconnected media have to be integrated into everyday life on different levels: personal and private, organisational, and national and supra-national levels.

This thematic issue combines domestication research, a research tradition in media studies developed in the late 20th century, and an empirical analysis of current, digital, and interconnected media. That is, this issue studies the use of digitally connected media such as vacuum robots, drones, and kitchen appliances with reference to the domestication paradigm in media and communication research, practice theory and other approaches aimed at examining digital media practices in everyday life. At the same time, it brings together an interdisciplinary set of scholars from media studies, sociology, anthropology, and human-computer interaction.

In this introduction, we want to look back and look forward. In the following section, we will present a brief review of themes and concepts in domestication research as an avenue into the research of current media and data practices; we also argue for the ongoing relevance of the approach. We will examine the metaphors of domestication and taming. Eventually, we then discuss praxeological and data-related aspects of media use not explicitly treated in domestication research before we give an overview of the contributions in this issue.

Back to the home: Re-visiting domestication theory

We suggest returning to issues and concepts that have been developed within domestication research in order to analyse how newly developed media are taken up in a number of contexts. This review is complicated by the fact that there are several approaches to the domestication of media technologies which more or less overlap. Maren Hartmann distinguishes two streams of the domestication approach, a British and a Norwegian or "Nordic" one (cf. Hartmann 2020).

The British stream is deeply rooted in Cultural Studies and focuses on the household and the "ontological security" (Giddens 1984) it provides, i.e., the trust in the consistency of one's own identity, the continuity of life, and one's immediate surroundings. Media, as a specific form of technology, are related to this ontological security: they are linked to everyday rituals and even if the ontological security is initially questioned by new media technologies (cf. Silverstone et al. 1992: 17), they lose their threatening character by becoming woven into the everyday (cf. Bausinger 1984: 349-350) – they become domesticated.

Consider the integration of television into a family's life (Silverstone 1994). While the evening news might deliver disturbing images from remote and violent events into the living room, it is nonetheless reassuring that the TV keeps churning out news at regular intervals. In that sense, the approach does not only examine the way media content is consumed, interpreted, and used, e.g., in identity making: it also looks at the interpretation of the media object itself. Thus, domestication research focuses on the "double articulation" of media as content and as object (Silverstone et al. 1992: 18). A TV set as an object has to be integrated into the household and its spatial setting in the same way as watching the news or other shows has to be integrated into the everyday activities within the household. Within the domestication framework, these everyday activities, chores, and routines have been considered as a part of the "moral economy of the household" (Silverstone et al. 1992); the domestication of media in turn has been seen as an adoption of these devices and services into the moral economy and, simultaneously, as an adaption of said economy to the devices' possible use scenarios. In focusing on the processes of evaluation of media and their content as a collective activity, this approach has highlighted not only the centrality of the interactions and negotiations within the household for everyday life; it has also hinted at the normative and practical work that informs a simple question about a supposedly simple act of consumption, such as "what to watch tonight".

The Norwegian stream also emerged in the 1990s as a strand of research based in science and technology studies that took shape at the University of Trondheim; in the beginning, this stream was independent of the work done in Britain. The studies from Norway are broader in scope: they are not limited to the household or media technologies, and they also consider taming as a society-wide rather than an individual or domestic process (cf. Sørensen 1994: 42; see also Hartmann 2020: 48-49). Nevertheless, they are similar to the British domestication studies because they (a) also use the term "domestication" and describe it as a process of technology appropriation (cf. Sørensen 1994), and because (b) the Norwegian studies also work empirically – above all ethnographically – and focus on the practices of users and their means of appropriating media technologies. This domestication school, which Hartmann (2020) calls 'Nordic' and to which, for example, a Finnish stream from the field of design research can also be attributed, is characterised not only by its user-centeredness but also by a greater openness with regard to the technologies studied (cf. Aune 2007; Löfström 2007; Østergaard Madsen/Kræmmergaard 2015).

With reference to the Nordic perspective, the focus on the household has been questioned. Domestication also happens outside the physical walls of the household (cf. Silverstone 2006: 234); the residential unit is then only the starting point for the mobility emanating from it (cf. Bakardjieva 2006: 68-70) as the domestic sphere can also be relocated through media to a café, the city park, or any other public or private place. In this way, dichotomies between the inside and outside of the home, between the private and the public sphere were dismissed in the early 2000s. However, focusing on the household allows to highlight the role of the ordinary in both media use and the co-constitution of the private and public spheres. This refers to the everyday life of the users, which, according to Bakardjieva (2006: 70), breaks the focus of the early works on media consumption and thus allows for different perspectives of analysis. The concept of everyday life, which she roots in Schütz/Luckmann's (1973) phenomenology, allows to shed light on the realities and practices of media use.

Similar questions about the way media content is received within the domestic sphere were posed in the field of (linguistic) "media appropriation". This field unites studies that inquire qualitatively how media content is appropriated communicatively and related to context (cf. Holly/Püschel 1993: 8). Ayaß (1993) characterises this research as an approach that rediscovers and takes into account the active role of the recipients. However, research on media appropriation acknowledges that there is an "interplay" between media texts (and therefore media industries and content creators) and the recipients (cf. Holly 2001: 17). Just like the domestication approach, investigations into media appropriation are fundamentally rooted in Cultural Studies (cf. Morley/Silverstone 1990; Holly/Püschel 1993: 8; Holly 2001: 18; Hartmann 2009) and obliquely refer to praxeological research as they question whether processes of appropriation are a rationally executed action (cf. Faber 2001: 32). Domestication and appropriation-orientated studies both work qualitatively, applying ethnographic and praxeological approaches; however, domestication focuses more on the embedding of media in the everyday life of household members while research on media appropriation tends to focus on the "reception" of media content and therefore gives weight to the media texts, contents, and their generation. Also, the latter sheds more light on *communicative* and hence linguistic practices of appropriation (cf. Holly/Püschel 1993: 7) while the configuration of the household as a social unit seems to be more important for domestication theory.

The above-mentioned approaches have in common that they in some way or other focus on the appropriation of media technology. While the metaphor of domestication is used prominently, we want to examine this metaphor in the following and argue to use the metaphor of "taming" instead before looking more in detail at connections of domestication research to other theoretical avenues.

Metaphors of taming and of domestication

We suggest using the term "taming" to describe the process of incorporation of media into a particular household or an individual's life. As Maren Hartmann (2022) has noted, domestication and taming both relate to anthropological processes and the making of first civilisations through the adoption of animal husbandry.[1] Domestication, in this regard, denotes the long-term process of

---

1 While animal husbandry is the more apt metaphor for the domestication of media technologies, the selection and cultivation of plant species, i.e., farming, has played an equally important, if not even more transformative role in the formation of early settlements and human civilisations (c.f. Childe 1951, 59; Scott 2017).

bringing animal species through socialisation and breeding into constant contact with human beings and under their control. Instead of following grazing animal herds, humans began to control animal movement and herd size and thereby animal sociality to a large extent. This fixation of animals in close and stationary proximity to humans is intertwined with the creation of human civilisation; this control, however, does not only relate to the individual animal but the procreation of the species as a whole. Humans have, to a certain degree, controlled how animals breed and thereby have become animal breeders themselves. Over long periods of time, domesticated species like the dog, the pig, the chicken, the horse etc. have come into being (cf. Childe 1951: 66-71). Taming, in contrast, relates to the individual animal and its adoption into a close human-animal relationship. In this sense, even animals that are members of domesticated species have to be trained or socialised not only into living with humans, but into following their commands. Dogs have to be house-trained and thereby told to do their business outside the home while young horses have to be brought to bear the weight of a human on their shoulders. Taming makes it possible to use animal power for human purposes – the pulling of ploughs, the protection of property – but also makes the individual animal docile. Pets as a social phenomenon showcase that domestication and taming can lead to the transformation of wild and ferocious animals into friendly companions which we do not keep for practical, but for emotional purposes. Pets do not do a human's work, instead, they have to be taken care of.

Following the above explanation, taming is an apt metaphor for how individuals incorporate media into their everyday lives. Media technologies do not come as something that is thoroughly wild into households, but as devices and services that have been created by humans with users in mind. Their adoption in households is an ongoing process, as is domestication, but individuals do not breed devices and services in any way over a long period of time, but tame individual animals, or use individual devices until they switch to a new device. That is, taming describes the process of adopting a particular animal into a domestic or professional setting. In the same way, the term can be employed to highlight the practical work of getting a particular medium – a particular phone or laptop, a particular service such as Apple Music – to work in a particular setting. While domestication describes the process that ends in the creation of a new species, taming has to deal with the individual animal with its idiosyncrasies and epigenetic makeup. In the same way, users have to come to terms not with a generic ideal-type phone, for example, but a *Samsung Galaxy A53* with 5G support, and a concrete product which might come with a faulty battery (cf. Silverstone 2006). While every individual has to cope with making the respective device their own, they are not alone in this endeavour, but can rely on peers, online forums, and YouTube tutorials to adapt the device to their needs and find creative ways to use it.

While domestication focuses on a long process that might only become tangible after hundreds of years, taming is a more concrete process that can be observed more easily. It begins and ends with an individual animal. It is a process that engages concrete individuals and animals, or in our case, media. The term "taming" suggests already that it is an ongoing activity, a process. Taming thus lends itself well to understanding media use as a practical problem. That is, individuals new to a certain medium have to come to terms with how to use it. They do not only have to understand how it is operated – how do I take a picture with a smartphone – but how this use is situated in a wider social setting – e.g., when wondering why one should take a picture in the first place and in wondering what kind of picture to publish on social media.

Media practices: A praxeological perspective on domestication

Referring to "taming" focuses on the ongoing process on media interaction. In this section, we want to tease out a few connections to other media and social theories that lie dormant in domestication research – among them similarities to practice theory and the sociology of evaluation and testing. While this is not always made explicit, the above-mentioned approaches to domestication have in common that they investigate media as part of social practices. They do not perceive media as text that has to be decoded or interpreted by a (single) user, but they (a) see this interpretation apply equally to technologies and media objects themselves and (b) highlight that this media use has to happen in a concrete time and place. Here, domestication – or taming – is not only performed by individuals, but it is always embedded in a social context. However, it is not only the situation or the local circumstances that influence the outcome of media involvement; rather, this outcome is the result of an activity, a process – the result of "practice". That is, interaction with media objects and media content is always embedded in an activity that is already ongoing, and it is this practice that constitutes the meaning media have in this situation. According to sociologist Stefan Hirschauer (2016), centring on practice allows us to see various "actors" as participants of social practice – with different levels or grades of activity and involvement (cf. Hirschauer 2016: 49). Not only humans are involved in practice, but also objects (like a toothbrush is involved in brushing teeth or a baton in conducting) and even more abstract things such as body postures, social configurations, or spatial environments. A media theory that positions social practice as a starting point before other entities such as media, interaction, or technology (Schüttpelz/Meyer 2017: 159) allows to inquire into the reciprocity of social cohabitation and media (see also Schüttpelz/Gießmann 2015).

Although Bassett's (2007: 63-67) criticism suggests that social practice is not sufficiently placed as the starting point of inquiry in domestication approaches, domestication research can be described as praxeological (cf. Silverstone 2006: 231): it examines the "accomplishment" (Garfinkel 1967) of interaction with media as a collective and ongoing process and as something that has to be achieved locally. In this sense, routines also consist of social practice (cf. Schüttpelz/Meyer 2017: 158). With regards to the participation of media, the practices of interest here are *media practices*: practices which are "situational, bodily, significative, processual, cross-media, infrastructural, historical and socio-cultural" (Dang-Anh et al. 2017: 7) and which are related and bound to (but not determined by) the situation in which they are carried out. According to Dang-Anh and colleagues (2017: 12), media become media in execution – in the practical accomplishment as media (cf. Gießmann 2018). They only come to the foreground of action in case of disturbance or breakdown of the practice carried out (cf. Krämer 1998).

While this focus on practice highlights the continuous and situative creation of media, domestication research also connects to another ongoing debate on the practical circumstance of evaluation. As stated above, Silverstone and colleagues conceive of households as being equipped with a particular "moral economy" (Silverstone et al. 1992). This term has been used in a number of ways in social research. One of its earliest uses was in a ground-breaking study in social history by E.P. Thompson (1966) on *the making of the English working class*. Thompson describes how protests over food prices took place in 18th and 19th century England: he suggests that the riots of that time against the rising price of bread were not simply taking place because rioters were no longer able to afford to buy bread, but because they saw the price hikes and the change in their access to local markets as an affront to an "old paternalist moral economy" (1966: 63). That is, the riots were not "simple responses to economic stimuli" (Thompson 1971: 76) but protests against something that was considered to infringe upon a shared moral understanding and traditional entitlements. Here, economic valuations and moral evaluations are intertwined. It is this aspect that is of interest to the domestication research tradition: this research examines how those two aspects are related to each other in households – the household as an economic and a moral unit:

The moral economy of the household is therefore both an economy of meanings and a meaningful economy; and in both of its two dimensions it stands in a potentially or actually transformative relationship to the public, objective economy of the exchange of goods and meanings. (Silverstone et al. 1992: 16)

Domestication research and the concept of a moral economy suggest that there is a common sense with household members regarding media usage and other issues and values. This consensus, however, is not there if one cares to look at it (Haddon, this issue), e.g., when a student and her father disagree whether or not it makes sense to listen to music while doing homework. Instead of framing household interaction about media as consensual, it makes sense to empirically examine how and if household members come to terms when evaluating certain media, or rather, certain media practices. In the above example, one could examine how student and father deal with their disagreement. Overall, the "moral economy of the household" connects to a more recent academic interest in the nexus of economy, practices, and evaluation as can be seen in a "sociology of valuation and evaluation" (Lamont 2012). Here as well the pricing and the judgement of goods and services is not seen as the simple outcome of market effects or of the sum of individual strategies, but as a cultural activity that is embedded in a certain (historical) situation. In this vein – and this might be the most prominent case of this type of sociology –, Boltanski and Thévenot (2006) have argued that actors do not only issue judgements or justifications strategically, as rational actors, but by doing so, the actors themselves are able to make sense of situations and the elements of these situations. Boltanksi and Thévenot write of an *économie des conventions* (cf. Diaz-Bone 2017) because they suggest that individuals have several frames of reference at hand to evaluate something – e.g., when we consider taking a plane or the train for a trip and taking time and financial aspects as well as environmental concerns into account. While Boltanski and Thévenot (2006) have analysed how these often conflicting forms of evaluation play out in concrete situations, the input of domestication research concerning the focus on the household adds more empirical depth to this endeavour. It also highlights that these evaluations are embedded in a history of shared interactions and conflicts as well as economic and moral commitments.

Domestication research also sheds light on the fact that not all households are created equal. It can be used to understand how social groups and actors deal with digital media in different ways. These ways can include macro-perspectives which are useful when analysing how social milieus, government agencies and other (collective) actors work together to domesticate or tame digital media technologies and infrastructures. From the beginning, domestication research has not focused on abstract users or the ideal-type nuclear family, but particular types of households, be them single-parent households or the elderly (Haddon/Silverstone 1995; Haddon/Silverstone 1996), a tradition that is still strong today (cf. Scheerder et al. 2019). That is, digital media come into households that are equipped to adapt those media to their needs in different ways: the elderly for instance are often seen as a segment of the population which is slow to adapt to the changing media landscape (Birkland in publ.). Yet, care work is one field in society which is on the forefront of digital change, with robots, apps and services aimed at senior citizens and their caregivers. Also, immigrants use digital means to stay in touch with their family and friends in their home countries. Teenagers use social media and other media outlets differently from their parents. Although parents and their children typically own smartphones, their use differs according to age, gender, and other aspects. As such, media technology use is part of a class- and culture-based way of life that Bourdieu has described as "habitus" (1984). As this habitus is shaped in families and other households, it remains relevant to study these micro-sites of media use. These different media habitus come to the fore in close-up examinations of everyday media practices. Also, the creative ways that users employ in media use – which have been the focus of Cultural Studies – can be understood as not pertaining to the individual user but to the user as an individual who uses media in a socially situated ensemble of a household which has created its own idiosyncratic media practices.

In sum, this perspective allows us to focus not only on the individual and their device(s), but their relation to the household which in turn is situated in a sociocultural entanglement of potentially conflicting moral and economic values.

Taming digital and mobile media

While the discourse on media and practices has been central in some way to Media and Cultural Studies, the involvement of data into everyday media use is a relatively new phenomenon. While the problems and benefits of the wide-spread use of interconnected and data-producing digital devices and services have been discussed since the advent of the Internet, we want to include data in our praxeological understanding of media use. In this sense, media practices also appear as data practices: the "co-operative" (Goodwin 2018) character of media practices also applies to data (cf. Burkhardt et al. 2022). Data are never 'raw' (cf. Gitelman 2013), they are never just 'given' (cf. Gießmann/Burkhardt 2014: 3), but closely connected to their local, situational, and representative context; therefore, they are tied to the practices carried out with, on, and through data (cf. Burkhardt et al. 2022).

To a large extent, data practices that correlate to domestic media practices are induced outside the home on servers. They are connected to a range of smart devices and remain somewhat opaque to users. Data processing is highly dynamic and household members are – to quote Hirschauer (2016: 51) – only one "participant" with an uncertain level of agency (cf. Neff/Nagy 2018; Habscheid et al. in publ.). With data flows in the picture, the domestic use of media is part of a global network that is, however remotely, connected to the local interaction with digital media. This has to be taken into account when analysing local practices.

Although the domestication research paradigm has been shaped with pre-digital and early digital devices in mind, this paradigm has certain elements that provide fruitful avenues of inquiry into the current media situation. Domestication research has been seen as old-fashioned as the focus on the household – of the some of the research – and the home as sites of media use have been side-lined by more mobile media use. While the mobilisation of media use is obvious in today's global prevalence of mobile and smartphones, it has to be noted that domestic media use – personal media use in domestic spaces and the socialisation of media users in and through families, roommates, partners, and friends – continues to be an integral part of 21st-century everyday life. The Covid-19 pandemic has highlighted the importance of the domestic sphere. But even before Covid-19, smartphone use took place inside the home; smartphone use was discussed among household members, including the payment for ongoing mobile data plans. Laptops, tablets, and iPods have been used at home as well. As such, questions that concern the domestic evaluation of media technologies are still relevant today. Another dimension of domestic media use is relatively new, however. The "Internet of Things" comes with a number of supposedly smart and interconnected household devices. These devices are domestic in that they add functionalities and automation to household appliances such as fridges, locks, and vacuum cleaners; they are also domestic in the sense that they are not battery powered and mobile, but stationary, such as smart speakers. They are designed to increase the interconnection of the home; they further blur the line between domestic and public places and media. While domestication research examined plans for smart homes (Haddon 1995) early on, it still has to fully explore questions to the related data practices that were not fully conceivable about 30 years ago.

The pandemic as well as new domestic appliances remind us that modern life is still connected to homes and households. The discourse around mobility and "digital nomads" (Hartmann 2019) has obscured that this new mobility is only possible against the backdrop of a still mostly sedentary lifestyle. Even though certain segments of society are commuting to work and changing their address ever so often, eventually, they still keep returning to a place they call home. Even if they do not feel at home in this place, they have to organise their everyday life in domestic spaces with family members, loved ones or roommates. This includes the integration of media into said life.

Bearing these aspects in mind, our interest in domestication research does not entail a simple return to a focus on purely domestic life, but it suggests looking at household interaction with media with reference to media use outside the home and to the household members' influence on each other's media use. In this vein, we follow Silverstone, Hirsch and Morley, and "aim [...] toward understanding the nature of the relationship between private households and public worlds and the role of communication and information technologies in that relationship" (Silverstone et al. 1992: 13). The focus on the collective adoption of media is another element of domestication research that seems worth applying to current research, too. While it is common sense in media studies that users do not simply adopt readings of a media text as suggested by its authors, many studies still focus on the individual reading and adoption of media, i.e., on the relation between an individual and a single medium, be it TV or a social-media platform. Other research traditions into media ecologies have emphasised how media use is always part of an ensemble of media (Cali 2017). Domestication research, however, has additionally suggested that media adoption is not only an individual task, but one that is mediated through the household in two ways: (a) individuals are socialised in households also in reference to their media use; whether certain media are present or not, the use in certain situations – e.g., the use of smartphones at the dinner table (Ferdous et al. 2016) – is discouraged. As household members spend time together, they have to negotiate how media – be them gaming consoles, phones, TV sets – are used. Also, as (b) households pool economic resources, they have to come to terms with the costs of new media, the rent they incur with reference to data plans, subscriptions to streaming services, and the electricity bill. Domestication research allows us to focus not only on the collective adoption of media but also on the meso-level, i.e., the household as a force field of conflicting and coincident interests, values and material circumstances.

Even though the focus on the household is still important, domestication no longer remains a solely private and domestic issue. While in the 20th century mass media were primarily used to take in information, entertainment, and the arts from the outside, current media technology – in light of the growing importance of data and platformed media – connects users to the outside world in several ways: with the Internet and even more so with social media, users provide information about themselves online to others. By liking, commenting, and posting content on social media platforms, news sites and forums, users make public and provide data about their interests, opinions, and site visits. On the other hand, working with smart-home technology, users can control smart home devices from outside their home. While social media allows individuals to publish their private lives to more or less controlled and platformed publics, smart home devices controlled via smartphone apps allow for the "externalization" of domestication and domestic media (Brause/Blank 2020). These processes all relate to data; this data and many more are collected and aggregated by a number of hosts and third parties. They become part of big data analytics which in turn are used for targeted advertisement or the training of machine-learning algorithms. As misuses of this data have become public, e.g., in the political micro-targeting through Cambridge Analytica during the 2016 American presidential election or as documented in the Facebook leak by Frances Haugen, users have to deal with the "moral economy" of data in their everyday dealings with technology. When they use data-hungry apps such as TikTok, they may face criticism from other household members. Also, on a macro-level, the problems arising from data collection, manipulation and privacy breaches have to be dealt with by governments, civil rights organisations, and regulators. Governments and secret services have to decide how to use the data being generated for their own purposes, too. As the GDPR of the European Union has demonstrated, the way data is treated is a concern among policy-makers and at least parts of civil society (Quinn et al. 2019).

As stated above, we suggest following a situational and ethnomethodological understanding of practice theory in the tradition of Garfinkel and Goffman (cf. Hirschauer 2016). Thus, media only become media through use and through media practices. "Taming" refers to the aspects that are highlighted by domestication research; the term allows to see how the realisation of media practices is itself contingent on a history of interactions between user and medium; in turn, these interactions are located and, to a certain extent, enabled, by the co-location and proximity of users and media in households. The "taming of data practices", then, describes the ways in which users deal with the data practices that come with today's media.

The articles in this issue

In bringing these various strands together, the articles in this issue analyse domestic and digital media and data practices with reference to the themes and concepts of domestication as well as practice-based research. All of them combine conceptual and empirical research into current data practices in and around households and domestic or amateur use.

The first set of articles examines domestic and digital media practices and the way they change what it means to watch TV, cook, and clean today. In revisiting one of the most prominent media of the 20th century – which has also been prominently discussed in domestication research (Silverstone 1994) – **Maren Hartmann** and **Vera Klocke** deal with the "material articulations" of watching television in the early 21st century. While content produced by and for TV stations – in news and entertainment – is still relevant today, it is no longer consumed only via TV sets and broadcast, but through video platforms, streaming services, and a set of varied devices. With a plethora of possibilities at their disposal, users seem more able than ever to accommodate television to their routines, rather than adapting their routines to the TV schedule and location. It remains to be seen what is left of TV "in times after TV". **Katharina Graf**, in turn, does not examine leisure practices but reproductive and culinary ones in the "smart kitchen". Her paper details how individuals integrate smart devices and digital aids and platforms into the processes of food procurement and preparation. In this way, Graf sheds light on often over-looked aspects of digitalisation, changing gender roles, and the impact of "warm experts" in the extended family which recommend certain digital kitchen aids. Taking on cleaning, another reproductive and domestic task, **Max Kanderske** discusses the triangulation of space, people, and "semi-autonomous agents" as relevant for processes of taming by investigating user experiences with domestic vacuum robots. The "netnographic perspective" as well as the perspective of "time geography" in this paper demonstrate one more methodological approach to investigating domestic media technologies in practice. Domestication does not only happen in the home, but outdoors as well. **Niklas Strüver** focuses on the strategies of Amazon to enlist companies into producing devices that are compatible with Amazon's Alexa voice assistant: he highlights how Amazon tries to tame and entice device manufacturers into and onto its platform in order to turn Alexa into the go-to infrastructure for the future smart home. In this way, Strüver illustrates how infrastructures and platforms allow for certain domestic practices to take place by pre-configuring which smart-home technology becomes interconnectable in the first place, and how.

Moving away from the more or less smart home, **Hendrik Bender** and **Marcus Burkhardt** shed light on the outdoor practices of civilian drone use. They show how the drone – originally a project of military research – was tamed and creatively re-appropriated by hobbyists and the maker community, and how this in turn provoked the commercial production and professional use of drones in movie production, agriculture and research. Through this co-operation of a number of actors and fields, the drone eventually became what it is today, a semi-autonomous quadcopter with a camera – and a novel way to produce data. Eventually, Bender and Burkhardt describe a build-up and enmeshment of amateur tinkering and professionalisation on the one hand and of exploratory use and regulation on the other.

The boundaries of the home and its outside are not fixed but negotiable. Two contributions review this negotiation: **Tanja Aal**, **Md Rashidul Hasan**, **Denis Kirschsieper** and **Claudia Müller** compare the use of traditional and new media by older adults in Bangladesh. Based on an exploratory interview study, they work out different influencing factors for taming media and technologies. In a conceptual reflection, **Cordula Endter**, **Florian Fischer** and **Tobias Wörle** examine the domestic media use by elderly people. They focus on the use of digital assistive technologies and consider the connection of material-spatial environments with concepts of age and ageing. In this way, they elaborate on the production of home-like qualities with regards to digital technology.

The two following papers are "entering the field" in that they are exploratory and shorter than the other papers in this issue. **Alexander B. Kucharski** and **Sebastian Merkel** deal with smart-speaker use of older users. They highlight how usage practices, subjectivities and values are co-produced in smart-speaker use. **Anne Weibert**, **Konstantin Aal**, **Sarah Rüller**, **Markus Rohde** and **Volker Wulf** focus less on data than on a social experiment with fabrics, digital devices, and memory. They showcase a participatory design study featuring immigrants to Germany in which the immigrants reflect on their understanding of home by quilting a tapestry out of textile fabric and digital components.

This issue also includes a conversation with **Leslie Haddon** who can be considered to be one of the founding figures of domestication research in Britain. He started off researching, among other things, "intelligent homes" (Haddon 1995) as they were called at the time and now focuses on children's media use (Haddon 2020). Our conversation deals with the timeliness and timelessness of domestication research, its role with regards to current digital media, academic discourses and research in media studies.

This thematic issue is based on a workshop done on the topic at Collaborative Research Centre (CRC) "Media of Cooperation" at the University of Siegen, Germany. As the whole of the CRC, the workshop was funded by Deutsche Forschungsgemeinschaft (DFG), the German Research Foundation.[2] We are especially grateful to Maren Hartmann who provided an inspiring keynote and comments during the presentations of the papers in progress. Without her, the workshop would not have been as productive. We also would like to thank the contributors

---

2   Gefördert durch die Deutsche Forschungsgemeinschaft (DFG) – Projektnummer 262513311 – SFB 1187

for the shared dedication in meeting the deadline for this publication as well as Katharina Hauptmann and Kirsten Wächter for their professional proofreading.

References

Aune, Margrethe (2007): "Energy Comes Home." In: Energy Policy 35/11, pp. 5457-5465.

Ayaß, Ruth (1993): "Auf der Suche nach dem verlorenen Zuschauer." In: Holly, Werner/Püschel, Ulrich (eds.), Medienrezeption als Aneignung. Methoden und Perspektiven qualitativer Medienforschung. Wiesbaden: VS Verlag für Sozialwissenschaften, pp. 27-41.

Bakardjieva, Maria (2005): Internet Society: The Internet in Everyday Life, London: Sage.

Bakardjieva, Maria (2006): "Domestication Running Wild. From the Moral Economy of the Household to the Mores of a Culture." In: Berker Thomas/Hartmann, Maren/Punie, Yves/Ward, Katie (eds.), Domestication of Media and Technology. Maidenhead: McGraw-Hill Education, pp. 62-79.

Bassett, Caroline (2007): The Arc and the Machine. Narrative and New Media, Manchester: Manchester University Press.

Bausinger, Hermann (1984): "Media, Technology and Daily Life." In: Media, Culture and Society 6, pp. 343–351.

Berker Thomas/Hartmann, Maren/Punie, Yves/Ward, Katie (eds.) (2006): Domestication of Media and Technology, Maidenhead: McGraw-Hill Education.

Birkland, Johanna (in publ.): "Domestication and Older Adults – Changing Definitions of Home and Family." In: Hartmann, Maren (ed.): The Routledge Handbook of Media and Technology Domestication, London: Routledge.

Boltanski, Luc/Thévenot, Laurent (2006): On Justification Economies of Worth, Princeton: Princeton University Press.

Bourdieu, Pierre (1984): Distinction. A Social Critique of the Judgment of Taste, Cambridge: Harvard University Press.

Brause, Saba Rebecca/Blank, Grant (2020): "Externalized Domestication: Smart Speaker Assistants, Networks and Domestication Theory." In: Information, Communication & Society 23/5, pp. 751-763.

Burkhardt, Marcus/van Geenen, Daniela/Gerlitz, Carolin/Hind, Sam/Kaerlein, Timo/Lämmerhirt, Danny/Volmar, Axel (2022): "Introduction." In: Burkhardt, Marcus/van Geenen, Daniela/Gerlitz, Carolin/Hind, Sam/Kaerlein, Timo/Lämmerhirt, Danny/Volmar, Axel (eds.): Interrogating Datafication. Towards a Praxeology of Data, Bielefeld: Transcript, pp. 9-36.

Cali, Dennis (2017): Mapping Media Ecology, New York: Peter Lang.

Childe, V. Gordon (1951): Man Makes Himself, New York: New American Library.

Couldry, Nick/Mejias, Ulises A. (2019): "Data Colonialism: Rethinking Big Data's Relation to the Contemporary Subject." In: Television & New Media 20/4, pp. 336-349.

Dang-Anh, Mark/Pfeifer, Simone/Reisner, Clemens/Villioth, Lisa (2017): "Medienpraktiken. Situieren, erforschen, reflektieren. Eine Einleitung." In: Navigationen 17/1, pp. 7-36.

Diaz-Bone, Rainer (2017): "Discourses, Conventions, and Critique – Perspectives of the Institutionalist Approach of the Economics of Convention." In: Historical Social Research 42/3, pp. 79-96.

Faber, Marlene (2001): "Medienrezeption als Aneignung." In: Holly, Werner/Püschel, Ulrich/Bergmann, Jörg (eds.): Der sprechende Zuschauer. Wie wir uns Fernsehen kommunikativ aneignen, Wiesbaden: Westdeutscher Verlag, pp. 25-40.

Ferdous, Hasan Shahid/Ploderer, Bernd/Davis, Hilary/Vetere, Frank/O'Hara, Kenton/Farr-Wharton, Geremy/Comber, Rob (2016): "TableTalk: Integrating Personal Devices and Content for Commensal Experiences at the Family Dinner Table." In: UbiComp '16. Proceedings of the 2016 International Joint Conference on Pervasive and Ubiquitous Computing, pp. 132-143.

Garfinkel, Harold (1967): Studies in Ethnomethodology, Englewood Cliffs: Prentice Hall.

Giddens, Anthony (1984): The Constitution of Society. Outline of the Theory of Structuration, Cambridge: Polity.

Gießmann, Sebastian (2018): "Elemente einer Praxistheorie der Medien." In: Zeitschrift für Medienwissenschaft 10/2, pp. 95-109.

Gießmann, Sebastian/Burkhardt, Marcus (2014): "Was ist Datenkritik? Zur Einführung." In: Mediale Kontrolle unter Beobachtung 3/1, pp. 1-13.

Gitelman, Lisa (2013): "Raw data" Is an Oxymoron, Cambridge: MIT Press.

Goffman, Erving (1983): "The Interaction Order." In: American Sociological Review 48/1, pp. 1-17.

Goodwin, Charles (2018): Co-Operative Action. Cambridge: Cambridge University Press.

Habscheid, Stephan/Hector, Tim/Hrncal, Christine (in publ.): "Human and Non-Human Agency as Practical Accomplishment: Interactional Occasions for Ascription and Withdrawal of (Graduated) Agency in the Use of Smart Speaker-Technology." In: Samira Ibnelkaïd/Iluiia Avgustis (eds.): Situated Agency: Embodied Action-Projection in Artifacted Social Interactions. Special Issue of Social interaction. Video-based studies of human sociality.

Haddon, Leslie (1995): "The Home of the Future Today. The Social Origins of Intelligent Homes." In: Esser, Josef/Fleischmann, Gerd/Heimer, Thomas (eds.): Soziale und ökonomische Konflikte in Standardisierungsprozessen, Frankfurt/M: Campus, pp. 89-104.

Haddon, Leslie (2020): "The Domestication of Touchscreen Technologies in Families With Young Children." In: Lella Green/Donnell Holloway/Kylie Stevenson/Tama Leaver/Leslie Haddon (eds.), The Routledge Companion to Children and Digital Media, Abingdon: Routledge.

Haddon, Leslie /Silverstone, Roger (1995): "Lone Parents and Their Information and Communication Technologies." In: SPRU/CICT report series No. 12, Brighton: University of Sussex.

Haddon, Leslie/Silverstone, Roger (1996): "Information and Communication Technologies and the Young Elderly." In: SPRU/CICT report series No. 13, Brighton: University of Sussex.

Hartmann, Maren (2009): "Roger Silverstone: 'Medienobjekte und Domestizierung'." In: Hepp, Andreas/Krotz, Friedrich/Thomas, Tanja (eds.), Schlüsselwerke der Cultural Studies, Wiesbaden: VS Verlag für Sozialwissenschaften, pp. 304-315.

Hartmann, Maren (2019): "Domestizierung, mobile Medien und anderes (un)häusliches mehr." In: Linke, Christine/Schlote, Isabel (eds.): Soziales Medienhandeln. Integrative Perspektiven auf den Wandel mediatisierter interpersonaler Kommunikation, Wiesbaden: Springer VS, pp. 101-116.

Hartmann, Maren (2020): "(The Domestication of) Nordic Domestication?" In: Nordic Journal of Media Studies 2/1, pp. 47-57.

Hartmann, Maren (2022): Domestication Theory or Domesticating Theory? Some Reflections on the Life of a Concept. Keynote at workshop "Taming Digital Practices – On the Domestication of Data-Driven Technologies", February 7, 2022, University of Siegen (unpublished).

Hirschauer, Stefan (2016): "Verhalten, Handeln, Interagieren. Zu den mikrosoziologischen Grundlagen der Praxistheorie." In: Schäfer, Hilmar (ed.), Praxistheorie. Ein soziologisches Forschungsprogramm, Bielefeld: Transcript (Sozialtheorie), pp. 45-67.

Holly, Werner (2001): "Der sprechende Zuschauer." In: Holly, Werner/Püschel, Ulrich/Bergmann, Jörg (eds.), Der sprechende Zuschauer. Wie wir uns Fernsehen kommunikativ aneignen, Wiesbaden: Westdteutscher Verlag, 11-24.

Holly, Werner/Püschel, Ulrich (1993): "Vorwort." In: Holly, Werner/Püschel, Ulrich (eds.), Medienrezeption als Aneignung. Methoden und Perspektiven qualitativer Medienforschung, Wiesbaden: VS Verlag für Sozialwissenschaften, pp. 7-10.

Krämer, Sybille (1998): "Das Medium als Spur und als Apparat." In: Krämer, Sybille (ed.), Medien – Computer – Realität, Frankfurt/M: Suhrkamp, pp. 73-94.

La Mettrie, Julien Offray de (1996 [1749]): Machine Man and Other Writings, Cambridge: Cambridge University Press.

Lamont, Michèle (2012): "Toward a Comparative Sociology of Valuation and Evaluation." In: Annual Review of Sociology 28, pp. 201-221.

Löfström, Erica (2007): "Visualizing Energy in Households: The Power Aware Cord as a Means to Create Energy Awareness." In: Proceedings of the European Network for Housing Research Conference, Rotterdam.

Morley, David/Silverstone, Roger (1990): "Domestic Communication – Technologies and Meanings." In: Media, Culture & Society 12/1, pp. 31-55.

Neff, Gina/Nagy, Peter (2018): "Agency in the Digital Age: Using Symbiotic Agency to Explain Human-Technology Interaction." In: Papacharissi, Zizi (ed.), A Networked Self and Human Augmentics, Artificial Intelligence, Sentience, London: Routledge, pp. 97-107.

Østergaard Madsen, Christian/Kræmmergaard, Pernille (2015): "The Efficiency of Freedom: Single Parents' Domestication of Mandatory E-Government Channels." In: Government Information Quarterly 32/4, pp. 380-388.

Quinn, Kelly/Epstein, Dmitry/Moon, Brenda (2019): "We Care About Different Things: Non-Elite Conceptualizations of Social Media Privacy." In: Social Media + Society 3/5, pp. 1-14.

Röser, Jutta/Müller, Kathrin Friederike/Niemand, Stephan/Roth, Ulrike (2019): Das mediatisierte Zuhause im Wandel. Eine qualitative Panelstudie zur Verhäuslichung des Internets, Wiesbaden: VS Verlag für Sozialwissenschaften.

Scheerder, Anique/van Deursen, Alexander/van Dijk, Jan (2019): "Internet Use in the Home: Digital Inequality From a Domestication Perspective." In: New Media & Society 21/10, pp. 2099-2118.

Schüttpelz, Erhard/Gießmann, Sebastian (2015): "Medien der Kooperation. Überlegungen zum Forschungsstand." In: Navigationen 15/1, pp., 7-55.

Schüttpelz, Erhard/Meyer, Christian (2017): "Ein Glossar zur Praxistheorie. 'Siegener Version' (Frühjahr 2017)." In: Navigationen 17/1, pp. 155-163.

Schütz, Alfred/Luckmann, Thomas (1973): The Structures of the Life-World. Evanston, IL: Northwestern University Press.

Scott, James C. (2017): Against the Grain. A Deep History of the Earliest States, New Haven: Yale University Press.

Silverstone, Roger (1994): Television and Everyday Life, London: Routledge.

Silverstone, Roger (2006): "Domesticating Domestication. Reflections on the Life of a Concept." In: Berker Thomas/Hartmann, Maren/Punie, Yves/Ward, Katie (eds.), Domestication of Media and Technology, Maidenhead: McGraw-Hill Education, pp. 229-248.

Silverstone, Roger/Hirsch, Eric/Morley, David (1992): "Information and Communication Technologies and the Moral Economy of the Household." In: Silverstone, Roger/Hirsch, Eric (eds.), Consuming technologies. Media and information in domestic spaces, London: Routledge, pp. 13-28.

Srnicek, Nick (2016): Platform Capitalism, Cambridge: MIT Press.

Sørensen, Knut (1994): "Technology in Use. Two Essays on the Domestication of Artifacts." In: STS Working Paper (2).

Thompson, E.P. (1966): The Making of the English Working Class, New York: Vintage.

Thompson, E.P. (1971): "The Moral Economy of the English Crowd in the Eighteenth Century." In: Past & Present 50, pp. 76-135.

Turow, Joseph/Couldry, Nick (2018): "Media as Data Extraction: Towards a New Map of a Transformed Communications Field." In: Journal of Communication 68/2, pp. 415-423.

Zuboff, Shoshana (2019): The Age of Surveillance Capitalism, London: Profile.

Field Research
and Case Studies

Rethinking Material Articulations of "Television" in Times After TV

Vera Klocke and Maren Hartmann

Abstract

Television today is a highly networked medium. The social practice of watching television is no longer bound to a specific device, but can take place on various devices, some of which only result in 'television' when they are brought together. In this article, these different material articulations that can accompany television are analysed through a domestication lens, with a particular emphasis on the concept of ontological security. It is argued that the material manifestations of routines are an important element in the development and maintenance of a household's ontological security and that it is precisely the linkages of the various devices that sustain this. Based on this analysis, we ask to what extent the concepts and categories of the domestication approach can be used, but also extended, in order to profitably apply them to the study of contemporary media households. It is argued that precisely the study of the 'old' medium of television, which is accompanied by a conceptual blurring, provides useful insights into current domestication processes of technology. The article draws on an ethnographic study in Berlin households, which used participant observation, thick description and visual methods to investigate the processes of media appropriation. This article argues that it is precisely this kind of time-intensive investigation that is necessary to capture the small things that are part of the material articulation of television today.

Keywords

television, double articulation, convergence, material articulations, ontological security, visual ethnography, video-reenactments

Introduction

Since television moved into households in the 1950s, it has been a domestic medium and an integral part of everyday life. Hermann Bausinger summed this up particularly well in his text "Media, technology and daily life" (Bausinger 1984), in which he describes media use as part of everyday action that is characterised by ambiguity. Bausinger therein establishes a connection not only between media-related and everyday actions, but also between different things in the living space, as a drawing in the German version of the article (Bausinger 1983) (Fig. 1) underlines (which comes with a numbered list of the pieces visible therein). While one television viewer is also discernible, the dominant aspects are the pieces of furniture, the media technologies as well as other things in the room. This arrangement illustrates a connection between the viewers' actions and the things and devices found in the living room. Both shape the space and the reception of television.

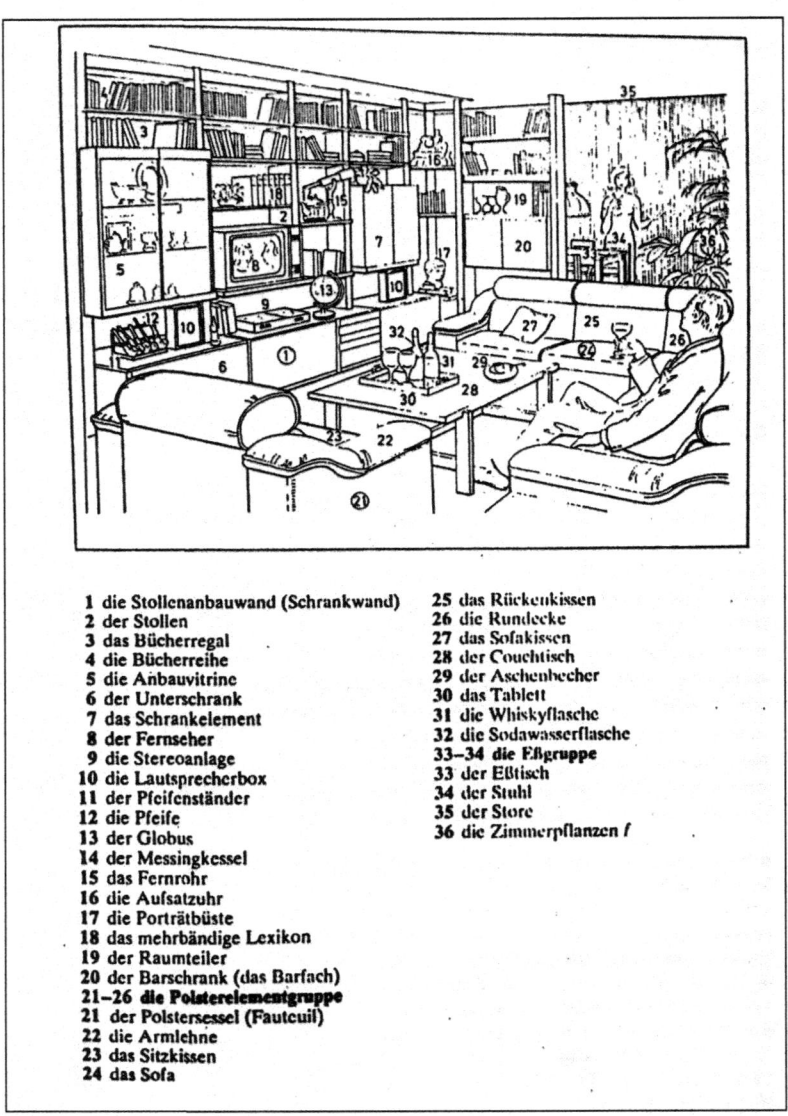

1 die Stollenanbauwand (Schrankwand)
2 der Stollen
3 das Bücherregal
4 die Bücherreihe
5 die Anbauvitrine
6 der Unterschrank
7 das Schrankelement
8 der Fernseher
9 die Stereoanlage
10 die Lautsprecherbox
11 der Pfeifenständer
12 die Pfeife
13 der Globus
14 der Messingkessel
15 das Fernrohr
16 die Aufsatzuhr
17 die Porträtbüste
18 das mehrbändige Lexikon
19 der Raumteiler
20 der Barschrank (das Barfach)
21–26 die Polsterelementgruppe
21 der Polstersessel (Fauteuil)
22 die Armlehne
23 das Sitzkissen
24 das Sofa
25 das Rückenkissen
26 die Rundecke
27 das Sofakissen
28 der Couchtisch
29 der Aschenbecher
30 das Tablett
31 die Whiskyflasche
32 die Sodawasserflasche
33–34 die Eßgruppe
33 der Eßtisch
34 der Stuhl
35 der Store
36 die Zimmerpflanzen f

Fig. 1: According to Bausinger, not only the television set itself, but all things and pieces of furniture are part of the media household (Bausinger 1983: 26).

This approach of seeing media, things and everyday actions as interwoven, is still groundbreaking today when it comes to examining media reception as part of everyday experience. Nevertheless, much has changed since the text was published in English in 1984. While for Bausinger the television set had a central place in the living room cabinet and was operated with the remote control as a matter of course (see Fig. 1), television has undergone a significant transformation, both medially and materially. People are no longer dependent on television sets to watch television, but can resort to projectors or mobile devices such as laptops, smartphones or tablets. Use has individualised, since the platforms have changed and the whole television 'market' has diversified immensely. Media content can be accessed via the sites of streaming providers and media libraries and consumed flexibly in terms of time and place. This is accompanied by an increased selection of devices that can be used for watching television. Media content has 'converged' into different devices (Peil/Sparviero 2017). The materialisation of such media, however, i.e. the devices, so our claim, are not necessarily interchangeable. Instead, they have become major players in the practice of 'television'. Paradoxically, the moment they have become interchangeable, they are instead used in unique and often rather rigid ways.

In this article we define what 'television' is, starting from a practice that acquires meaning in the context of the domestic sphere and is closely linked to the space and environment in which it takes place (Morley 1986). This means that we illuminate television as a social practice that can now take place on quite different devices. And it is precisely these different material articulations of television that we are interested in. We call it 'television' in order to avoid a clear-cut distinction between the social practice of 'watching television' and the material articulation of 'the television set'. Just like Anna McCarthy, we want to preserve the 'dialectical qualities' of television 'as an object in space and as a relationship between spaces', thereby emphasizing its *"flexibility* as an environmental media apparatus" (McCarthy 2001: 14). It is exactly the axis where practices and material articulations meet that we are concerned with here - therefore it is simply 'television.' It is the constant (and everchanging) recombination of these practices and materialisations that we assume characterises television today. Sometimes, this is an attempt to copy earlier versions of 'watching television' even though the technical set-up has changed. Sometimes, it could simply be considered a new way of a social engagement that is technically supported in diverse ways. The question we pose is whether – with these changes in the devices that can be used for television – the relationships of the devices to the other (media) things and furniture in the living space also change. An examination of these connections allows us to a) develop an understanding of current media households and b) classify the material articulation of television and the resulting role of the materialities' in television as a social practice. It is precisely the study of this 'old' medium of television, which is accompanied by a conceptual blurring, i.e. the axis of practices and technologies, which has the potential to provide useful insights into technology domestication processes in the 21st century, since TV today is a much more interconnected and fragile medium.

The paper draws on an ethnographic study in Berlin households that used participant observation, thick descriptions and visual methods to investigate the processes of media appropriation (Klocke unpublished manuscript). While this kind of time-consuming ethnographic research has taken a back seat in recent years in research on domestication, we argue that it is precisely this meticulous investigation that is necessary to understand the processes of media appropriation. Using this material, we show what relationships the devices used to watch television enter into with other devices and things, and examine the extent to which these influence the processes of media appropriation and the social practice of watching television. In a further step, we use the domestication approach, and in particular the question of ontological security, to investigate what role this diversity of devices plays for the households studied. Thus, our research has shown that – although there have been many developments in the field of television – for many users it is primarily a matter of holding on to something that has been around for a while. And this desire for security is closely linked to the material constructions of television, albeit in sometimes paradoxical forms. In this way, we also reflect on the extent to which the concepts and categories of the domestication approach can be used, but also extended, to profitably apply them to the study of contemporary media households.

Material articulations of networked technologies

Our title suggests that we study 'television' in times after TV. This might require at least a brief explanation. The constituting characteristic of television (signals that are transmitted and can be received exclusively with a television set (Hasebrink 2002: 46)) disappeared with its digitalisation. People alternate between linear and networked content, including the reception of short video snippets and social media content. These different types of content are very closely linked. A division into 'television' and 'non-television' would therefore not be useful to examine the media appropriation processes of television.

Domestication research has become a well-established framework that helps to analyse media appropriation processes in everyday life (see Berker et al. 2006; Hartmann 2023). Empirical studies on domestication have appeared in many areas and some have also developed the conceptual framework further (see e.g. Huang/Miao 2020; Winther/Bell 2018; Brause/Blank 2020). Nonetheless, the need to continue this updating process remains prevalent. The domestication framework managed to provide an alternative to other television studies at the time of its emergence in the late 1980s, early 1990s. Up to this point, communication and media studies had mainly focused on media texts and neglected the context of media appropriation (Livingstone 2007). Domestication instead emphasised user engagements with media in a rather specific environment: the home (mostly in Western contexts, primarily perceived as a family home).

Bausinger (1984), already referenced above, was more than once taken as a reference point in the early formulations of the domestication concept. In his text, Bausinger at some point describes a standard weekend day in the life of a German family (Familie Meier). His focus is particularly on the role that media played therein - or rather, the role it did not play (when things do not work out according to plan). Bausinger manages to underline that the motifs behind media usage are often not media-based, such as when "the mother sits down next to her eldest son and wachtes the sports review with him. It does not interest her, but it is an attempt at making contact" (Bausinger 1984: 349). Television is a basis for communication and its offerings often used to build the basis for the structures of everyday life. In this sense, 'television' was indeed different back then, albeit only to an extent. It still today provides many 'attempts at making contact', but the offerings are far less pre-structured, far less place- and time-bound. This is both a technological and a social question, since lifestyles, work structures and family set-ups have also shifted. While David Morley and Roger Silverstone back then emphasized the connective power of television, linking the structures of domestic life to the (symbolic) participation in the national community (Morley/Silverstone 1990: 55), this connection has become more frazzled. This is also visible in the material set-up, another core emphasis in the domestication approach.

In contrast to many other television studies approaches, which either looked at the ideologies in media production or at specific genres and their perception, one of the core emphases of domestication has always been the material nature of media consumption, i.e. its embeddedness in issues of consumption with an emphasis on technologies. As both technology and content, the media (and especially television) are "doubly articulated", as emphasised by Silverstone:

Television is both object and medium within this domesticity. Our choice of technology, our incorporation of it into the private spaces, times and practices of our homes is paralleled by the same kind of choices that we make with respect to programmes and the work we do on them both inside and outside our domestic space: to make them our own. (Silverstone 1994: 175)

The first articulation refers to the object status of media technology within the living space. These objects, which according to Morley already have an immanent symbolic meaning, move into the domestic sphere and are in turn appropriated there by the owners. In this process, meanings are assigned to them by the users.

In the first place, the TV set (along with all the other technologies in the household) is already a symbolic object, qua item of household furnishing, a choice (of design, style, etc.) which expresses something about its owner's (or renter's) tastes, and communicates that choice, as displayed by its position in the household [...]. (Morley 2006: 181)

The second articulation refers to the status of technology as a mediator of media. It implies the study of the appropriation processes of the medium, i.e. the symbolic level[s] of media content.

In the empirical studies that have taken place within the domestication approach, the material dimension of media technologies has been examined with a view to various aspects. James Lull, for example, has described how television sets are used as altars around which residents place identity-creating objects and images (Lull 1991: 65–66). Corinna Peil's study on mobile communication in Japan shows that devices are also modified, for example with tags and stickers, to express the identity of their owners (Peil 2011: 320). Another focus is the examination of devices in terms of their place in spaces. Morley, for example, attributes a family's low television viewing time to the fact that the furniture is not aligned with the device (Morley 1986: 118) and Thorsten Quandt and Thilo von Pape describe the different media technologies in the living space as being in competition with each other (Quandt/von Pape 2010: 332). Nonetheless, the 'nitty-gritty' of the material aspects was not always at the forefront of domestication research, despite its emphasis in the framework. Early domestication work took pictures of the rooms where technologies were placed in the homes and had respondents fill in lists of technologies around. These and other materials were then used in the interviews. Nonetheless, the symbolic meanings were ultimately given more room in the studies.

In our study, we are primarily concerned with the interconnections between the devices and how these connections shape the practice of television. The materially networked nature of these media also potentially links back to early criticism of television research ignoring the social nature of media appropriation.

For this question of the social in networked media, we focus here on the question of ontological security, which featured fairly prominently in early domestication research (e.g., Silverstone 1994: 19). While originally it was the moral economy of the household that was closely linked to the question of how ontological security is created and upheld, our research seems to point at a slight shift. First of all, single households pose the challenge of locating the moral economy – as do mobile media when they are used outside of the home. However, the moral economy has always been a socially negotiated instance (see e.g. Leslie Haddon's early work on the question of the acquistion PC into family homes; Haddon 1988). Additionally though, it appears to us that this has become radically more complex and is actually the cause of additional stress and insecurity.

For the material side of things, we follow Saba Brause and Grant Blank (2020) and their study on smart speaker assistants (SSAs). They asked, "What use genres have been created to domesticate SSAs?" (Brause/Blank 2020: 751), wanting to understand "the role the devices play in users' lives" (ibid.: 752). To do so, they use Maria Bakadjieva's notion of use genres, guiding users "to make the technology effective and meaningful in their specific situations" (ibid.: 753). While convenience and entertainment were identified as use cases by other authors, Brause and Blank additionally identify "companionship, self-control and productivity, health care support, better sleep, peace of mind and improved accessibility" (ibid.: 757) as use genres. Brause and Blank's extension of the domestication concept is called "externalisation" and defined as "the impact of networked devices in each other's domestication.' This extension is indeed helpful for framing domestication processes around devices that are spatially distributed and interactive (such as smart speakers). This focus helps to pay attention to "the implications of the networked, dispersed, always-on and possibly remote characteristics of connected home technologies" (ibid.: 759). However, while the authors outline that their sample predominantly consisted of self-reported technologically proficient users (7 out of 12), they themselves define the users' proficiency as a limitation of the study rather than an advantage. They do therefore not further regard it. In our study, the users are also technologically savvy; it is a core characteristic that they all share (albeit to different degrees). However, this does not mean that they are only equipped with new devices. Rather, they are often concerned with maintaining the ritual of watching television, which often involves a mixture of older and newer media. This maintenance of the practice of 'watching television' is closely related to the question of ontological security in the household as we will discuss below. The connection of the devices to each other plays a crucial role in this.

Ontological security in insecure times

In the following, we will explore the notion of ontological security in the context of its material articulations. Our claim is that the material manifestations of routines, of networks and similar settings support the more general experience of media use as an important element in the development and upkeep of ontological security. This has become more complex in recent years. We use both the domestication approach as it has been developed in British media studies and the Nordic interpretation in the social studies of technology (see also Berker et al. 2006; Hartmann 2020). Broadening these approaches helps to connect the individual case studies presented here with a more general question of ontological security as a societal concern.

The case studies show that people sometimes accept elaborate set-ups in order to stick to their usual form of television. These superstructures have become an integral part of their television practice and play an essential role in ontological security. Due to their pettiness, however, these set-ups also become fragile, which in turn can lead to a threat to the order.

Silverstone (1994 19) outlines:

ontological security is sustained through the familiar and the predictable. Our common-sense attitudes and beliefs express and sustain our practical understandings of the world, without which life would quickly become intolerable. Common sense is sustained by practical knowledge and expressed and supported by a whole range of symbols and symbolic formations.

These commonsense attitudes and beliefs are partly developed in their practical and thus their material manifestations. Ontological security is a key concept for understanding domestication processes because it underlines a key motivation to use media in the first place (and is therefore a key attribute of culture more generally). There is an element of reassurance involved in ontological security – of letting oneself (and ultimately the world) know that things are ok. In the context of media use, ontological security, although key to the domestication framework, is partly problematic (see Silverstone 2006; Hartmann 2023). It often reinforces the existing rather than allowing the new to emerge. And while the familiar and the predictable are necessary (the term security clearly points to this), they also limit the opportunity for change. The upkeep of ontological security might ultimately prevent users from exploring the full potential of media (see Feenberg 1999: 107). At the same time, it is key to our ability to lead our lives (Giddens 1984: 64). It is a crucial concept for understanding the logics of modernity and the constitution of what we consider society in the Global North. On many levels, however, ontological security is increasingly turning into ontological insecurity, on an individual, but also on a social and even a societal level (see e.g. Agius/Bergman Rosamond/Kinnvall 2020). The use of media is only one aspect therein, but quite an important one; and increasingly so.

One area where this is beginning to be debated is the field of disconnection studies, a new research field in recent years (see e.g. Syvertsen 2020; Treré/Natale/Keightley 2020). In this context, Annette Markham recently outlined that disconnection is a potential cause for ontological insecurity (Markham 2020). We tend to agree: despite all claims that people suffer from an over-use of media or reassurances that they would like to reduce media consumption, they tend to rely or even depend on their media use. Taking 'the media' away causes discomfort. It is the symbolic security blanket (or rather the lack of it) that Silverstone explored in his take on *Television and Everyday Life* (1994). He suggests that "our media, television perhaps preeminently, occupy the potential space released by blankets, teddy bears and breasts (...), and function cathectically and culturally as transitional objects" (ibid.: 11). The void that begins to exist once the baby is starting to move away from the mother (in Donald Winicott's understanding of child development – see e.g. Winicott 1953) is first filled with other transitional objects (such as the aforementioned blanket or bear), but later 'becomes' television and/or other media. These objects help to build one's own sense of self, one's independence. Sometimes, however, they do not get abandoned or overcome (in the original sense of transition), but they instead remain and occupy an important place in our lives.

But let us briefly return to the question of why ontological security is linked to media use. We begin by returning to Silverstone (1994: 16), who wrote about "the deeply felt needs of audiences and viewers for continuity; needs that are in turn made more pressing perhaps by virtue of the increasingly stressful or threatening world in which we live; a world which is, of course, for most of us only seen on television". Not only does television (or 'the internet') deliver the world to us, but this world is increasingly stressful. Nonetheless, we also rely on the media to provide just that: information about the world out there, a reassurance that we are 'in the know' and 'on top of things'. Being left out, not knowing what is going on, implies major stress for many people. But why does avoidance not help if the media do create the feeling of fear in the first place? Silverstone's claim underlines this in very helpful terms when he states that "those needs are being massaged or reinforced by the programmes themselves which, in almost every case, are involved in the creation and mediation of anxiety and in its resolution" (ibid.). It is not only the *creation* and *mediation*, but particularly also the *resolution of anxiety* which is key here. The mediated version of the world, albeit highly problematic and potentially threatening, also allows its (temporary) closure – it allows us to shut it off. This can be the literal pressing of a button, but it can also be the knowledge that the next programme will start in five minutes and deliver a less threatening image. After all, we can always switch to another channel or open another app. Our claim is that it is not only in media use as such (and our dealings with the 'wild' content through routines and order), but particularly in the material set-ups that the respondents in our research found their sense of security. During times where the ontological insecurity on this societal level is rising (through international conflicts and wars, through climate change, etc.), media use in its material manifestation is potentially even more relevant than before.

The sometimes complex practices related to these material settings seem to reassure these rather well-equipped users of their ability to control their (little) world, but also bring moments of insecurity (see below). These point to the potential abyss behind the carefully constructed set-ups. Markham emphasises that we tend to cover this up quickly again, i.e. "if we're disconnected in one way, we find other ways of being in the world". She nonetheless goes on to explain that "this moment highlights a fracture in our ontological security" (Markham 2020: 3). In contrast to people who left the television on all day long in earlier times, it is the lack of responses, the missing dialogical interaction that looms large nowadays when disconnectivity occurs. While the media allow us to consume the carefully constructed notions of social coherence, of collective signifiers, we – as users – are co-creators in this process. This increases the pressure to perform. Plus, as Markham outlines, it is the phatic nature of the communication in the digital sphere that actually builds the basis for our co-construction of the world and ourselves. Only when we can rely on this, i.e. only if the ontological security feels fairly secure, can we build on this and actually envision a future (Browning 2018). But all this relies on the technologies not failing us: "this process incorporates multiple agential nonhuman elements in what is often glossed as ubiquitous, or 'always on' internet" (Markham 2020: 4).

In summarising a whole range of theoretical approaches to the question of the construction and performance of self, Markham outlines that

Self is interactional in that it is built repeatedly in response to the mirror of the other's perceptions, it is a temporary outcome of cyclical dynamics of structure and agency, and it is stabilized through structured and organized routines so that what was once a negotiation of meaning (negotiation of identity) or a subject position, becomes an objectified, reified Self. This is not to say the Self remains obdurate or unchanging. But that it feels good to know who we are. That's the simple explanation of ontological security. (2020: 10)

This quote provides a brief, albeit concise explanation of ontological security and its challenges. What appears in the material below are indeed 'structured and organized routines', embedded in networks of technological gadgets. They have been put in place by the users themselves, sometimes as vast and complicated technological networks, sometimes without any visible link to anything (simply using WiFi). The habits and routines that build thereon, are simultaneously shaped by and shaping the technologies.

The study and its methodology

This article is based on the study of thirteen media households, conducted by Vera Klocke between 2018 and 2021 (Klocke unpublished manuscript). Over a period of three years, these households were visited regularly. Participant observations served to understand the appropriation processes of the devices. From the observations, thick descriptions emerged in which the processes of media appropriation were brought to the fore. They are following Bausinger's description, who explained that the meaning lies, so to speak, in the process itself (Bausinger 1983: 61). In addition, visual methods such as sketches, photos, 3D renderings and video re-enactments were used.

The households were selected with a view to a diversity of devices used to watch television. In a second step, households were selected with regard to domestic situation, age, sexuality and social class. Care was taken to include both individuals living alone and individuals living together. Nonetheless the selection is not representative. Thus, most of the participants in the study have relatively good financial resources – compared to the average in Berlin.

At least five participant observations took place in each of the sampled households from 2018 to 2021. During these meetings, we watched television together. The observations were noted and were subsequently summarised into thick descriptions. The writing style was oriented towards conveying the atmosphere of the households and making it aesthetically experienceable through the writing (Miller 2008). In addition to the observations, conversations were conducted, which were recorded and transcribed. Parts of these conversations were in turn incorporated into the thick descriptions. Within the thick descriptions, the role of media technologies is not only described, but also analysed. Thus, the descriptions also form part of the data analysis. The thick descriptions proved to be particularly useful with regard to the representation of the processes of media appropriation. In addition, methods such as video re-enactments and 3D renderings were added to visually document and investigate the materiality of the media technologies as well (see Klocke unpublished manuscript). The video-reenactments in particular underlined the connections between the various media technologies. In them, the owners were asked to comment on processes such as switching on the devices and plugging in cables. This approach was inspired by the work of anthropologist Sarah Pink, who invites people in their households to reenact certain processes of their media use (Pink 2004). This procedure enabled us to record media use in minute detail and to trace the material contexts and modes of operation.

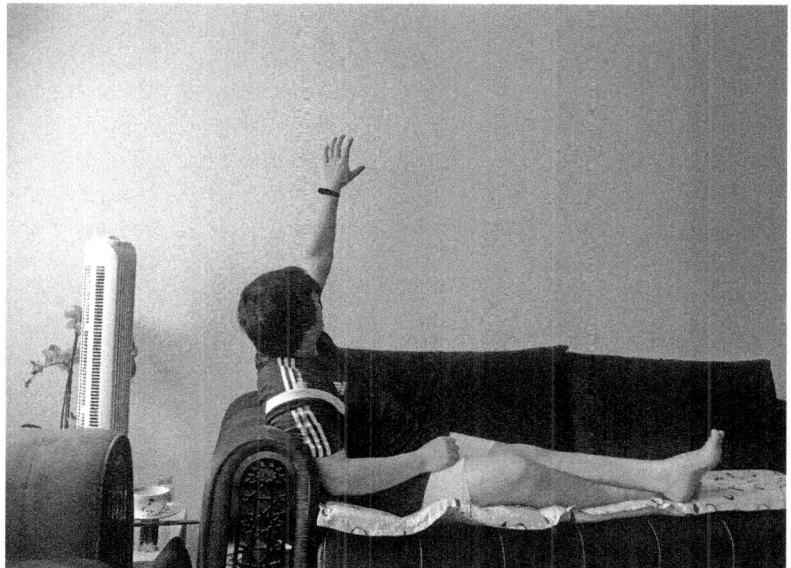

Fig. 2: *An informant describes where he plans to hang his TV. He has furnished his flat with the device in mind, even though he did not own one at the time. (own image)*

Another visual method that has proven to be profitable is the recreation of living spaces as 3D renderings, which also appear in this text. They were used to recreate the living spaces and explore the relationship between media technology and interior design. While the re-enactments serve as a method of data generation, the 3D renderings primarily serve to recreate and document the spaces. In addition, they also offer insights as they allow researchers to move back into the spaces after leaving the field.

The comforting powers of television set-ups

An ethnographic study of living spaces shows that watching television can be accompanied by a certain number of (technical) devices. Based on our sample, this applies above all to households in which people try to hold on to their familiar television sets because of nostalgia or sustainability. They invest time, but also technical skills, to watch films and series from the internet on their stationary TV sets. This may have to do with the fact that their TVs are not internet-enabled and need to be connected to other devices in order to play content from the internet. However, it may also relate to households where the TV sets are internet-enabled. Here, people use additional equipment because they find it too inconvenient to operate their smart TVs. People put up with these set-ups because they want to watch television in the familiar setting and on the television set to maintain an existing order. These attachments stabilise their everyday lives and provide a reified form of leisure time and 'being at home'. One informant, Nicole, whose set-up we'll talk about in more detail next, says of the quality of her TV, "It didn't change my old habits, it didn't change my TV habits." This reliance on a stable set-up is an important element in the build-up and maintenance of ontological security. Unchanging familiarity is exactly what it needs to become a basis for everyday rituals, which in turn form the basis for the exploration of the world 'out there'. Television sets also provide this reliability and so in many households the set-up-practices themselves have become a ritual. This is the case with our 47-year-old informant Nicole, who lives alone in a large two-room flat. She works as an employee in the cultural sector and comes home every night at the same time to watch television in order to "wind down". She watches TV by connecting her laptop, which she takes out of her work bag when she arrives, to the TV with a cable. Nicole only watches TV like this, which also has an effect on the seating area: The cables which she uses to connect the two different (temporal) eras, 'television' and 'internet', are always readyily available on the sofa. The following excerpt from the thick description of her household illustrates how Nicole sets up her television situation.

Nicole throws herself on the sofa and picks up the TV's remote control, which is lying on the sofa. On the remote control, she presses the 'VMem' button, which stands for 'Video Memory'. The TV comes on with a crackling sound, but it takes a while before an image is displayed. In the meantime, she opens her MacBook, presses the 'On/Off' button and enters her password. With a swiping motion of the fingers of her right hand, she switches from the work screen to her 'leisure desktop'. This is what Nicole calls the desktop she uses in her spare time. She has set up a total of two. The other desktop is called the 'work desktop'. Her leisure screen is characterised by the fact that Netflix is always open there.

She connects the laptop to the charging cable and the power socket. In the meantime, the TV has switched on, which means that the screen surface is a dark shade of blue. When this happens, Nicole presses the 'Menu' button on the remote control and selects 'HDMI-5'. Actually, the 'VMem' key causes a direct switch to the HDMI-1 input, but the corresponding cable, which is also still in the cable tube, is broken. Therefore, Nicole has to take a small work around and select 'HDMI-5', i.e. another HDMI input, in an additional step. She has always planned to change the cables, but now the detours have become a fixed part of her routine, so there is no particular reason to change anything. When the TV is on, she plugs in the HDMI cable, which lies on the sofa, first into an adapter and then into the corresponding input of the laptop. Her new MacBook does not have an HDMI input, so she needs the adapter. It is important to first set the HDMI channel on the TV and only then plug in the cable, otherwise the laptop often does not play the sound via the TV. When the connection is established, Nicole sometimes calls up her watch list on Netflix, where she has saved films and series she wants to watch. Most of the time, however, she simply continues with episodes of a series she has already started.

These set-ups and connections between the different devices are fragile and need to be adjusted again and again as the devices change. Nicole performs the procedures routinely; they have become part of what Nicole associates with 'watching television'. The order of the procedures – such as the relatively late connection of cable and device as the sound will not be transmitted otherwise – indicates how much knowledge the individuals have acquired regarding their set-ups. The desire to watch content from the internet on the TV set turns the users into experts, some of whom are meticulously familiar with the procedures and modes of operation of their specific devices.

Fig. 3: HDMI cables ready on the sofa are an important part of Nicole's television practice. (own image)

In the process, users often feel a sense of satisfaction when they have found a solution to a technical problem. In return, they are willing to invest time in developing the strategy. One 39-year-old man says he had imagined the construction of his projector to be easier but now that it has worked out, he is also proud:

It's just a bit more complicated because I couldn't get the sound out there, so I kind of fiddled around with it for a month until I was satisfied and here I can only get the picture and the sound out separately. And that's why I had to put it in here and then there are two different versions. The audio box is back there. But it took months of research until it worked like that.

Now, the structure and thus the materialised routines are stable. Nevertheless, disruptions keep occurring because the number of connections and interconnections leaves the structure vulnerable. Repeatedly interferences occur that cannot be identified by the users. At the same time, however, it is precisely these disruptions that in turn enable a better understanding of the superstructures. Latour described that it is only at the moment of the disturbance that the functioning of the previously impenetrable black box becomes visible. He illustrates this using the example of a broken overhead projector. Only after the rushed technicians have opened the device do the actors inside become visible (Latour 2000: 223). Our emphasis, however, reveals the issue of insecurity arising from exactly such instability. If the cable has become my umbilical cord, any severance thereof will cause pain and anxiety (sometimes barely visible, sometimes on a fundamental level). As Markham (2020) outlined, disconnectivity is not easy to bear. It implies more than the technical disconnection; ultimately, it is about participation in society.

The investigation of the households shows that the degree of fragility increases with the number of devices and the connections among them. In a household with a family watching via a projector, all family members become nervous when an error message appears on the screen or the sound suddenly cuts out. When a problem occurs, it can be due to a variety of reasons. It can be the many possible nodes, such as cable crossings, but also the WIFI router that fails all of a sudden. These technical disruptions have a long tradition in the history of television. There also used to be problems when satellite dishes were misaligned or when the connection from a VHS player to a TV set was interrupted. We would argue, however, that the disturbances we are talking about have a different quality even if it is not a radical change because they do not primarily take place in the inner workings of individual technical devices but tend to affect the network, which consists of various devices that are often needed in order to watch television. This means that there is a multitude of intersections outside the devices which are made and checked by the owners themselves. More needs to be done to maintain the illusion of television.

In the event of a disruption, people are left perplexed and often have no idea where to start looking for a solution. This is evident in the aforementioned household where a family is trying to watch TV via a projector that is connected to many other devices, such as a smartphone, HDMI cables and Fire-TV-sticks.

13-year-old Matthias selects the film 'Bolt' via the smartphone and the 'Fire TV' operating application. The 'Disney' logo then appears, but without sound. The children shout, "louder, louder!' and Jan, the father, frantically presses the remote control on the audio bar, but it does nothing. Jan looks perplexed at the technology in his hands. 'You don't have to hear anything yet,' Jan says. 'Yes, you do!' the children shout, 'there's always a sound!' The father unsuccessfully presses on his smartphone. The ten-year-old Leyla stands in front of the big screen and tries to press the 'play' button that is displayed at the bottom of the screen in pause mode. As she does so, she makes the screen move. 'Yes', Jan says, leaning over the remote controls. 'That would be most convenient if this were a touchscreen.' He looks at the devices in his hands, which do not tell him what the mistake might be.

Thus, not only the technical equipment, but also the procedures represent a black box that functions according to invisible parameters. The state of blackboxing can be described on two levels. On the one hand, it refers to the more or less material black box and, on the other, to the practice of blackboxing. This means that not only the technical devices, but also the "ways of thinking" and practices elude the view from the outside (Latour 2000: 372). In this respect, the living room and the everyday routines of the domestic sphere can also be described as a process of blackboxing. Only the moments of interruption offer the possibility to gain insights into the 'black box' of routines in front of the devices. The ideas about how to spend the evening would otherwise be hidden.

In the household where the family is attempting to watch the film "Bolt" via the projector, the material contexts are closely linked to the shared reception of the family. The individuals would not make this effort to watch television alone. In addition, the set-up works exclusively with the father's smartphone, without which 'television' cannot take place. The material stabilises the ontological security of the household in the sense that it also protects the time spent together as a family.

Television as a materialised habituation

We have argued that television is accompanied by a high degree of material density and that it is precisely this material and its connections that play an important role in the ontological security of households, since routines do materialise in them. But of course, although various devices can be used to watch television, there are also uses that are limited to a single device. In these cases, too, the social practice of watching television is accompanied by a multitude of choices that come with uncertainties. On which of the devices should television be watched?

This uncertainty is particularly evident in households that do not rely on a permanently installed television set, but on mobile devices that have to be set up repeatedly. These uncertainties and insecurities relate not only to social practice and the processes of negotiation in everyday life, but also, on a larger scale, to the design of the living space. Without the visible and available material of television, some of the people interviewed say they do not know exactly how to furnish their living spaces.

This is the case for Hanna, a 49-year-old woman, who lives alone and watches TV on her laptop every night. To do so, she carries it from the living area to the sleeping area and unfolds it on the bed. Here, as for many other people, the uncertainty is intensified by the temporal detachment from a linear television programme. Hanna watches television "some time in the evening". Since she often works from home, the spheres of work and leisure are hardly separated. This is reinforced by the device on which work emails also pop up when Hanna is watching a series on Netflix.

She tries to deal with this mode of uncertainty by establishing routines. Hanna tries to watch television at about the same time each evening, for example, in order to establish a rhythm, but this only works to a limited extent. While David Gauntlett and Annette Hill, concerning linear television, noted that users oriented their everyday appointments such as dinner to the intrinsic time of the medium of television (Gauntlett/Hill 1999: 23), a contrary observation can be made here. Users of time-flexible content adapt their television consumption to other temporal markers, such as those set by mealtimes and the end of work. However, since these working times are quite flexible, especially for people who work via their laptops and from home, people like Hanna have to make autonomous decisions about how they organise their time, which is something they feel is demanding. This polychronicity has been described elsewhere as one of the challenges facing us right now (see e.g. Neverla/Trümper 2019).

This personal responsibility also relates to the design of living spaces. Without a television set, there seems to be no institutionalised centre with which pieces of furniture can align, and so Hanna describes not knowing where to put her sofa. She has deliberately entered into this uncertainty because it is important to her to also decide against the furnishing paradigms that often go hand in hand with having a television set. She rejects the devices as a status symbol and yet longs for a spatial order that can come with them. This ambivalence of television also relates to the question of what content is considered 'television'. While Hanna grew up with the awareness that television (here in its original one-directional form) is not intellectually demanding and thus a waste of time, she enjoys the series and films from streaming providers, which she perceives as high quality. Although television sets, which are often associated with the past, can also play internet content, Hanna continues to associate the sets with a waste of time and a prestige symbol of a social class to which she does not feel she belongs.

For Hanna, not owning a television is an essential part of ontological security, as it is an important part of her self-conception. Instead of resorting to a device that is important for this one activity of watching television, for her it is about the availability of media content, which the laptop can ensure in its flexibility. Ontological security can thus be found in possession and non-possession alike.

Fig. 4: The laptop, which is used by its owner for work but also for watching television, has not made its way into the furnishings. It is arranged on the bed almost every day (own image).

In this multi-layered uncertainty, she is helped above all by two aspects traditionally associated with television: on the one hand, the live-broadcast-experience and, on the other, watching together with family and friends (Morley 1986). Hence, while she always wonders whether she should really watch the kind of content that she can access flexibly at any time, she can relax particularly well during live broadcasts. On an evening when she watched the live broadcast of a television match, she commented: "That's what we all strive for. To be in the moment, to be in the now, and football is such a catalyst for that feeling, because the players are in the now and the spectators are in the now, and maybe at the same time we are watching history being made."

Hanna does not question the time she spends watching television when she knows about a group of people doing the same. This also applies to the actual presence of people with whom she watches together as illustrated in this extract from a thick description:

Hanna applies different standards to 'watching something' depending on whether she does it alone or with others. She would never see watching programmes together with other people as a waste of time. Anything that is social is viewed positively. When she watches animal films with her parents, she calls it 'nice' and a 'different quality because then you also share it with the others and talk about it'. When she watches something with her partner on Sunday mornings in bed, it is also great to get lost in. Only when she consumes the programmes alone she evaluates how much time she spends on them and how they make her feel. She seems to ask herself at every moment, 'Is this the life I wanted?'.

Significantly, for Hanna and for some of the other interviewees, this shared practice takes place primarily on fixed devices that are not, however, part of their everyday lives. In these fixed settings, they seem to be able to relax particularly well because the communal time runs along fixed and ritualised lines that also have something to do with the set-ups. Even though the constellation with the laptop is a fixed ritual of Hanna's, which also includes other things like her teapot and a cushion that she always fixes in the same way between the wall and her back, the television and the rituals and routines have not manifested themselves spatially or materially. So the set-up has to be done by her anew every evening. This makes television an ambivalent experience for Hanna, because it confronts her – in alignment with communal situations that are also television – with watching mainly alone. By acting against her moral compass, which forbids her to watch alone or to watch television in general, there seems to be a disruption of security.

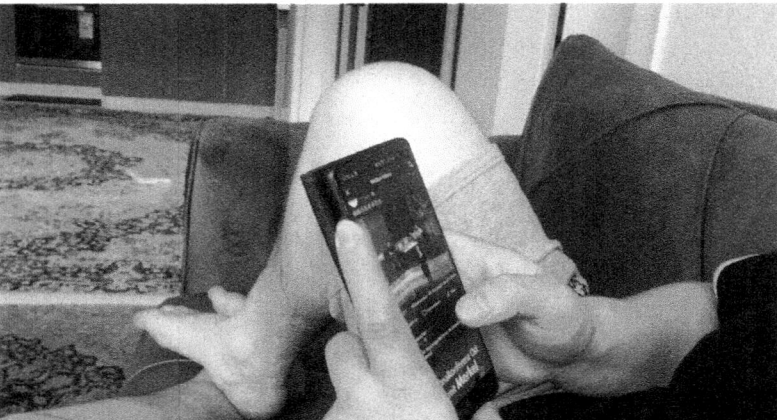

Fig. 5 + 6: For Paul, who watches content exclusively on his smartphone, 'watching TV' both in and out of the living room looks relatively similar. (own images)

In a household where a couple live together in a flat and both watch content exclusively on their smartphones, consumption is highly individualised. Both Paul and Nila are in their mid-20s and are very attached to their devices, which they use to communicate but also serve as their only source of video and film content. While both have an equally close relationship with the devices, the smartphones seem to threaten the processes of the living space at the same time.

Around 7 pm, Paul returns from work as a geriatric nurse. Stepping through the front door, he goes straight to the bathroom to take a shower while his wife Nila spreads a tablecloth on the floor and places plates on it. Paul comes into the room with his smartphone in hand. He talks about work and that he has to leave in a minute, sits down puts the smartphone on his left knee and opens the YouTube app on his smartphone. Nila admonishes her husband with glances. Her own smartphone is out of her reach on the sideboard. Paul scrolls. In between eating, then scrolling again. The YouTube, Facebook and Google apps are opened again and again, but still evoke the same behaviour: Scrolling. When stressed, he says, watching videos quickly on his smartphone calms him down. After eating, Paul goes to the sofa and continues scrolling. Later, we leave the flat together and I accompany him to his second job as a security guard. In the metro he takes out his smartphone again. Watching videos but especially scrolling continues: YouTube, Facebook and Google. There is little difference between his media reception and his sitting position in the flat or while riding the underground.

'Television' is always in Paul's pocket and enables him to withdraw into his own "symbolic space" (van Rompaey/Roe 2001: 356), while the removal of the medium is a source of discomfort for him.

The same is true for his wife, who – if not during meal times – also watches videos on her smartphone. Nevertheless, his watching while eating, which he describes as stress relief, influences the communication in the living room. Nila repeatedly tries to restore order, which she sees in danger because of the smartphone. However, this discussion builds on a power imbalance given that he is the main breadwinner and states that he needs the mobile phone to recover from this work that supports them both financially. These gendered dynamics are an issue in several of the households studied. In this context, (mostly female) parties can be observed who perceive the technological devices as a threat to community and communicative exchange.

Here, the mobility of the device (on the lap while eating, on the road) poses a challenge to the attempt to create device-free time. The moral economy has to balance many things here: questions related to spare time and how to fill it, economic relations, and the idea of quality time. The actually well-distributed access (everyone has theirs) becomes a problem right there, because in contrast to the past, it is not the remote control that is being fought over as the content-determiner, but the time without devices.

Conclusion

In the domestication approach, media technologies were initially understood as a threat to ontological security, because "media disengage the location of action and meaning from experience" (Silverstone/Hirsch/Morley 1992: 20). The media, which came into the domestic sphere as disruptive factors, were to be adapted to the conditions and values of the household, i.e. its moral economy (e.g. Silverstone/Morley/Dahlberg/Livingstone 1989; Silverstone/Hirsch/Morley 1992). At the same time, these negotiation processes were also understood as reciprocal; the household members and the moral economy were also changing in this process of appropriation. Nonetheless, the need to domesticate was seen as a reaction to the wild nature of media technologies in their double articulation: they entered the home as foreign objects with content attached (see e.g. Silverstone 1994). Hence the need to tame, to adapt the technologies (nowadays the 'digital practices', as the title of this special issue suggests) to the culture and values of the households. Eventually, however, the understanding of the domestication process began to shift and media technologies – even if they can still pose a threat and sometimes need to be tamed – were seen to provide the opportunity to potentially provide ontological security to both individuals or groups "wherever they happen to be" (Silverstone 2006: 233). Hence digital media can threaten and provide ontological security at the same time. This (ambivalent) potential has grown as digital media have become increasingly personalised and have allowed the creation of content through users.

While watching television has always been a social practice and has always been based on specific material settings (as well as their enactments), the practice and the context have become more complex and more threatening thanks to the increasing digitalisation. It is a change first of all on a 'quantitative' level: more technological options (especially also in terms of their connectivities), but also a wider set of social practices related to media consumption. While not watching television used to be a possibility for social distinction (e.g. Sicking 2000), this question has become much more complex, as the aforementioned debate on digital detox underlines (e.g. Syvertsen 2020). General disconnection is not a real option but causes another level of ontological (in)security. These range from the infamous FoMo (Fear of Missing Out) to questions of employability and social disconnectivity. As the material presented here has underlined, the domestication question of a moral economy, of internal and external debates surrounding media use, sometimes nonetheless reflects old judgemental schemes (TV is not good for you), while also carrying the just-mentioned weight of negotiations of new versions of ontological (in-)securities.

We are not suggesting that the material set-ups described and analysed above provide the answer to these threats. However, they point to the need to take them into close consideration in the study of domestication processes. Their complexity often provides (and requires) additional layers of appropriation. These additional practices, however, might in and of themselves also provide security. At the same time, they increase the threat of ontological insecurity. Thus they provide routines and visible manifestations of belonging; instead of the above-mentioned (security) blanket, it is now the cable or adapter that signals consistency and the promise of connectivity in the established and well-versed setting. Although they are not desired objects, but rather almost invisible background objects, the materiality of cables and similar technologies inscribes itself into routines so that it sometimes even begins to dominate the social practise of television. This happens, for example, when cables have a shaky contact, and the complete 'television' set-up no longer works. As the examples above have shown, these practices often involve social decisions, i.e., reassurance takes place in negotiations with friends, family, partners. Even in households where two people have different media routines, their understanding thereof and reference to each other reinforces their position. The question of disconnectivity and the inability to 'solve' the perceived dependence through this, simply underlines the power of a new practice of 'television': a practice that is both old and new. As we have seen, it often adheres to outdated practices, 'pretending' that it is still television 'as we know it'. In order to keep up this illusion, many steps are taken and particular materialities established. This is a form of externalisation, as Brause and Blank (2020) called it, where the domestication of one device (or related paraphernalia) always has to been seen in relation to the domestication of other devices. This is the point where stability and instability meet; the new materialities, thanks to their networked nature, are rather fragile and do not always work as planned. At the same time, they offer a sense of a long-established practice, thereby increasing the sense of the already-known, the familiar. The tension between the old and the new constitutes the challenge to domestication that will probably accompany many technologies yet to come.

References

Agius, Christine/Bergman Rosamond, Annika/Kinnvall, Catarina (2020): "Populism, Ontological Insecurity and Gendered Nationalism: Masculinity, Climate Denial and Covid-19." In: Politics, Religion & Ideology 21/4, pp. 432-450.

Bausinger, Hermann (1984) [1983]: "Media, Technology and Daily Life.' In: Media, Culture & Society 6/4, pp. 343-351.

Bausinger, Herrmann (1983): "Alltag, Technik, Medien." In: Pross, Harry/Rath, Claus-Dieter (eds), Rituale der Medienkommunikation. Gänge durch den Medienalltag, Berlin: Guttandin & Hoppe, pp. 24-36.

Berker, Thomas/Hartmann, Maren/Punie, Yves/Ward, Katie J. (eds.) (2006): Domestication of Media and Technology, New York: Berkshire.

Brause, Saba Rebecca/Blank, Grant (2020): "Externalized Domestication: Smart Speaker Assistants, Networks and Domestication Theory." In: Information, Communication & Society 23/5, pp. 751-763. Doi:10.1080/1369118X.2020.1713845

Browning, Christopher S. (2018): "'Brexit.' Existential Anxiety and Ontological (In)security." In: European Security 27/3, pp. 336-355.
Feenberg, Andrew (1999): Questioning Technology, London: Routledge.
Gauntlett, David/Hill, Annette (1999): TV Living. Television, Culture and Everyday Life, London: Routledge.
Giddens, Anthony (1984): The Constitution of Society, Cambridge: Polity Press.
Haddon, Leslie (1988): "The Home Computer: The Making of a Consumer Electronic." In: Science as Culture 1/2, pp. 7-51.
Hartmann, Maren (2008): "Domestizierung 2.0: Grenzen und Chancen eines Medienaneignungskonzeptes." In: Winter, Carsten/Hepp, Andreas/Krotz, Friedrich (eds.), Theorien der Kommunikations- und Medienwissenschaft. Grundlegende Diskussionen, Forschungsfelder und Theorieentwicklungen, Wiesbaden: VS Verlag, pp. 401-416.
Hartmann, Maren (2020): "(The Domestication of) Nordic Domestication?" In: Nordic Journal of Media Studies 2/1, pp. 47-57.
Hartmann, Maren (ed.) (2023): The Routledge Handbook of Media and Technology Domestication. London: Routledge.
Hasebrink, Uwe (2002): "Modi linearer und nicht-linearer Fernsehnutzung." In: medien & zeit. Kommunikation in Vergangenheit und Gegenwart 27/2, pp. 44-52.
Huang, Ying/Miao, Weishan (2020): "Re-domesticating Social Media When It Becomes Disruptive: Evidence From China's 'Super App' WeChat." In: Mobile Media & Communication 9/2, pp. 177-194.
Klocke, Vera: unpublished manuscript.
Latour, Bruno (2000): Die Hoffnung der Pandora. Untersuchungen zur Wirklichkeit der Wissenschaft, Frankfurt am Main: Suhrkamp.
Livingstone, Sonia (2007): "On the material and the symbolic: Silverstones doppelte Artikulation von Forschungstraditionen in den New Media Studies." In: Neue Medien & Gesellschaft 9/1, pp. 16-24.
Lull, James (1991): Television, Reform and Resistance, London: Routledge.
Markham, Annette (2020): The Ontological Insecurity of Disconnecting – A Theory of Echolocation and the Self. https://www.academia.edu/44577011/The_Ontological_Insecurity_of_Disconnecting_A_Theory_of_Echolocation_and_the_Self (accessed 06/04/2022)
McCarthy, Anna (2001): Ambient Television: Visual Culture and Public Space, Durham: Duke University Press.
Miller, Daniel (2008): The Comfort of Things, Cambridge: Polity Press.
Morley, David (1990): "Domestic Communication - Technologies and Meanings." In: Media, Culture and Society 12, pp. 31-55.
Morley, David (1986): Family Television. Cultural Power and Domestic Leisure, London: Comedia Publishing Group.

Morley, David (2006): "Television. Not So Much a Visual Medium, More a Visible Object." In: Chris Jenks (ed.), Visual Culture, Reprint, London: Routledge, pp.170-189.

Neverla, Irene/Trümper, Stefanie (2019): "As Time Goes By: Tracking Polychronic Temporalities in Journalism and Mediated Memory." In: Maren Hartmann/Elizabeth Prommer/Karin Deckner/Stephan Görland (eds.), Mediated Time, Cham: Palgrave Macmillan, pp. 219-236.

Peil, Corinna (2011): Mobile Communication in Japan. On the Cultural Infrastructure of Mobile Phone Appropriation, Bielefeld: Transcript.

Peil, Corinna/Sparviero, Sergio (2017): "Media Convergence Meets Deconvergence." In: Sergio Sparviero/Corinna Peil/Gabriele Balbi (eds.), Media Convergence and Deconvergence, Basingstoke: Palgrave Macmillan, pp. 3-30.

Pink, Sarah (2004): Home Truths: Gender, Domestic Objects and Everyday Life, Oxford: Berg.

Quandt, Thorsten/von Pape, Thilo (2010): "Living in the Mediatope: A Multimethod Study on the Evolution of Media Technologies in the Domestic Environment." In: The Information Society 26/5, pp. 330-345.

Röser, Jutta/Müller, Kathrin Friederike/Niemand, Stephan/Roth, Ulrike (2019): Das mediatisierte Zuhause im Wandel. Eine qualitative Panelstudie zur Verhäuslichung des Internets, Wiesbaden: Springer VS.

Sicking, Peter (2000): Leben ohne Fernsehen, Wiesbaden: DUV.

Silverstone, Roger/Morley, David/Dahlberg, Andrea/Livingstone, Sonia (1989): Families, Technologies and Consumption: the Household and Information and Communication Technologies. CRICT discussion paper, Centre for Research into Innovation, Culture & Technology, Brunel University. available at http://eprints.lse.ac.uk/46657/

Silverstone, Roger/Hirsch, Eric/Morley, David (1992): "Information and Communication Technologies and the Moral Economy of the Household." In: Roger Silverstone/Eric Hirsch (eds.), Consuming Technologies: Media and Information in Domestic Spaces, London: Routledge, pp. 15-31.

Silverstone, Roger (1994): Television and Everyday Life, London: Routledge.

Silverstone, Roger (2006): "Domesticating Domestication: Reflections on the Life of a Concept." In: Thomas Berker/Maren Hartmann/Yves Punie/Katie J. Ward (eds.), The Domestication of Media and Technology, Maidenhead: Open University Press, pp. 229-248.

Syvertsen, Trine (2020): Digital Detox: The Politics of Disconnecting, Bingley: Emerald.

Treré, Emiliano/Natale, Simone/Keightley, Emily (2020): "The Limits and Boundaries of Digital Disconnection." In: Media, Culture and Society 42/4, pp. 605-609.

van Rompaey, Veerle/Roe, Keith (2001): "The Home as a Multimedia Environment: Families' Conception of Space and the Introduction of Information and

Communication Technologies in the Home." In: Communications 26/4, pp. 351-370.

Winicott, Donald Woods (1953): "Transitional Objects and Transitional Phenomena." In: International Journal of Psychoanalysis 34/2, pp. 89-97.

Winther, Tanja/Bell, Sandra (2018): "Domesticating In Home Displays in Selected British and Norwegian Households." In: Science & Technology Studies 31/2, pp. 19-38.

Wright, Katharine A. M./Haastrup, Toni/Guerrina, Roberta (2021): "Ontological (In)security and Covid-19: Reimagining Crisis Leadership in UK Higher Education." In: Critical Studies on Security 9/2, pp. 171-178.

Cyborg Cooks: Mothers and the Anthropology of Smart Kitchens

Katharina Graf

Abstract

Future kitchens are increasingly imagined as smart. Wired food processors offer a choice of recipes and prepare food for busy cooks while smartphones or intelligent fridges promise to shop online autonomously. Whatever the futuristic image, so-called "smart technology" is depicted as rescuing domestic cooks too busy or inexperienced to cook. Social anthropology is suspicious of such one-directional and hegemonic visions of technological impact on everyday life and ideally positioned to explore the entanglements of social, cultural, economic and political dimensions in increasingly digitally mediated human-machine interactions in the home. Yet, an ethnographic understanding of how humans and kitchen technologies interact in this rapidly changing context is surprisingly scarce. In this research paper I address this gap from an anthropological perspective on domestic food practices in urban and rural Germany through the feminist notion of the cyborg cook. In doing so, I engage with and challenge the above futurist visions as well as scholarly debates around the smart home and the domestication of digital technologies. I draw on multisensory participant observation of domestic cooks' interactions with the digital kitchen robot Thermomix to demonstrate that smart kitchens are already a reality and that cyborg cooks are firmly established among us. I argue that especially mothers should be considered as early adopters of digital technologies in diverse domestic kitchens and contest the assumptions in futurist visions and in the literature that women, including those from cultural or class minorities, are tech-averse marginal users.

Keywords

domestic cooking; smart home; digital kitchen technologies; feminist technology studies; Germany

Introduction

"The kitchen is dead" a much-cited report recently declared (Jo at Cookpad 2018), stating that cooking robots and app-controlled delivery services predestine us to a kitchen-free future. In fact, as an architect argues in a Swiss report about kitchens, "we ought to be glad that kitchens are still built at all" (Vollenweider 2006, author's translation). Others argue that kitchens are morphing into new status symbols (Rützler/Reiter 2017): such "hell's kitchen[s]" are becoming ever bigger and high-tech, yet often unfit for "real" cooking (Matzig 2016). Yet others assume that future domestic cooks, who grow up using digital technologies, will re-centre their social life around the smart kitchen (GfK 2017: 91-102). According to these visions of designers and marketers, app-controlled smart fridges assist the cook in ordering food while connected food processors empower him or her to quickly prepare elaborate dishes from scratch. Whatever the futuristic image, so-called "smart technology" is invariably depicted as coming to the rescue of domestic cooks who are too busy or inexperienced to cook. Social anthropologists are suspicious of such one-directional visions of technological impact on everyday life and ideally positioned to explore the complex entanglements of cultural, economic and political dimensions in human-machine interaction in the domestic kitchen, an interaction which is increasingly digitally mediated.

The research project upon which this paper is based is an ethnographic study of how digitally assisted cooks actually cook in what could be called the digital age: a time that is marked – but not necessarily determined – by a growing presence of digital technologies, virtual connectivity and a perceived acceleration of life (Wajcman 2015; Koch 2017). While the knowledge of nutrients in food, of beneficial and detrimental diets, or of how consumer choices reflect social status is growing steadily, there is scarcely an anthropological understanding of how cooks know how to cook in this rapidly changing context (Sutton 2016). This gap is especially noticeable in Germany (Leonhäuser et al. 2009: 28-35; Barlösius 2016: 30-31). At the same time, Germany has been at the forefront of scientific and technological development in food for more than a century and is reputed globally for producing a vast range of household appliances, increasingly including digital ones, and is changing domestic cooking worldwide. This paper is motivated by exploring this double tension between futuristic visions of food preparation and everyday experience on the one hand, and between global reputation and domestic practice in Germany on the other. Like other feminist scholars studying technology and everyday life, I seek to "question this implicit division between cutting-edge technologies and existing technologies, the spectacular and the ordinary" (Wajcman 2015: 3) through an ethnographic lens.

More recent domestication theory provides a useful starting point for describing the use of and interaction with digital technologies in the home, for instance, in tracing the negotiations between people and things as households rework their "sense of self" (Silverstone 2006: 236f) and the role of "warm experts" in collaboratively producing knowledge that straddles the bodily and the digital (Bakardjieva 2005: 98f); I also challenge this concept and the conclusions that especially scholars of the smart home are making. In particular, and in contrast to the other contributions to this special issue, this paper questions the basic tenet of domestication theory, namely, that users of (digital) technology are separate entities in the daily practices of engaging with it. I do so through introducing the notion of the "cyborg cook". Since cyborgs are part human and part machine, and because they have been a productive element in feminist critiques of technoscientific processes and debates, they help me do two things in this paper. First, to study how cyborg cooks defy boundaries of any kind and highlight the connections between people and things, between humans and machines. Second, because of that, to challenge the conclusion of smart home scholars that the digitally connected home is increasingly male-dominated (Chambers 2016: 167; Strengers/Kennedy 2021; Kryger Aagaard 2022).

Combining a phenomenological approach with a materialist understanding of human-machine collaboration, in the first section I will introduce my research design, asking how humans and digital technologies interact in contemporary kitchens in Germany. My multi-sensory immersion in what I call everyday cyborg practices seeks to overcome the above-mentioned double tension. Based on the thick description of human-machine interaction in domestic kitchens, in the second section I will then conceptualise domestic cooks as cyborgs, a "cybernetic organism, a hybrid of machine and organism, a creature of social reality as well as a creature of fiction" (Haraway 1991: 149). Thus, when sourcing, processing, preparing, serving and disposing of food with tools, a cook becomes more than human (and always has been): a cyborg cook. At a time when human-machine interactions are increasingly digitally mediated, this feminist concept is well suited to consider bodily and digital knowledge as equally constitutive elements of domestic food practices. In the third section, which dissects the continuous gendering of domestic food work, I will continue to describe cyborg cooks in interaction with digital kitchen robots to illustrate that smart kitchens are already more reality than fiction. I demonstrate that mothers in particular are not marginal users of smart home technologies but should instead be considered as early adopters. In the final section on diverse kitchens, I will address some of the intersectional power relations in futurist visions around cooking and built into digital technologies, and advocate for diversifying our understanding of contemporary smart kitchens. I will conclude with a call for more immersive ethnographic attention to everyday cyborg practices.

Research Gaps and Research Design: Studying Cyborg Practices

Until now, food research in Germany has focused largely on verbal data gathered via interviews (e.g., Leonhäuser et al. 2009; Häußler/Meier-Gräwe 2012; Brombach 2017; Klünder 2020) or on survey-style consumer research which relies mainly on recall studies (Max Rubner-Institut 2008; Gose et al. 2016). However, interviews alone can neither capture everyday practices and non-verbal aspects of cooking adequately, nor can they account for the growing role that non-human actors, especially widespread digital technologies such as kitchen robots or smartphones, have in domestic food work. Although some smaller, isolated studies explore the use of smartphone apps for dieting (Kofahl 2016), online shopping (Klyanitskiy 2018) or digital provisioning (Cajic/Brückner/Brettin 2021), to date no published research seems to focus ethnographically on the use of digital technologies in everyday food preparation in Germany. This stands in contrast to the fast-growing ethnographic attention to digital food practices in largely anglophone contexts (e.g., Rodney et al. 2017; Lewis 2020; Schneider/Eli 2021). To address this gap in the German context, I am relying on anthropological approaches to embodied knowledge, especially around food, which are inspired by phenomenology, and which examine concretely how humans and non-humans collaborate in making food. As the short overview below suggests, this body of research questions and widens the human-centric understanding of experience as proposed in earlier research on lived experience and practical knowledge. At the same time, such materialist approaches to food still understand lived experience as the basis upon which thinking and knowing is premised.

Inspired by Tim Ingold's (2011[2000]) work on bodily skill and ways of knowing, food anthropologists such as David Sutton (2014) highlight the sensory and non-verbal dimensions of practical ways of knowing without neglecting the social and symbolic dimensions of bodily knowledge. This ethnographic work draws on the phenomenological premise that doing and knowing are one and the same thing in everyday practices such as cooking (Merleau-Ponty 2001[1945]). By attending not only to the bodily knowledge of humans but also to the constitution of more-than-human interactions, more materialist food scholars demonstrate further that food work and eating necessarily straddle the boundaries between human and non-human, and between organic and non-organic (e.g., Paxson 2013; Abbots 2017; Elton 2019). Similarly, my research focuses on boundary-crossing practices within more-than-human environments which increasingly include digital technologies. This theoretical and methodological approach thus goes beyond the implicit emphasis on the narratives and discourses that are centred in interview-based research, and even beyond observation and a form of participation that is premised on the visual (Graf 2022). I expressly also rely on my multi-sensory experience of human-machine interactions across everyday life both online and offline, something which I call cyborg practices.

Concretely, since early 2022 and probably lasting until early 2024, I have been joining the daily cyborg practices in ten diverse kitchens in urban and rural homes in western Germany; these visits have been complemented by interviews in the kitchens of another ten households as well as expert interviews with market and trend researchers, software engineers, policy makers and online influencers across Germany, Austria and Switzerland.[1] Concerning the choice of households, diversity means a number of things for reasons that will also be explained throughout the paper. First, as the notion of cyborg practices highlights, I engage with all actors in the making of a meal, including machines, algorithms and the food itself. Social and cultural diversity also matter. Those ten households that allowed me to join through participant observation are spread across all income groups; half have children, and the other half are single- or two-person households. Most of the households include members with a background in migration, sometimes with a distinct ethnic identity and distinct cultural food practices. I have also been working with households of minority sexual and gender identities, households that are strikingly absent in representative studies around food and the home in Germany. Of course, different forms of diversity intersect among my research participants, each combining into unique cyborg practices that should be understood more as portraits of a diverse society rather than as strictly representative samples.

Through the ethnographic focus on experiences, rather than on public or private discourses, and on ordinary but diverse kitchens, rather than imagined ones, the study of cyborg practices allows to bridge the double tension between futuristic visions of cooking and the global reputation of German domestic technology on the one hand, and between everyday experience and domestic space on the other.

Furthermore, by focusing on the interaction between humans and machines in everyday contexts, I consider bodily and digital knowledge as equally constitutive elements of cooking practice and thereby unravel the "smartness" of digital technologies in daily life. As I will show, bodily and digital practices combine in the interaction with digital kitchen robots that take over key tasks of processing and cooking food, but also in algorithms embedded in smartphone apps that conveniently propose recipes, ingredients or takeaway meals to the domestic cook and predict future shopping or cooking practices. Needless to say, my research has revealed that certain humans or machines also resist interaction. To that end, I work not only with households that own a digital kitchen robot, but also with those that do not. In either case the question is no longer simply what happens to

---

1   The sampling of participating households was not limited to pre-determined locations but rather based on reachability from Frankfurt/Main to allow for repeated visits; two-hour train rides one-way being the upper limit. Households are based in three *Bundesländer*: Hesse, Rhineland-Palatinate and North Rhine-Westphalia.

the embodied knowledge of domestic cooks with the rise of so-called intelligent kitchen appliances, smart kitchens or app-controlled food deliveries. Rather, as I will demonstrate in the following section, different forms of knowledge interact and mutually stimulate or inhibit one another in everyday cooking.

The Ethnography of Cyborg Cooks and Feminist STS

The first ethnographic case I would like to present here is that of Inge. Inge[2] is a mother of three and married to Marco, a second-generation German Italian. Although her own Latin American roots figured prominently in our conversations, Marco's food heritage was much more dominant in this middle-class family's everyday foodways. This impact became tangible one day when Inge prepared pizza, a weekly staple food in her household. When I arrived around noon on a regular weekday in spring 2022, she informed me that she had already prepared the dough in her Thermomix Model TM6 (elsewhere in Europe known as Bimby), a digital kitchen robot made by the German firm Vorwerk that not only blends and kneads ingredients but also weighs, grinds, chops, ferments, cooks or steams food.[3] Cooking with it is described as guided cooking because, via the integrated screen, the digital assistant tells the cook what to do step by step (see figure 1) according to a recipe chosen from among thousands of options. Inge explained that since she had not managed to make pizza the previous weekend, her children were increasingly impatient to eat it and she had to prepare it on this weekday instead. Preparing food with the Thermomix, as she did multiple times every day, did not feel like it infringed upon her part-time wage work, Inge told me. It allowed her to continue working or do other things while the machine worked for her. Since she had tried and tested this recipe so many times, she knew exactly how to make it; where to follow and where to divert from the machine's guided cooking to achieve the right kind of dough.

We went into the kitchen, and she began to process the leavened dough; portioning it with her hands she worried that it was much smaller than usual. Then, Inge told me that neither her husband, nor her eldest and youngest children would join us: "It will be just Christiano [her 8-year-old son], you and me." This would make things easy, she rejoiced, as three pizzas could be more easily moved around the oven to bake each to the perfect level of crispness. It also meant she could use mozzarella cheese, which her lactose-intolerant husband would not eat. As she continued to flatten the dough with a rolling pin, she explained that her husband, who used to assemble and knead the pizza dough before they owned the

---

2   Pseudonyms are used and household details anonymised throughout this paper when requested by research participants.
3   For more information, please visit the Thermomix website: https://www.thermomix.com/tm6/ (last access: 30/11/2022).

Thermomix, had identified semolina blended with normal white flour as the ideal combination to shape the dough. Assuring herself that I liked it, too, Inge decided to use canned tuna as a topping besides tomato puree and cheese, and, while rubbing her belly, that she would also prepare rocket lettuce and cherry tomatoes for the two of us, "to make it lighter and help digesting". Although worried that the pizza would not be as good as usual as it had leavened for only about one hour, Inge was pleased with the result.

Fig. 1: *Interacting with the Thermomix (photograph by the author)*

The making of this meal bespeaks the ordinary cyborgness of contemporary cooks. To argue with domestication theorists, it involves negotiations of a new "sense of self" of the people and things of a household within a larger sociotechnical frame of values, something that Roger Silverstone and his colleagues described as the "moral economy of the household" (2006: 236f). Inge is given a choice of recipes coded by software engineers to work with this machine but improves or adapts it according to her own embodied knowledge and the preferences or needs of each family member for any given meal. She incorporates the digital sensors of the machine to measure the ingredients, relies on its motor to work the heavy dough but employs her bodily feeling for the yeast when deciding to portion and roll the pizza base. Moreover, her husband's skills have become a part of Inge's; her children's and guest's taste preferences are reflected in the meal choice and the pizza topping. If attending carefully to the described scene – to the multiple technologies, practices and bodies that make this particular meal on that particular day – it is soon clear that they all are protagonists; and there are many more that cannot be mentioned here.

I offer this case to argue that domestic cooks cannot be (and never should have been) considered as bounded individuals, but are rather composed of a complex material and social web of technologies, practices and bodies, better described as cyborg cooks. Cyborgs cooks are part human and part machine, they "live between the material and the digital. Their selves extend beyond the boundaries of physical bodies, their sensory capacity and ways of knowing about the world blinking across handheld devices and wireless networks, flickering as avatars, photographs..." (Hartblay 2018: no page). In short, cyborg cooks are no longer fiction but very tangible creatures inhabiting contemporary kitchens in Germany and elsewhere (Truninger 2011; Ascione 2014). In meshing bodily engagement with the artificial intelligence of the tool, cyborg practices are creating entirely new forms of knowledge in increasingly smart kitchens, while society fails (or refuses?) to notice them.

Early on, feminist historians of technology revealed the gap or tension between futuristic visions and everyday experiences concerning domestic technological development and challenged the widespread notion of technological determinism. Ruth Schwartz Cowan's (1983) study shows how the introduction of electric kitchen technologies in ordinary homes during 20th century America – hailed as facilitating and speeding up domestic tasks – reorganised women's domestic work rather than reducing it. This reorganisation was due mainly to two things: first, to the shift from largely subsistence economies centred around joint family labour in the home, garden and field to more urban market economies centred around predominantly male wage work outside the home throughout the 19th century; second, to servants and children no longer contributing significantly to domestic work for a number of reasons. Thus, while men and children worked less in the home, women ended up working more. Other scholars show that while new kitchen technologies were marketed as intelligent machines taking over most work, this marketing wrongly suggests that all a female cook has to do is press buttons and set timers. An analysis of instruction manuals for microwave ovens shows that a cook still relies on bodily knowledge to assess the size, cut and shape of meat in order to use the machine successfully (Silva 2000; see also Cockburn/ Ormrod 1993; Graf 2022). Chiming in with a growing scholarly interest in (digital) science and technology in everyday life (Beck 1997; Bakardjieva 2005; Michael 2006), these studies and the cases of Inge and other domestic cooks I have been working with demonstrate how technological developments, including failure or redefinition are less a total institution than part of a complex socio-technical system, whereby technology and cultural, economic and political processes mutually shape each other in everyday life. These transformations are negotiated with a household's "sense of self that could be justified, more or less, with respect to traditions and the articulation of value" (Silverstone 2006: 236).

Yet, much as they have been doing so for more than 150 years, the futurist visions of the smart home and kitchen still promise a cook's liberation from the drudgery of daily food work through intelligent appliances (Berg 1999; Wajcman 2015; Strengers/Kennedy 2021). The marketing of the "smart" kitchen and the simplistic vision depicted above can thus be considered the latest reincarnation of technological determinism. Although such visions create aspirations and move people, they do so in often unpredictable and non-linear ways and involve users and non-users alike (Pinch/Bijker 1984; Nickles 2002; Truninger 2011). The case of Inge shows that it becomes increasingly difficult, even futile, to determine who the cook is as digital kitchen robots and so-called "guided cooking" enter domestic kitchens.

Domestic cooks are not simply users of digital technologies but become cyborgs in both interacting and collaborating with their digital kitchen technologies to achieve a certain result based on a bodily and shared taste knowledge of what is considered to be a good meal (Graf 2022). In other words, cyborg cooks combine bodily and digital ways of knowing and achieve more-than-human or superhuman abilities in doing so. These cyborg practices do not necessarily alter existing ways of processing or handling food. For instance, Inge and other cooks I have been working with learned to use digital kitchen robots to make the meals they had previously prepared but saving themselves some of the physical labour and reducing the uncertainty of success. Although the Thermomix TM6 has a programming function to adapt or create one's own recipes, my research participants simply remembered the little steps of deviation from a pre-programmed recipe such as replacing an ingredient, adapting quantities or using a certain function or step for a different dish. Equally, the touch, smell or sound of food as it transforms into a meal were combined with the digital sensors of the machine to increase accuracy and reliability.

But algorithms and codes also create new forms of knowledge. The algorithms in recipe apps such as Vorwerk's Cookidoo or Whisk helped my research participants get new ideas that matched their interests, taste preferences or levels of skill. Shopping apps speed up online shopping or the selection of a meal each time a cook uses a digital service to order food or a meal. Thus, knowledge and convenience are collaboratively achieved between humans and machines. Just as cyborg cooks learn more with each meal planned, processed, prepared and eaten, so do the algorithms that track their choices and digital practices. While the public rightly calls for more critical scrutiny of "food codes" and demands more regulation in digital realms around food production, distribution and consumption (Deiniger/Haase 2021), I propose instead to study the broader "algorithmic systems", the "intricate, dynamic arrangements of people and code" (Seaver 2019: 419). Based on his anthropological foray into music recommendation algorithms, Nick Seaver cautions us against black boxing codes and algorithms as untransparent and dangerous. Focusing on algorithmic systems as heterogenous sociotechnical systems allows us to understand the dynamic and imprecise nature of what are often informal ad-hoc processes.

Thus, as algorithms are fed more digital data with each interaction, ethnographic attention is required to study how algorithms contribute to shaping cyborg practices and a cyborg cook's engagement with new forms of knowledge. At this stage of my research, it is yet too early to say how algorithms and the assumptions made by app developers and software programmers around consumers and their needs or preferences are built into cooking apps or kitchen robots. Given the messiness of everyday life, the context specific human-machine interactions and the recurrent imperfections and glitches that inevitably accompany the incorporation of new technology in everyday life as I will show below, I would be careful to assume that smart kitchen technologies simply work. Without wanting to dismiss the legitimate warnings about the commoditisation of digital food data or of "Big Mother" in increasingly smart homes (Lewis 2020: 171; Sadowski/Strengers/Kennedy 2021: 8), I doubt that digital kitchen technologies like smart fridges or cooking robots will collect complete or even legible data about domestic food practices, and that this data in turn allows software engineers or marketers to draw straightforward conclusions. I also suggest that we take seriously and try to understand why so many domestic cooks do not perceive their digital food practices as risky or problematic.

Nevertheless, it is clear that the technoscience that informs, creates and enables digital kitchen technologies is biased by gender, class and/or race, as Yolande Strengers and Jenny Kennedy (2021) show with respect to smart home voice assistants such as Alexa or Google Home. Thus, although the notion of the cyborg cook seeks to undo various boundaries and instead highlights interactions as well as (dis)connections, studying how people and code interact in cooking still requires attending to the multiple power relations underlying digital domestic practices similar to Haraway's feminist notion of the cyborg.

Cooking Mothers: Marginal Users or High-tech Superhumans?

The scholarship on food and cooking is fairly united in arguing that today's cook is still predominantly female, and likely a mother (e.g., Glucksman/Nolan 2007; Cairns/Johnston 2015; Bowen/Brenton/Elliott 2019). Despite the domestic science movement and a modernist intervention in domestic design a century ago, both of which have been contributing to transforming practices and perceptions around domestic labour until today – if not to altering the underlying values associated with the home as I pointed out above – women remain responsible for domestic cooking across cultures and continents. This also seems to hold true in digitally assisted cooking (Lewis 2020: 107, 116). Contemporary cooks in Germany are no exception (e.g., Leonhäuser et al. 2009; Häußler/Meier-Gräwe 2012; Brombach 2017): Despite women's education, wage work and various reform movements, everyday cooking remains largely a mother's work. Men cook mostly for leisure during weekends or as professionals (e.g., Frerichs/Steinrücke 1997; Baum 2012; Ray 2016). Importantly, as this and the next section will show, mothers, with their detailed knowledge of food and the wider material and social context within which it is prepared, remain expert practitioners even as digital cooking robots are taking over some of their work.

While this overview suggests a saturated research field, the gender, ethnicity and class of cooking in Germany are less well studied, certainly with regards to digital kitchen technologies. In contrast to the doubly burdened female cook described in the above-mentioned literature, the 21st century cook circulating in the German imagination is a digital native who relies on a smartphone app to order dinner via drone delivery, asks her intelligent fridge to replenish her stocks via online shopping or downloads a recipe onto his wired food processor to cook from scratch (GfK 2017). According to market research, the generations of Millennials and iBrains (ibid.) who grew up using digital communication technologies are keen to depart from "conventional" cooking and harness new technologies to cook. This one-directional vision is problematic on at least two accounts. First, by omitting the question of who the future high-tech loving cook is, it remains blind to questions of gender, age, class, race and ethnicity and thus for social inequality and the uneven distribution of digital literacy as highlighted in the contributions by Weibert et al. and Kucharski/Merkel to this volume. Second, by assuming the use of digital communication technologies is directly translatable into the use of digital technologies for cooking, it disrespects the context-specific socio-material construction of scientific knowledge and technologies and the complex entanglements of cultural, economic and political dimensions of their (dis/mis)uses. Even more problematically, it hides from view those who make sci-fi happen every day in their kitchens.

To begin with – and perhaps not surprisingly –, in the households examined, women, especially mothers, remain responsible for and carry out most routine domestic food work, certainly during the working week from Monday to Friday. This holds true across socio-economic and cultural backgrounds and irrespective of the specific food practices. What might seem more surprising, though, is that the women in my study are more avidly acquiring and interacting with digital kitchen technologies than men. Whereas most male domestic cooks in both family and single-person households highlighted the use of their hands and bodies in our interviews and often explicitly rejected digital technologies when planning, processing and/or preparing food, mothers in particular emphasised that digital technologies saved them time and effort in what they perceived as often stressful everyday routines. Although I also study the widespread use of smartphones and apps in this context, in the following I remain focused on digital kitchen robots like the Thermomix. Indeed, many women recounted how they had acquired a kitchen robot when having their first child in order to "free the hands", as Anna, a representative and self-employed saleswoman of the Thermomix and a mother herself, confirmed in an interview.

What is more, when owning a digital kitchen robot, women cook more – a finding that resonates with Cowan's argument from nearly 40 years ago. Inge's ambivalent conclusion during one of our conversations sums up a trend that other interviews confirm: "It's funny, I don't cook less since we have owned the Thermomix, I cook more!" Inge used the example of making pizza and pasta dough as a prime example of this: "Before we had the Thermomix, Marco used to knead the dough, it's hard work. But now the Thermomix does this work, so Marco no longer makes any dough at all." Crucially, her husband also no longer does the work around dough-based meals such as shaping, portioning or processing it, none of which can be done with a kitchen robot and which is now done by Inge. Just as older domestic technologies like the microwave were touted to liberate women from the drudgery of daily food work, digital kitchen robots similarly reorganise previously complementary gendered work in the home, while standards of hygiene and appreciation of homemade foods rise simultaneously, leading to less work for men but "more work for mother" (Cowan 1983). On the one hand, my female research participants all emphasised how the robot saved them time and physical effort. On the other hand, they also reported to be spending more time cooking than they did before owning it, because the machine provides them with the possibility of doing so. This is due to both a longstanding emphasis of eating together in family households in Germany (Mintel 2005; Brombach 2017) and a renewed valuation of homemade foods and homecooked meals across middle-class Germany and other highly industrialised countries, a renewal that emerged with the onset of the Covid-19 pandemic in spring 2020. Once again, for better or worse, mothers end up working more to feed their families.

But I also want to propose an important positive spin to this finding, one that moves on from Cowan's pessimistic portrayal of middle-class mothers tricked into more domestic work by advancing a more experience-based vision of mothers as high-tech and more-than-human cyborgs. Thus, although the domestic media practices of mothers are often hidden from sight, they are anything but marginal as Chambers (2016) or Strengers/Kennedy (2021) suggest. Rather, I argue that especially female domestic cooks should be considered as early adopters or heavy users of digital technologies.

The decision to explore, buy and interact with a digital kitchen robot in all of the households I have worked with and that own a digital kitchen robot (nine out of seventeen households interviewed and visited at the time of writing), was made by women, often against their partner's explicit scepticism. Anna, the Thermomix saleswoman, confirmed that in the vast majority of cases her female clients use her cooking demonstrations – the standard way of selling the Thermomix/Bimby in Europe (Truninger 2011; Ascione 2014) – to convince their husbands to make the investment of ca. €1,300. Women also install and maintain their Thermomix and solve problems related to it, often with the help of the saleswoman who sold them the machine in the first place and who stays in touch with most of her clients via social media. Thermomix saleswomen are frequently friends or relatives and could be considered as "warm expert[s]" who "mediate[s] between the technological universal and the concrete situation" (Bakardjieva 2005: 99). Indeed, the entire marketing structure and after-sales service around the Thermomix is largely in the hands of women, who are bonding through friendship and mutual trust (and defy standard marketing procedures based on one-click online purchases, remote customer services and planned obsolescence).

Cyborg practices involving the Thermomix – though perhaps less so the more conventionally marketed comparable kitchen robots – are thus challenging the commonplace assumptions and depictions of women, especially mothers, as tech-averse and dependent on their male counterparts to envision, set up and maintain a smart kitchen. On the contrary, my research suggests that kitchens in Germany are already smart and female cyborg cooks are firmly established among us. However, their needs and ideas for adequate technologies are rarely addressed in designing and marketing futurist visions of the smart home and kitchen: men have been and still are leading the technical and academic work on smart home technologies (Strengers/Kennedy 2021: 9). It is to the aspect of diversity when imagining the smart home and kitchen that I will turn to in the following.

Disconnected Cyborgs: Diversifying the Smart Kitchen

While advocating for the cyborgness of female cooks in what are already smart kitchens, it is equally important to highlight the intersectional power relations inherent in digital technologies and how they affect who can become a cyborg and under what conditions. The case of Diana is illustrative. A mother of German origin with two young children, married to a second-generation German Moroccan man, she is what could be called a reluctant cyborg. Her mother-in-law gifted her the latest Thermomix model in early summer 2022 "to finally learn how to cook Moroccan food for the family" as Diana recounted somewhat wearily during our interview in her home at the end of summer. Although keen to use it, within those months she had used the robot only occasionally and so far not with great satisfaction or success. She had just started to work part-time again and wondered when she would find the time to learn how to use it. She felt the gifted machine ought to be used "since it is so expensive and I do want to learn to make Moroccan meals". She had not yet benefitted from a personalised cooking demonstration, because her mother-in-law had purchased the machine via her sister-in-law, thus distancing the usual direct contact between customer and saleswoman; she lacked a "warm expert" (Bakardjieva 2005). In this lower middle-class household, forced to move to a cheaper neighbourhood outside of Frankfurt after the birth of their children and stuck with a kitchen that Diana repeatedly complained was too small, the Thermomix occupied the only free counter space and appeared quite out of place (figure 2). Indeed, although the Thermomix is also being marketed to lower-income households through various payment schemes, including the option to receive the robot for free if selling it to four other households, in Germany it targets largely white, middle-class consumers who are more likely to be connected to warm experts.

Fig. 2: *Covered Thermomix on reduced countertop space (photograph by the author)*

Furthermore, Diana was surprised to find no suitable recipes when searching for typical Moroccan dishes like *harira* [a thick tomato-based soup] or *loubia* [a cream of white beans]. Instead, her sister-in-law shared a pdf via smartphone containing a poorly photographed Moroccan cookbook published with the French Thermomix of the previous model. Since her sister-in-law, who grew up eating and cooking Moroccan food and speaks French, incorporated the Thermomix in her routine food preparation so successfully, Diana's mother-in-law decided it had to be a suitable gift. However, Diana did not speak French, and she also struggled to apply the recipes in the pdf and designed for use with the previous model to her own German-language machine. Stuck with an expensive machine that blocked her reduced counter space and unable to access Moroccan recipes via the German-language recipe collection, Diana was at a loss as to how to interact with the Thermomix while feeling increasingly pressured to do so by her in-laws.

Diana's cyborgness was hampered by a number of things. First, she had only limited access to the relevant networks of knowledge via the machine itself and the wider socio-material environment in which she could learn how to combine bodily and digital knowledge, largely due to linguistic barriers and a lack of warm experts. Second, as a German domestic cook and wife of a Moroccan German, she operated within two different moral economies of the household: her Moroccan in-laws asking her to incorporate their practices and broader values around food in her own family's daily practices. Taken together, this case points to the disconnections that also mark techno-scientific fields such as domestic cooking and underlines the double tension between imaginations and everyday experience on the one hand and global reputation and actual practices on the other. The machine itself as well as its software, support networks and digital recipes were clearly not designed with users like Diana in mind, confirming what other scholars have highlighted with respect to the highly gendered, class-based and racialised imaginations and designs of smart home technologies as predominantly male, middle-class and white (Berg 1999; Chambers 2016; Strengers/Kennedy 2021; Kryger Aagaard 2022).

Through the circulation of not only gendered, but also class-based and racialised visions of the smart home and kitchen as well as their material manifestations in science and technology, certain food practices are normalised while others are marginalised, for instance, what is considered as healthy food, appropriate kitchen size and appliances or access to recipes and food knowledge in cookbooks, websites or apps. In anglophone contexts public figures such as Michelle Obama or Jamie Oliver hope to teach a lifelong love for home-grown foods and cooking among young children, assuming – like social reformers before them – that good cooks make for good citizens (Hollows/Jones 2010; Biltekoff 2013). The German public also wonders whether domestic cooks will finally cook and eat what science recommends (e.g., Gose et al. 2016; Sarah Wiener Foundation 2019). These discussions, which bespeak the double tension I addressed above, are implicated in assumptions about class and ethnicity. Although income and educational status are considered in some related studies (e.g., Frerichs/Steinrücke 1997; Leonhäuser et al. 2009), they rarely interrogate how gender intersects with class, ethnicity or culture and thus risk marginalising alternative values and practices (Dyer 1999; Wilcox/Kong 2014).

Conclusion

In sum, then, futurist imaginations and scientific and technological development contribute to standardising the perception of the ideal cook; not only is she decidedly no superhuman cyborg, she also is not poor, a person of colour or otherwise diverse. It is no accident, feminist technology scholars argue, that the development of science and technology and the gender question have emerged in parallel in Western society (Cockburn/Ormrod 1993; Bray 2007). Wajcman argues that "Western technology, like science, is deeply implicated in [the] masculine project of domination and control of women and nature" (2010: 146) and I would add a long list of intersecting power relations. Although a growing body of work demonstrates how certain notions of femininity, but also of class and race, have been reconfigured over the last century, ranging from modernist re-designs of kitchens as women's *Taylorized* workspaces to cooks as domestic scientists (e.g., Bell/Kaye 2002; Freeman 2004; Heßler 2009), with a broader societal wish to emancipate cooking from gendered, class-based or racialised conceptions of domesticity, these movements often have the opposite effect. Women, the poor or the migrant today are rarely positively associated with technology, and their kitchens are scarcely considered as the forefront of futurist ideals or of scientific and technological development (Parr 2002; Carney 2015). Against this background, it does not surprise that so-called digital natives, when transposed into the futurist smart kitchen, are rarely explicitly gendered or tethered to "traditional" images of the domestic cook as hard-working, let alone a poor mother in a culturally diverse household. Perhaps it is because mothers, often intersecting with minority cultural and class backgrounds, are currently revolutionising contemporary kitchens, that we refuse to notice that cyborgs are among us.

As this paper has demonstrated, the notion of the cyborg cook allows to conceptualise the many elements that contribute to the preparation or consumption of a meal and does not limit itself to identifying the cook as purely human, nor simply as female, middle-class and/or white. Although some concepts of domestication theory prove useful when understanding domestic negotiations and knowledge reproduction around and with digital technologies, the underlying tenet of domestication theory – i.e. that a technology user is separable from the technology and the technoscientific web enabling its existence – seems absurd when confronted with the notion of the cyborg. Since this research started with cyborg practices through experiencing the interaction between humans and machines – between the skilled touch of the cook and the intelligent machine that measures or blends ingredients – it has to be reconsidered who the cook is. By breaking with multiple dichotomies – between humans and non-humans, between and women and men, but also between rich and poor, and between ethnic majorities and minorities – cyborgs enable an awareness of the culturally, economically and politically constructed differences of groups and the variety of cyborg possibilities and practices. Depending on gender, income, cultural background, age and experience, the cyborg cook will likely be made of very different organic and non-organic materials, and the ingredients that go into a meal will be correspondingly diverse.

This paper also problematised visions of smart homes and the role of digital technologies therein through an immersive and multi-sensory foray into everyday practices around cooking in Germany. It sought to provide an anthropological perspective on the "taming" of digital practices in contemporary homes. Through grounding the use of digital technologies in diverse contemporary kitchens, it challenged the double tension or division between futuristic visions around domestic food preparation and the reputation of Germany as a high-tech nation on the one hand, and between everyday experiences and actual practices on the other. In contrast to the public imagination of the smart kitchen as a place of the future that is increasingly male-dominated, the multi-sensory ethnography of cyborg practices illustrates that contemporary kitchens are already smart and that especially mothers should be considered as cyborg cooks; a material and social web of multiple technologies, practices and bodies. The ethnographic cases thus contribute to previous scholarship on domestic technologies and the smart home in two ways. First, they confirm that although digital technologies like the Thermomix alleviate and alter some of the daily workload, women, especially mothers, are still largely responsible for everyday domestic food work. Second, rather than considering domestic cooks as bounded individuals or distinctly separable from the technology they use or from digital forms of knowledge such as algorithms or codes, this paper suggested that they should be understood as cyborg cooks when interacting and connecting with machines and their wider social and material environment to prepare the daily meal. Doing so, this paper showed furthermore how contemporary kitchens are already smart, and that female cooks, especially mothers should thus be recognised as the drivers of socio-technical change that they are in everyday domestic life.

In other words, when adopting the perspective of the kitchen, the story of the smart home and domestic IoT can become a story of female and other marginalised cooks' mastery of technology – contrasting with the perspectives told in the literature and the news around the smart home warning us of the increasingly male control of domestic technology. Without wanting to suggest that we have overcome the 1950s ideal of white, middle-class and heteronormative domesticity and its implicit division of labour within the home (Cowan 1983; Strengers/Kennedy 2021: 3), the smart kitchen and cyborg practices within it help to nuance and complicate narratives around perpetuating gender norms and the perceived and actual marginalisation of certain groups in our society, without at the same time silencing and/or reproducing the power imbalances that lead to these narratives. To better understand the constantly changing field of the connected smart home and its human and nonhuman inhabitants, more immersive ethnographic attention to everyday cyborg practices is needed. Ultimately, the notion of the cyborg cook and the anthropology of the smart kitchen presented here advocate for a more diversified understanding of who cooks in Germany and how they are doing so every day.

Acknowledgements

I would like to express my deep gratitude to my research participants who made this study possible by sharing their everyday food practices with me and inviting me to join them in their homes and kitchens. I also owe big thanks to my research assistants Angela Friedrich and Tessa Wiederholl for helping me organise the ethnographic materials. I would further like to thank the organisers and participants of the authors' workshop at the University of Siegen for providing the time and space to discuss my work at an early stage of my research. I am particularly grateful to the two anonymous reviewers as well as Niklas Strüver and David Waldecker for their thoughtful and productive critique, which greatly helped shape this paper. I would also like to thank the faculty members at MIT Anthropology in Cambridge, Massachusetts, who gave me the opportunity to present and discuss my research and arguments in this paper further.

I have no conflict of interest to declare. Of course, any omissions or faults that might remain are solely to blame on me. Research for this paper was possible due to funding from the Deutsche Forschungsgemeinschaft (project number 452339143).

References

Abbots, Emma-Jayne (2017): The Agency of Eating: Mediation, Food, and the Body, London: Bloomsbury.
Ascione, Elisa (2014): "Mamma and the Totemic Robot: Towards an Anthropology of Bimby Food Processors in Italy." In: McWilliams, Mark (ed.), Food and Culture: Proceedings of the Oxford Symposium on Food and Cookery 2013, Blackawton: Prospect Books, pp. 62-69.
Bakardjieva, Maria (2005): Internet Society: The Internet in Everyday Life, London: SAGE.
Barlösius, Eva (2016): Soziologie des Essens: eine sozial- und kulturwissenschaftliche Einführung in die Ernährungsforschung, 3rd edition, Weinheim: Beltz Juventa.
Baum, Stephanie (2012): "HausMANNskost: eine Analyse des Kochens aus der Perspektive sich wandelnder Männlichkeit." In: Rückert-John, Jana/Schäfer, Sabine (eds.), Geschlecht und Ernährung, pp. 66-82.
Beck, Stefan (1997): Umgang mit Technik: kulturelle Praxen und kulturwissenschaftliche Forschungskonzepte, Berlin: Akademie Verlag.
Bell, Genevieve/Kaye, Joseph (2002): "Designing Technology for Domestic Spaces: A Kitchen Manifesto." In: Gastronomica 2/2, pp. 46-62.
Berg, Anne (1999): "A Gendered Socio-Technical Construction: The Smart House." In: MacKenzie, Donald/Judy Wajcman (eds.), The Social Shaping of Technology, 2nd edition, Buckingham: Open University Press, pp. 301-11.
Biltekoff, Charlotte (2013): Eating Right in America. The Cultural Politics of Food and Health, Durham: Duke University Press.
Bowen, Sarah/Brenton, Joslyn/Elliott, Sinikka (2019): Pressure Cooker. Why Home Cooking Won't Solve our Problems and What We Can Do About It, New York: Oxford University Press.
Bray, Francesca (2007): "Gender and Technology." In: Annual Review of Anthropology 36, pp. 37-53.

Brombach, Christine (2017): "Meals and Eating Practices within a Multigenerational Approach: A Qualitative Insight Study." In: International Journal of Clinical Nutrition and Dietetics 3, 122 (online). URL: https://www.graphyonline.com/archives/IJCND/2017/IJCND-122/ (last access: 29/11/2022)

Cajic, Sandra/Brückner, Meike/Brettin, Suse (2022): "A Recipe for Localization? Digital and Analogue Elements in Food Provisioning in Berlin. A Critical Examination of Potentials and Challenges from a Gender Perspective." In: Sustainable Production and Consumption 29, pp. 820-830.

Cairns, Kate/Johnston, Josée (2015): Food and Femininity, London: Bloomsbury.

Carney, Megan (2015): The Unending Hunger. Tracing Women and Food Insecurity Across Borders, Oakland: University of California Press.

Chambers, Deborah (2016): Changing Media, Homes and Household: Cultures, Technologies and Meanings, London: SAGE.

Cockburn, Cynthia/Ormrod, Susan (1993): Gender and Technology in the Making, London: SAGE.

Cowan, Ruth Schwartz (1983): More Work for Mother. The Ironies of Household Technology from the Open Hearth to the Microwave, New York: Basic Books.

Deininger, Olaf/Haase, Hendrik (2021): Food Code. Wie wir in der digitalen Welt die Kontrolle über unser Essen behalten, Munich: Antje Kunstmann.

Dyer, Richard (1999): "Making 'White' People White." In: MacKenzie, Douglas/Judy Wajcman (eds.), The Social Shaping of Technology, 2nd edition, Buckingham: Open University Press, pp. 134-37.

Elton, Sarah (2019): "Posthumanism Invited to Dinner. Exploring the Potential of a More-than-Human Perspective in Food Studies." In: Gastronomica: The Journal of Critical Food Studies 19/2, pp. 6-15.

Freeman, June (2004): The Making of the Modern Kitchen: A Cultural History, London: Berg.

Frerichs, Petra/Steinrücke, Margareta (1997): "Kochen – ein männliches Spiel? Die Küche als geschlechts- und klassenstrukturierter Raum." In: Dölling, Irene/Krais, Beate (eds.), Ein alltägliches Spiel: Geschlechterkonstruktion in der sozialen Praxis, Frankfurt/Main: Suhrkamp, pp. 231-55.

Jo at Cookpad (2018) Is the Kitchen Dead? Cookpad blog post. URL: https://medium.com/cookpadteam/is-the-kitchen-dead-d7c44597b1f3 (last access: 29/11/2022)

Growth from Knowledge (GfK) (2017): Neue Muster in der Ernährung: die Verbindung von Genuss, Gesundheit und Gemeinschaft in einer beschleunigten Welt. GfK Consumer Panels und Bundesvereinigung der Deutschen Ernährungsindustrie, Erlangen: Druckhaus Haspel.

Glucksman, Miriam/Nolan, Jane (2007): "New Technologies and the Transformations of Women's Labor at Home and Work." In: Equal Opportunities International 26/2, pp. 96-112.

Gose, Maria/Krems, Carolin/Heuer, Thorsten/Hoffmann, Ingrid (2016): "Trends in Food Consumption and Nutrient Intake in Germany between 2006 and

2012: Results of the German National Nutrition Monitoring (NEMONIT)." In: British Journal of Nutrition 115, pp. 1498-507.

Graf, Katharina (2022): "Taste Knowledge: Couscous and the Cook's Six Senses." In: Journal of the Royal Anthropological Institute 28/2, online early view. URL: https://rai.onlinelibrary.wiley.com/doi/full/10.1111/1467-9655.13708 (last access: 29/11/2022)

Haraway, Donna (1991): Simians, Cyborgs and Women. The Reinvention of Nature, New York: Routledge.

Hartblay, Cassandra (2018): Cyborg: theorizing the contemporary. URL: https://culanth.org/fieldsights/cyborg (last access: 29/11/2022)

Häußler, Angela/Meier-Gräwe, Uta (2012): "Arbeitsteilungsmuster bei der Ernährungsversorgung von Familien: Persistenz oder Wandel?" In: Gender – Zeitschrift für Geschlecht, Kultur und Gesellschaft 4/2, pp. 9-27.

Heßler, Martina (2009): "The Frankfurt Kitchen. The Model of Modernity and the 'Madness' of Traditional Users, 1926-1933." In: Oldenziel, Ruth/Zachman, K. (eds.), Cold War Kitchen: Americanization, Technology, and European Users, Cambridge: MIT Press, pp. 163-84.

Hollows, Joanne/Jones, Steve (2010): "'At Least He's Doing Something': Moral Entrepreneurship and Individual Responsibility in Jamie's Ministry of Food." In: European Journal of Cultural Studies 13/3, pp. 307-22.

Ingold, Tim (2011[2000]): The Perception of the Environment. Essays on Livelihood, Dwelling and Skill, Oxon: Routledge.

Klünder, Nina (2020): Die Ernährungsversorgung in Familien zwischen Zeit, Alltag und Haushaltsführung: eine Mixed-Methods-Untersuchung, Weinheim: Beltz Juventa.

Klyanitskiy, Alexander (2018): Wenn Lebensmitteleinkauf online geht: eine vergleichende Forschung der Kundenerwartungen und Erfahrungen in vier Städten. Unpublished BA Thesis, Goethe Universität Frankfurt.

Koch, Gertrud (2017): "Einleitung: Digitalisierung als Herausforderung der empirischen Kulturanalyse." In her (ed.), Digitalisierung: Theorien und Konzepte für die empirische Kulturforschung, Cologne: Halem, pp. 7-20.

Kofahl, Daniel (2016): "Ernährungsbezogene Selbstvermessung: Von der Diätetik bis zum Diet Tracking." In: Duttweiler, Stefanie/Gugutzer, Robert/Passoth, Jan-Hendrik/Strübing, Jörg (eds.), Leben nach Zahlen: Self-Tracking als Optimierungsprojekt, Bielefeld: transcript, pp. 123-40.

Kryger Aagaard, Line (2022): "When Smart Technologies Enter Household Practices. The Gendered Implications of Digital Housekeeping." In: Housing, Theory & Society (online preview). URL: https://www.tandfonline.com/doi/full/10.1080/14036096.2022.2094460

Leonhäuser, Ingrid-Ute/Meier-Gräwe, Uta/Möser, Anke/Zander, Uta/Köhler, Jacqueline (2009): Essalltag in Familien: Ernährungsversorgung zwischen privatem und öffentlichem Raum, Wiesbaden: Verlag für Sozialwissenschaften.

Lewis, Tania (2020): Digital Food. From Paddock to Platform, London: Bloomsbury.
Max-Rubner-Institut (2008) Ergebnisbericht Teil 1: Nationale Verzehrsstudie II. Bundesforschungsinstitut für Ernährung und Lebensmittel, Karlsruhe. URL: https://www.bmel.de/SharedDocs/Downloads/Ernaehrung/NVS_Ergebnisbericht.pdf?__blob=publicationFile
Max-Rubner-Institut (2008) Ergebnisbericht Teil 2: Nationale Verzehrsstudie II. Bundesforschungsinstitut für Ernährung und Lebensmittel, Karlsruhe. URL: http://www.bmel.de/SharedDocs/Downloads/Ernaehrung/NVS_ErgebnisberichtTeil2.pdf%3Bjsessionid=A759E5EE16CAE4B49CD0B00876EA168A?__blob=publicationFile
Matzig, Gerhard (2016) Hell's Kitchen. Süddeutsche Zeitung online. URL: https://www.sueddeutsche.de/kultur/statussymbole-hell-s-kitchen-1.3174377 (last access: 29/11/2022)
Merleau-Ponty, Michel (2001[1945]): Phenomenology of Perception, reprint, London: Routledge.
Michael, Mike (2006): Technoscience and Everyday Life, Maidenhead: Open University Press.
Mintel (2005): Eating Habits: Scratch versus Convenience Cooking – Pan-European Overview. Mintel Group, London. URL: http://reports.mintel.com/display/139432/
Nickles, Shelley (2002): "'Preserving Women': Refrigerator Design as Social Process in the 1930s." In: Technology and Culture 43/4 pp. 693-727.
Parr, Joy (2002): "Modern Kitchen, Good Home, Strong Nation." In: Technology and Culture 43/4, pp. 657-67.
Paxson, Heather (2013): The Life of Cheese. Crafting Food and Value in America, Berkeley: University of California Press.
Pinch, Trevor/Bijker, Wiebe (1984): "The Social Construction of Facts and Artefacts. Or How the Sociology of Science and the Sociology of Technology Might Benefit Each Other." In: Social Studies of Science 14/3, pp. 399-441.
Ray, Krishnendu (2016): The Ethnic Restaurateur, New York: Bloomsbury.
Rodney, Alexandra/Cappeliez, Sarah/Oleschuk, Merin/Johnston, Josée (2017): "The Online Domestic Goddess. An Analysis of Food Blog Femininities." In: Food, Culture and Society 20/4, pp. 685-707.
Rützler, Hanni/Reiter, Wolfgang (2017): "The Kitchen of the Future: Somewhere Between Sci-Fi and Social Design." In: Van der Meulen, Nicolaj/Wiesel, Jörg (eds.), The Culinary Turn. Aesthetic Practice of Cookery, Bielefeld: transcript, pp. 57-62.
Sadowski, Jathan/Strengers, Yolande/Kennedy, Jenny (2021): "More Work for Big Mother: Revaluing Care and Control in Smart Homes.' In: Environment and Planning A: Economy and Space 0/0, online early view, pp.1-16. URL: https://journals.sagepub.com/doi/10.1177/0308518X211022366

Sarah Wiener Foundation (2019): Für gesunde Kinder was Vernünftiges zu essen. URL: https://sw-stiftung.de/startseite (last access: 20/06/2019).

Schneider, Tanja/Eli, Karin (2021): "Fieldwork in Online Foodscapes: How to Bring an Ethnographic Approach to Studies of Digital Food and Eating." In: Leer, Jonatan/Krogager, Stinne Gunder Strom (eds.): Research Methods in Digital Food Studies, London: Routledge, pp. 71-85.

Seaver, Nick (2019): "Knowing Algorithms." In: Vertesi, Janet/Ribes, David (eds.), DigitalSTS: A Field Guide for Science and Technology Studies, Princeton: Princeton University Press, pp. 412-422.

Silva, Elizabeth (2000): "The Cook, the Cooker and the Gendering of the Kitchen." In: The Sociological Review 48/4, pp. 612-28.

Silverstone, Roger (2006): "Domesticating Domestication. Reflections on the Life of a Concept." In: Berker, Thomas/Hartmann, Maren/Punie, Yves/Ward, Katie J. (eds.), Domestication of Media and Technology, Berkshire: Open University Press, pp. 229-248.

Sutton, David (2014): Secrets from the Greek Kitchen: Cooking, Skill, and Everyday Life on an Aegean Island, Berkeley: University of California Press.

Sutton, David (2016): "The Anthropology of Cooking." In: Klein, Jakob/Watson, James (eds.), The Handbook of Food and Anthropology, London: Bloomsbury, pp. 349-69.

Strengers, Yolande/Kennedy, Jenny (2021): The Smart Wife: Why Siri, Alexa, and Other Smart Home Devices need a Feminist Reboot, Cambridge: MIT Press.

Truninger, Monica (2011): "Cooking with Bimby in a Moment of Recruitment: Exploring Conventions and Practice Perspectives." In: Journal of Consumer Culture 11/1, pp. 37-59.

Vollenweider, Alice (2006): "Eigentlich muss man froh sein, dass überhaupt noch Küchen gebaut werden." In: Spechtenhauser, Klaus (ed.), Die Küche: Lebenswelt, Nutzung, Perspektiven, Basel: Birkhäuser, pp. 17-20.

Wajcman, Judy (2010): "Feminist Theories of Technology." In: Cambridge Journal of Economics 34, pp. 143-52.

Wajcman, Judy (2015): Pressed for Time. The Acceleration of Life in Digital Capitalism, Chicago: University of Chicago Press.

Wilcox, Hui Nui/Kong, Panyia (2014): "How to Eat Right in America." In: Food, Culture & Society 17/1, pp. 81-102.

Domesticating Motile Media
The Routes and Routines of Vacuum Robots

Max Kanderske

Abstract

The automation of household chores is no trivial task – it necessitates a carefully orchestrated interplay between domestic spaces, people and semi-autonomous agents which have to be aligned in just the right way to facilitate a smooth flow of operations. iRobot, the manufacturer of the Roomba vacuum robot, acknowledges this when they promise that their app not only controls the robot, but also allows it to "[...] clean the way you want by learning and adapting to your home and lifestyle", emphasizing that the robot must account for a certain spatial arrangement as well as a certain everyday routine. The Roomba and similar products are usually labelled and sold as "domestic robots", likewise denoting their 'field of work' in both a spatial and practical sense. Going beyond the notion of the domestic robot, this article draws on the domestication framework (Berker et al. 2006; Silverstone 1996, 1994) to shed light on the various processes that eventually lead to them becoming domesticated robots that fit into the everyday life of their human and non-human co-habitants who also become attuned to them in the process. In doing so, the article expands the domestication discourse to media, whose motility, that is, their capability for self-induced movement, is rooted in their ability to sense, and ultimately map, their environments. By weaving netnographic (Kozinets 2020) findings and interview material into short vignettes, the article analyses the multiple levels on which the robotic domestication process unfolds – or fails to unfold. In doing so, the domestic space to which the robot becomes adjusted reveals itself to be constantly changing as a growing infrastructure comprised of IPAs and apps like IFTTT (If This Then That) is introduced by the homeowners, promising greater connectivity and control but demanding more sophisticated practices of domestication and re-domestication in return.

Keywords

media geography, motile media, domestication, smart home, IoT, sensing, mapping

Domesticating robots

T. lives with her two cats in an apartment with vinyl flooring. Before her vacuum robot, "Henry", which is named in reference to a well-known British brand of vacuum cleaners, is allowed to start the cleaning process, T. meticulously prepares each room, taking extra care to create an unobstructed workspace in which the robot can perform its duties without getting stuck. As she has been using her robot for an extended time, she is well aware of the common navigational pitfalls and routinely moves chairs and lightweight items like backpacks, shoes and charging cords out of the robot's way. While Henry vacuums, T. usually works alongside it, performing other household chores. After the robot is done, she restores the room to its original arrangement. T. is aware of some areas in her flat which pose problems for the robot's navigational capabilities and irregularly cleans these spots with a hand-held vacuum cleaner. As one of her cats once 'got into a fight with the robot', both cats now keep a respectful distance.[1]

As this vignette illustrates, the automation of household chores is no trivial task, but one that necessitates a carefully orchestrated[2] interplay between domestic spaces, their various human and non-human inhabitants and the (semi-) autonomous technologies in question. iRobot, the manufacturer of the Roomba vacuum robot acknowledges this, when they promise that their app not only controls the robot, but also allows it to "[...] clean the way you want by learning and adapting to your *home* and *lifestyle*." In emphasizing that the robot has to account for a certain spatial arrangement – the home – as well as a certain everyday routine – what they dub lifestyle –, the company evokes two categories routinely employed by domestication scholars in order to explain how the mutual adaption unfolds between media technologies and households. Within the domestication approach (Silverstone 1994; Silverstone/Haddon 1996; Berker et al. 2006)[3] to media studies, *objectification* describes the process of placing objects within the domestic environment with which they establish a functional and aesthetic relationship. *Incorporation* describes how the technologies are used and become embedded within

---

[1] The vignettes strewn throughout the article are condensed from empirical research carried out both on- and offline. A more detailed description of the methodology follows in the section on "Routes and Routines".

[2] I employ the term "orchestration" in the colloquial sense of "harmonious organization". For the orchestration of platform ecosystems, see Strüver in this volume.

[3] As vacuum robots like iRobot's Roomba usually operate within the confines of domestic space, I will primarily focus on the British strand of domestication theory (Silverstone/Haddon/Morley), and less on the STS-based Nordic strand which neither limits itself to the domain of the household nor to media technologies in particular. Rather, it expands the notion of 'taming' to processes of technology adoption on a societal level (Hartmann 2020).

the day-to-day lives and routines of the household members. As Roger Silverstone, one of the fathers of the domestication approach, poetically puts it:

"Objectification and incorporation are the strategies, or maybe, if one is true to de Certeau, the tactics, of domestication. Objectification and incorporation involve placing and timing. The complexities and instabilities of domestic life, both well established and essentially fragile, move to meet the new arrival." (Silverstone 2006: 234)

Extending Silverstone's thought, this article sets out to answer the question of what happens when the new arrival likewise *moves*.

Without analysing the opening vignette in too much detail for now, it should be self-evident that robots which move through home space semi-autonomously are subjected to vastly different patterns of adaption and use – both in a spatial and temporal sense – when compared to the more or less stationary media technologies which initially sparked the discourse around media domestication, like the TV. I posit that there are two distinct benefits to bringing the domestication approach to bear on the subject of robotic vacuum cleaners. First and more obviously, these concepts provide a tool for analysing how iRobot's flagship product Roomba and similar domestic robots become *domesticated robots* through what Silverstone (2006) calls 'active consumption', an ongoing "form of engagement in material culture" (ibid: 232) enacted on and within domestic geographies. Second, engaging with self-moving media through this perspective promises to foreground questions of (im)mobility as an aspect that crosscuts all other dimensions of domestication.

Before the afore-mentioned processes of *objectification* and *incorporation* can unfold, *commodification*, which comprises the 'outside elements' of product design, marketing research and public policy (Silverstone 2006: 233), and *appropriation*, that is, the process of purchasing the technological object and bringing it home have to be completed. During *conversion*, the members of the household mobilise the technology as part of their identities (Haddon 2017: 2) when engaging with the outside world. This can include displaying and presenting it, but also obtaining technologic literacy and engaging in the discourses facilitated by and surrounding the object (Silverstone 2006: 234).

In order to grasp how movement – or a lack thereof – affects the domestication process, the first section of the article will reflect if and how increasingly mobile and connected media technologies pose a challenge to the ways in which commodification, objectification, incorporation and conversion unfold. In doing so, the article expands the domestication discourse to media, whose motility (McKosker 2016; Bender 2018; Kanderske/Thielmann 2019), that is, their capability for self-induced movement, is rooted in their ability to sense, and ultimately map, their environments. The next section will provide a brief historical overview of how vacuum robots in general and iRobot's Roomba in particular ended up as common household appliances. After this cursory glance at the initial phase of commodification, the following sections will analyse the ways in which vacuum robots become adapted – or fail to adapt – to households and vice versa. Methodologically, this involves the analysis of vignettes describing various domestication scenarios which have been synthesised from empirical material gathered via interviews and netnographic (Kozinets 2020, 2015) findings. The theoretical groundwork laid out in the first section will serve to contextualise and interpret these vignettes, foregrounding key aspects of the domestication of motile media.

From furniture to motile media

To provide a clear understanding of how this contribution fits into the domestication discourse, I will take a moment to take stock of how various forms of media (im)mobility have been reflected by domestication scholars. The goal of this exercise is to identify the ways in which mobile and motile media productively strain established concepts of domestication, providing an updated theoretical framework to contextualise the empirical observations of the following sections.

I Media as furniture

Conceptualizing media as physical objects within the home space has been a mainstay of domestication theory, most prominently as one half of media's double articulation (Silverstone 1994) as both material artifacts and content providers. Especially within the field of television studies, positions that put a stronger emphasis on media as artifacts placed within domestic micro-geographies can be found, as the title of David Morley's (1995) seminal article "Television – Not So Much a Visual Medium, More a Visible Object" attests. Morley argues that the positions from which the TV can be seen and – perhaps even more importantly be heard – reveals more about the medium's role within the home than the engagement with its programming ever could. He illustrates his case with the TV's replacement of the hearth as the "totemic centrepiece" (Morley 2002: 87) within the "centre of the symbolic space of the family home" (ibid). While focusing on media technology's *position* can be useful to trace spatial changes in media usage, like the TV and telephone's "slow penetration of the home from more public to more private spaces" (Morley 2005: 29), it is also a highly reductive approach. As Monique Miggelbrink notes in her work on 'the furniturisation of media'[4] (2018), other tangible aspects of media objects have to be taken into account as well, most importantly their *cases* which act as interfaces between the technology inside it and the home (Miggelbrink 2018).

---

4   Original title: "Fernsehen und Wohnkultur – Zur Vermöbelung von Fernsehgeräten in der BRD der 1950er- und 1960er-Jahre".

From a perspective of media-as-furniture[5], the movement – or placement – of media is theorised as a singular event happening outside of recurring domestic routines. This placement oftentimes engenders further interior re-arrangements up to changes in the overarching architectural patterns of home spaces (Spigel 1992). In this context, the close relationship between media and furniture, in which various kinds of furniture are specifically designed to enter a liaison with certain media and their accessories, e.g. 'telephone tables' or 'TV stands' (Miggelbrink 2018), suggests that both exhibit similar mobility patterns. This understanding of mobility is underpinned by the etymology of French 'meuble' and its derivative German 'Möbel', both being rooted in Latin 'mobile'. Mobility here emerges as a) a relational property referring to the fact, that even furniture, which often remains unmoved for years at a time, still exhibits more mobility than immovable property and b) a category inextricably linked to the (media) practices of placing and re-arranging by which media are granted temporary mobility. In these cases, both the adaption of the commodified media technology and the adaption of the household environment are not continuous but one-time events related to furnishing and moving homes.

Both Morley and Miggelbrink emphasise that the TV produces various frictions and dislocations around the home, with other pieces of furniture literally having to 'make room' to accommodate television sets (cf. Spigel 1992). While the opening vignette showcased that domestic robots likewise command the movement of furniture and even members of the household like pets[6], significant differences in the resulting mobility patterns can be observed. We will return to the question of how these practices of 'making room' differ from the media-as-furniture approach after attending to another step in the mobilizations of media – the introduction of mobile ICTs into the household.

II Mobile Media

Since the 2000s, domestication research has tried to come to grasp with the particularities of mobile media which seem to call into question several of domestication theory's central categories at once. Mobile ICTs, for example, appear less as furniture – or even material objects – and much more as software, rendering the process of commodification more complex by adding application updates into the mix. Likewise, permanent connectivity to the outside world and its inhabitants puts the notion of the household as a spatial enclosure to the test. As David Morley notes, "individualised media, such as the mobile phone, now contribute

---

5   There has also been work on the inverse relation of furniture-as-media, see Hackenschmidt/Engelhorn 2014.
6   While the status of companion animals is still contested, an emerging body of sociological literature suggests that companion animals are increasingly being seen as "members of the family" (cf. Laurent-Simpson 2021; White 2019).

to a radical dislocation of domesticity" (Morley 2007: 7), or at least to a partial deterritorialisation of domestic space. These developments feed into the destabilisation of "the fundamental 'territorial' and 'sedentary' precepts of twentieth century social science" (Hannam et al. 2006: 2), bringing about a theoretical re-orientation that has been variously termed as 'mobility turn' or 'new mobilities paradigm' (Sheller & Urry 2006). In the case of media that are "Always-On/Always-On-You" (Turkle 2008), their position and usage patterns within domestic spaces seemed to be less important than their relationship to the human body and its immediate vicinity, resulting in them being described as 'wearables' or, more recently, 'near-body technologies' (Kaerlein 2018). Describing the impact of this mobilisation of media on domestication theory, Roger Silverstone observes a shift from the objective realities of the household to a more phenomenological understanding of the home:

"The notion of home is as a projection of self, and as something that can be carried with you; [...] a notion of home that attaches to the keypad of a mobile phone or blackberry, a technological extension of the self, and one which means that you are never out of reach, never disconnected. It is a notion of home that is performed on a daily basis through interaction rituals both with other individuals and with the technologies that enable those interactions." (Silverstone 2006: 242)

Despite mobile media's penchant for accompanying their users to places beyond the home and their ability to establish and uphold a growing number of connections to the outside, there seems to be, at least for most of us, an irreducible rest of living to be carried out within our physical homes – a fact that we have been made painfully aware of during the COVID-19 pandemic. Accordingly, David Morley contends that "despite all the talk of 'postmodern nomadology'", most people's "[...] 'horizons of action' – that sense of scale on which they can act meaningfully in the world – are still very limited" (Morley 2006: 23). This echoes geographer Torsten Hägerstrand's (1970) insight that most people's mobility patterns can be described in terms of tightly constrained space-time prisms centred around what he refers to as a 'home base'.

As will become clear when we turn to analysing the Roomba's routes and routines, both the concept of limited movement centred around a physical home base and the notion of 'home' being performed through interactions that increasingly rely on a "[...] capacity to extend the domestic beyond the confines of the household" (Silverstone 2006: 242) are useful when talking about motile media. Even though domestic robots can move semi-autonomously, their total range of movement is usually restricted to the physical boundaries of the home. At the same time, their ongoing domestication depends on several connections to the outside at once, that is, to both external software providers, as well as members of the household who can remotely instruct and monitor their domestic robots at home via their smartphones.

III Motile Media

The term 'motility' originates from the realm of biology where it refers to "the ability of living systems to exhibit motion and to perform mechanical work at the expense of metabolic energy" (Allen 1981: 1). It has been incorporated into the sociological discourse on mobility by Kaufman et al. (2004), who posit that motility, understood as "the capacity of entities (e.g. goods, information or persons) to be mobile in social and geographic space [...]" (ibid: 750), constitutes a sort of 'movement capital' (ibid: 752) in a Bourdieusian sense.[7] Having made the jump from living things to goods and information, the concept finally was introduced into media geography discourse by McCosker (2015) and Bender (2018).[8] They employed it to describe drone's "'autonomous' or self-sustaining vertical and lateral movement" (McCosker 2015: 3), which differentiated the visuality of flying cameras from that of mobile phones which – unable to move of their own accord – depend on their user's capability for motion. In applying the term more broadly to robotic actors that carry out the task of navigating their surroundings by mapping them via sensor technology, Kanderske/Thielmann (2019) highlight the entwinement between the robot's capabilities for sensing, sense-making, and movement. Akin to Tim Ingold's wayfarers who "know as they go" (Ingold 2000: 229–230), domestic robots "map as they clean", as the manual of iRobot's Roomba J7 model puts it. Robotic *movement* emerges as a central factor in the production of knowledge about interior spaces, even if it means crashing into an obstacle headfirst before changing course, as the first generations of vacuum robots were wont to do. Here, the notion of the case-as-interface introduced by Miggelbrink takes on a new life, as the case – in the form of the front-facing bumper-sensor that can sense if the robot has collided with an obstacle – literally becomes the means for gathering information about the environment.

As we will see, what domestic robots can perceive (and what they cannot) informs how (and if at all) they can carry out their task of cleaning the home space. This dependency on sensory hardware stems from the fact that navigating is a fundamentally relational task in which the navigating actor's position and possible course can only be determined within a system of external reference

---

7   Hege Høyer Leivestad provides a critique of this 'economic understanding' of the term and the market-based vocabulary surrounding it. She advocates for an anthropological approach to motility that may "[...] direct us toward those situations and positions of temporality where mobility is yet-to-be-realized, yet-to-be-completed, or not-intended-to- happen" (Høyer Leivestad 2016: 146–147).

8   To be precise, this is a re-introduction into the field of media studies. In his 1997 book "Open Sky", Paul Virilio employs the term to describe man – and not media (!) – as "[h]aving been first mobile, then motorized, man will thus become motile, deliberately limiting his body's area of influence to a few gestures, a few impulses, like channel-surfing" (Virilio 1997: 17).

points (Sprenger 2022). From this perspective, the home has to be understood as a kind of environment (Sprenger 2019) or sensor media milieu (Scholz 2022) that is constantly sampled by various sensing technologies which render particular parts of it (in)visible and (in)actionable.

Having conceptualised vacuum robots as motile sensory media in this way, we can proceed to assess how these considerations come to bear on domestication theory's central categories of objectification and incorporation. The trajectory of mobilisation outlined above suggests that a media technology's position in space can no longer serve as the central unit of analysis when trying to assess how its objectification is playing out. Instead, we have to account for *positional changes over time*, that is, the paths that motile media follow through the domestic environment. Tracing these movements through space *and* time blurs the categories between routes and routines, between objectification and incorporation. This understanding is supported by the etymology of the word 'routine', which – as Ehn and Lofgren (2009: 100) point out – is actually the diminutive of 'route', "the making of small paths in everyday lives". Sarah Pink and Kerstin Leder Mackley, who analyse domestic routines from a mobility studies perspective, equally arrive at this conclusion, when they suggest to fundamentally understand routines as routes, foregrounding movement through the home as an inevitable quality of domestic routines (Pink/Leder Mackley 2016: 19). Consequently, routes and routines will serve as the central units for analysing how domestic robots' movements become integrated – or fail to integrate – into the spatial and temporal arrangements that make up the household.[9]

Could media formerly be liked to furniture due to them occupying more or less fixed locations within the home space for extended periods of time, the shift towards mobile media that move in unison with the body and, ultimately, media that work out their own paths in relation to the environment and the task at hand necessarily entails changes in how these media become incorporated in our daily activities both spatially and temporally. From the perspective of mobility practices, the singular act of 'making room' for media objects gave way to integrating mobile media into pre-existing movement routines, and finally to moving alongside media that follow their own routines semi-autonomously. Consequently, the emergence of sensor-based motile media forces media geographers and domestication scholars to refocus on the relationship between media and their surroundings, taking into account their routes and routines as well as the (bodily) interactions they become part of both within and outside of domestic geographies.

---

9   Likewise, time geography has long been interested in patterns and rhythms of movement through time and space, representing them as 'paths' and 'bundles' (cf. Hägerstrand 1970).

Robots enter the home space

Each domestication process starts with the production of the media technology in question (Silverstone 1994: 83). Consequently, we will begin our investigation at the point in time at which vacuum robots are about to first enter the home space. In his seminal work "Television and Everyday Life", Roger Silverstone notes that domestication is not a linear process moving towards a definite end point. Rather, commodification and active consumption form a cyclic structure in which one process feeds back into the other, prompting a constant re-negotiation of the media-as-products and their incorporation into household spaces and routines (Silverstone 1994: 124). It follows that domestication has to be understood as an ongoing accomplishment, a long-term process that cannot be reduced to the one-off events of initial product design and adoption (Haddon 2006: 3). At all times, there are (at least) two overlapping trajectories of domestication at play, which share a relation akin to that of ontogenesis and phylogenesis: the first one being enacted on the level of individual devices and home spaces while the second, wider one, which has also been described as a technology's 'career' (Haddon 2006), unfolds across multiple cycles of commodification and consumption. While there is no definite end point to this cycle, it is possible to identify the point at which the career of domestic vacuum robots took off.

The first generation of domestic cleaning robots can be traced back to 1985. At that time, Hitachi completed their HCR-00 prototype, which already possessed various sensors to track its own position in relation to obstacles and navigated the domestic space with the help of a map generated during the journey (Prassler et al. 2016: 1730). While a multitude of vacuum manufacturers developed equally ambitious proof-of-concepts and prototypes, most of these domestic robots never actually set foot in the home space, as the built-in sensory technology drove up prices and manufacturers did not want to compete with their own handheld products (ibid). Notably, iRobot kick-started the domestication cycle for cleaning robots by means of a calculated technological downgrade: Even though its simple sensor setup – the Roomba featured only bumper and infrared sensors – made the Roomba seem navigationally inept when compared to its predecessors, it made the device cheap enough to actually claim a spot within household budgets. Prassler's and colleagues' (2016: 1732) laconic statement that "if you want to sell a domestic appliance, better sell it for a price that is known for domestic appliances" thus serves as a reminder that while better sensory systems might ease the process of adaption towards the actual physical terrain of the home, manufacturers also have to navigate the economic and affective terrains of household budgets and potential buyers' openness to experimentation.

Domestication scholars have long played with the dichotomy of 'wild' and 'tame' objects, likening the process of media domestication to "[...] the domestication of the wild animal: that is a process by which such an animal is accustomed 'to live under the care and near the habitations of man'" (Silverstone 1984:

83). A look into iRobot's history reveals that the company's robots can equally be described as having moved "[...] from being fringe (wild) objects to everyday (tame) objects embedded deeply in the practices of daily life" (Baym 2010: 45). Before turning to service robots, iRobot had initially developed the PackBot, a series of military robots used for reconnaissance purposes in hazardous environments, which proved instrumental in the search for survivors in the aftermath of the September 11 attacks.[10]

Engaging with the Roomba's pre-domestic genealogy has revealed two trajectories in the 'taming' of motile sensory platforms. From a technological point of view, the robots moved from expensive proof-of-concept prototypes to affordable appliances that households were willing to take a gamble on. Considering their domain of application, they moved from unbounded, messy and dangerous outside environments like minefields and disaster areas to the safe and comparably ordered confinements of domestic space.

Routes and routines

As has been pointed out above, understanding sedentary media's objectification usually revolved around their position, that is, around certain points in space. Motile media's self-induced movement shifts the focus from points to lines, from positions to routes and routines. Studying the development of routines, though, is no easy task. As Thomas Berker notes with regard to domestication processes, "[t]his kind of research, done thoroughly, demands a longitudinal approach – spanning several years and including a broad range of participants. Longitudinal studies are scarce, mainly because of their high demands on research resources. The toolbox of qualitative research methodologies, however, provides shortcuts. (Berker 2011: 261). Berker goes on to outline his chosen shortcut of treating "[...] designers, builders, and users as experts for what has happened in the past and what is happening now [...]", allowing him to re-trace a process of domestication that unfolded over the span of several decades. While this article equally draws on the experiences of user-experts which have been rendered accessible through interviews, it also employs netnographic methods (Kozinets 2020, 2015) that treat YouTube, various forums and social media sites like Reddit as digital archives in which instructions for and stories of adapting several generations of domestic robots to the home space have been conserved. Borrowing a method from qualitative social research and ethnography, all information gathered online and offline within the field have been synthesised into vignettes[11] to present relevant scenarios

---

10 iRobot's company history can be found at https://about.irobot.com/History [last accessed July 03, 2022].
11 The expressiveness of a vignette depends on its degree of rich description of concrete details and allows the reader to act as a co-analyst of the study (Pentenrieder 2018: 3).

and situations in a condensed form (cf. Pentenrieder 2018). In doing so, I closely follow geographers Martin Dodge's and Rob Kitchin's example of using 'home-coding vignettes' to describe exemplary patterns of media distribution and use in households (Dodge/Kitchin 2009: 1353). Each vignette is then analysed[12] and brought into dialogue with the existing research literature on domestic robots. Especially in the fields of human – robot interaction and human – computer interaction, a plethora of surveys regarding the integration of vacuum robots into household routines have been generated during Roomba's initial popularisation in the 2000s. For example, Sung et al. (2008) provide insight into the demographic of domestic robot owners and describe how forming an intimate bond with the robot affects the technology's adoption (2007). Forlizzi (2006) provides rich ethnographic accounts of the technology's user practices and Forlizzi and DiSalvo (2007) contrast a handheld vacuum cleaner with the Roomba, outlining how the latter challenges established patterns of cleaning. While, naturally, these articles cannot take into account recent developments like the improvement of the robot's navigational capabilities, the integration into wider sensor media/smart home ecologies and the growth of online communities around testing and optimizing domestic robots, they nevertheless provide fundamental insights into the early domestication history of vacuum robots.

Flattened geographies of cleaning

Before R. lets his older Roomba model work in the living room, he uses a handheld vacuum cleaner to clean the upholstery consisting of a sofa and two armchairs. Having applied the brush nozzle, he uses the opportunity to give the surfaces of tables and cupboards a cursory cleaning. As he spots a cobweb in the corner of the room, he makes use of the vacuum's extending handle to remove it. Finally, R. picks up the carpet at the center of the room, placing it on the sofa during the cleaning process, as his Roomba is scared of the dark surface which gets misidentified as a precipice by the robot's internal 'cliff sensors'. Looking to remedy the situation, R. has taken to the web. Even though online tutorials suggest 'blinding' his robot by putting a thick layer of scotch tape over its cliff sensors, R. does not want to implement this solution, as his home features a wide staircase and he has seen multiple YouTube videos of vacuum robots falling to their untimely end. Having read the robot's manual, R. regularly performs basic maintenance on it by wiping its sensors and emptying its dust bin.

While several empirical studies have investigated the ways in which vacuum robots change existing cleaning patterns – e.g., from scheduled cleaning to "opportu-

---

12 The difficulty with this method is striking a compromise between letting the vignettes guide the analysis and pre-structuring the findings for the reader's convenience.

nistic cleaning" (Forlizzi 2007: 132) –, there is still a lack of detailed descriptions of how the actual practice of vacuuming is transformed by the introduction of robots. I will follow two clues from geography to attempt an analysis of this transformation. In doing so, I will combine Hägerstrand's (1970) insight that much can be learned about mobility by paying attention to the specific factors that restrict movement with recent calls to conceptualise the spaces of geography as volumes rather than areas (Elden 2013) and attend to verticality (Graham 2016). While the two-dimensional maps produced by newer vacuum robots suggest otherwise, established accessories for handheld vacuum cleaners such as the "crevice nozzle" and the "extension wand", but also common cleaning tactics like cleaning dust in a top-down fashion, testify to the fact that domestic micro geographies consist of intricate three-dimensional surfaces that make cleaning a spatially challenging process. Nevertheless, the manufacturers of domestic robots forward their own understanding of cleaning, recasting the practice within the technical limitations of the robot. In their advertisements, vacuum cleaning takes place on strictly two-dimensional surfaces that have to be connected as seamlessly as possible, ideally without any noticeable height differences. As the vignette shows, this flattening of the domestic geography is at odds with the imaginary of fully automated household chores peddled by the manufacturers, as it necessarily precludes many surfaces from being cleaned. Consequently, the robot's domestication process usually entails a re-distribution of cleaning work along the vertical axis, in which the human actors oftentimes keep working alongside or – to be precise – above the robot.

R.'s turning to the net to find a solution to the Robot refusing to clean the carpet serves to foreground that domestication processes usually involve additional sources of information that contextualise and explain the technology in question. As Silverstone (2006: 234) succinctly puts it, "[m]achines and services do not come into the household naked". In the context of early domestication research, this mainly meant packaging and user manuals. Nowadays, the bulk of informational material, a slew of paratextual overcoats, to extend the metaphor, can be encountered online. That these paratexts are usually consulted in moments of crisis, i.e., when the robot does not behave as expected, speaks to the old STS adage that malfunctions provide insights into technology's regular workings by momentarily lifting the lid off otherwise black-boxed processes. In this case, it prompts R. to engage with the inner workings of the robot's sensory hardware, effectively forcing him to take a decision between the robot's ability to clean the carpet and its ability to safely operate next to the stairs. Here, various processes summarised under the term *conversion*[13] can be observed at the same time. As

---

13   E.g., displaying or demonstrating the media technology, developing skills and literacies, participating in discourses and discussions, taking pride in one's ownership etc. (Silverstone 2006: 234).

R. participates in the online discourse surrounding the robot's functionality, he gains what could be called 'sensor literacy', that is, insight into the way the motile robot finds its way through R.'s home.

Lastly, the notion of 'blinding' the robot harks back to the taming of animals, which is commonly employed as a reference point within domestication discourse. Here, it invokes a comparison with blinders, tools that have traditionally been used to keep domesticated animals from balking at environmental distractions. The suggested solution of taping over the cliff sensor equally limits the way in which the robot can establish a sensory relationship to its environment, leading to a change in its navigational behaviour.

Roombarisation

Whereas "making room for TV" – which is also the title of Lynn Spigel's (1992) seminal work on TV appropriation – mostly followed the media-as-furniture pattern in which moving and re-arranging are spaced-out one-off events, making room for vacuum robots is more akin to continuously baby-proofing the domestic environment. Why this is necessary becomes clear if we conceptualise the Roomba's activities as a continuous test of the environment, in which each movement cycle of the robot not only cleans the area of operation, but inadvertently also probes its boundaries, checking for objects to get stuck on or fall down from as it moves through space. Consequently, the users carry out preparatory practices – often subsumed under the term "Roombarisation" (cf. Sung et al. 2007) to increase both robot safety and cleaning efficiency. As the previous vignettes have shown, these activities can range from gathering items from the floor, to returning furniture to the position in which the robot initially mapped the room, to closing doors, prohibiting the robot or other members of the household from interfering with each other, up to removing or replacing household items that are deemed incompatible with the robot.

As noted above, vacuum robots necessarily flatten the practice of vacuum cleaning. Nevertheless, height, most importantly vertical space for manoeuvring, still plays an important role in the robot's adaption to the domestic environment and vice versa. When it comes to making sure that the robot does not get stuck in cramped spaces, three common patterns of adaption can be identified: 1) modifying the domestic geography to better accommodate the robot. This is usually achieved via "furniture risers" or other forms of DIY furniture modification usually recommended in the context of online tutorials and troubleshooting guides for Roomba use.[14] 2) Modifying the robot to extend the sensor range

---

14 A popular tutorial for installing DIY furniture risers can be found on https://www.instructables.com/Furniture-risers-Help-cleaning-droids-catch-more-d/ [last accessed 08.07.2022].

upwards, providing the robot with increased awareness of dangerously small spaces. A gamut of suggested solutions presents itself online, ranging from more improvised methods like gluing popsicle sticks to the bumper sensor to replacing parts of the case with community-produced 3D-printed parts sold on DIY marketplaces like Etsy.[15] 3) As we will see in a vignette below, there are users who prefer to limit the robot's area of operations to easily navigable spaces instead of exerting additional efforts towards mutual adaption. These approaches showcase once more that understanding the *objectification* of motile media goes beyond questions of positionality. It requires attending to the changing geometrical relationships of bodies moving through space and to the complex interplay between the surfaces and shapes modified during the practice of roombarisation.

These examples – as well as the case of R. not wanting to blind his robot's cliff sensor – show that total adaption is oftentimes not feasible. Modifications that ease operation in one area can produce frictions within other parts of the robot's operational domain or necessitate a cascade of further modifications, highlighting the need for careful evaluation. This decision-making process is also informed by an underlying economy of effort and time. To extend the biological metaphor, both robot and users work to find a niche in the household, in which the ratio between perceived effort and time savings is deemed acceptable. From this perspective, manufacturers' ongoing efforts to increase the robot's sensory capabilities can be read as attempts to reduce the need for additional manual adaption, broadening the robot's niche in the process.

Infrastructurisation

As D. regularly works late shifts, she has scheduled her vacuum robot to clean during the hours of the night when she is away. Returning to her home, she was surprised to find that the robot had cleaned only a small part of the flat before getting stuck in a corner. As it turns out, her Roomba, a model that primarily relies on its RGB camera for finding its way around the flat, gets disoriented easily in the dark. Being conscious of energy conservation, D. took to the net to find a way to solve the problem without leaving the lights on the whole night. Having tried various online tutorials, D. finally managed to create a schedule that lights up each room for the cleaning process via ITTT (If This Then That), an app that facilitates interoperability between various smart home devices. She explains that setting up her schedule involved measuring the time the robot usually spends in each room and setting up the order of rooms to be cleaned within iRobot's mapping application, leaving all doors open to enable free movement between rooms.

---

15   E.g. https://www.etsy.com/de/listing/1065660333/bumper-extender-v2-fur-roomba-und-andere [last accessed July 08, 2022].

By highlighting the need for both adequate lighting conditions and an external app to organise the cleaning process in relation to other smart home devices, D.'s nightly routine raises the question of the infrastructural preconditions of automated vacuum cleaning. Adopting Star's and Ruhleder's (1994: 113) way of asking *when*, that is, in the context of which practices, a thing emerges as an infrastructure instead of asking *what* an infrastructure is, we can assert that in the context of D.'s scheduling practice, the infrastructural background is comprised of a Wi-Fi network, the ITTT app and her smart lights, in addition to infrastructures already present in earlier descriptions, like the robot's base station (connected to the power grid), iRobot's own app and possible permanent modifications to the domestic environment, like furniture raisers. These infrastructures shape the way in which Roomba's routes and routines, and consequently its adaption to the home space and vice versa, unfold. Notably, Star and Ruhleder themselves link the occurrence of an infrastructure to the creation of an – albeit transient and relational – home, in which a larger-scale technology, like the ITTT app or Roomba's networked machine vision feature, in our case, affords local practices, like the scheduling of an autonomous cleaning routine:

"That is, an infrastructure occurs when local practices are afforded by a larger-scale technology, which can then be used in a natural, ready-to-hand fashion. It becomes transparent as local variations are folded into organizational changes, and becomes an unambiguous home – for somebody. This is not a physical location nor a permanent one, but a working relation – since no home is universal." (Star/Ruhleder 1994: 114).

While it is certainly possible to address the robot's infrastructural needs in a more simplistic fashion – some users reported placing night lights in every room to reach sufficient lighting conditions for cleaning – it is noticeable that other motivations, like energy conservation, the expectation of a 'sufficiently smart' solution or the joy of tinkering with the available options regularly drive the creation of complex smart home routines like in D.'s case.

Another way of shaping the domestication process via infrastructurisation is regularly described by owners of older Roomba models, who employ "virtual walls" consisting of two small base stations attached to the doorframe, to limit the robot's movements. These illustrate an ongoing trajectory of virtualisation concerning the infrastructural background of operating motile media: Where the early, bumper-based robots had prompted the practice of physically fencing them in by closing doors or erecting cardboard barriers, the virtual wall's base stations remain integrated into the environment, but already enforce their boundaries via electromagnetic signalling. Users of newer models, like D., can limit their robot's domain of operation by drawing a corresponding zone on their phone, marking a shift from modifying the physical home itself towards enacting changes on the cartographic model created by the robot.¹⁶ The introduction of IoT infrastructures also highlights that once 'smart' devices start talking to each other, tracing the domestication of singular media no longer provides us with the whole picture. Rather, we have to take into account how the process of domestication unfolds across media ensembles (Morley 2007: 7) or media ecologies of "digital domesticity" (Kennedy et al. 2020). Here, questions of interoperability and platformisation come to the fore, as the interplay between robot and smart environment is coordinated via cross-platform automation applications such as ITTT or intelligent personal assistants positioned as central nodes within the network (cf. Strüver in this volume).

Connecting to the outside

S.'s family keeps two dogs who regularly spend time alone while the other family members are at work/school. Having bought their Roomba while one of the dogs was still a puppy, the family decided on a model that can recognise and evade pet waste with its on-board RGB-camera and has advanced capabilities for mapping and navigation. S.'s family controls the robot via the app, which, besides allowing to select which rooms to clean, also provides the functionality to restrict the robot's access to certain areas of the flat. As S. usually is the first to leave the home in the morning, his partner messages him once she and the kids have left the family home, so that S. can set the robot to work via the app. S. chooses the rooms to be cleaned via the map generated by the robot's initial mapping run, trusting that the other family members have left the doors of their rooms open to provide a continuous working area for the robot.

The object recognition feature mentioned above already comes pre-loaded with a library of common objects to be found within the home space. Here, the idea of an idealised or intended dwelling inscribes itself into the domestication process, with the objects deemed to be the most common – or indeed most problematic, like loading cables and pet waste – being those that first get the treatment of being rendered recognisable to the robot. At the same time, newer models come with the capability to take a picture of the obstacle and can remotely ask the user via the app how to interact with it. As the advertisement on iRobot's homepage states: "When it first spots them, it will send you a photo so that you can tell it to avoid or clean around the obstacle in the future. It doesn't just learn your home; it reacts to it in real time."¹⁷ This feature is notable, as it evokes a new kind of agency in which the medium proactively contacts the user to advance the process of adaption. Whereas

---

16   Another parallel with animal husbandry presents itself here as emerging practices of virtual fencing are supposed to restrict the movement of cattle to a designated area without the need for erecting physical barriers in the environment (Friedrich 2020).
17   https://www.irobot.com/en_US/wi-fi--connected-roomba-j7plus-self-emptying-robot-vacuum/J755020.html [last accessed June 22, 2022].

earlier media literally had to wait until users 'made room' for them, motile media are able to 'make the first move' introducing a new dynamic into the domestication process.

The continuous fine tuning to the intricacies of the home outlined above is a prime example of domestication being a long-term process (Haddon 2003), an ongoing accomplishment that goes way beyond the initial act of adoption. As software updates and continuous (re-)training of machine learning models prompt changes in the robot's behaviour, the feedback loop of consumption and commodification dramatically speeds up. iRobot's P.O.O.P. (Pet Owner Official Promise)[18] guarantee is exemplary for this dynamic. It also tipped the scales in S.'s decision to purchase the pricier model whose advanced object recognition capabilities underpin the feature. The cycle runs as follows: users experience a problem, for example the robot, testing the environment for hazards as it goes, inadvertently distributing pet waste through the home. The users make their grievance public, often in the form of security or baby camera footage released on video on demand sites. If the problem occurs frequently enough or gets amplified by a viral video garnering attention of the media, the manufacturer is pressured to come up with a solution – in this case the training of an image recognition model – which gets injected back into the robot. The result of this complex chain of operations, which involves the extraction of image data from the home space, the off-site training of machine learning models and the eventual (re-)introduction of additional software into the home space, is a domestic robot that has become adapted to cohabitating with pets without turning its job into an unhygienic mess – a "housebroken robot", as S. proudly told me. Even though the robots are updated more or less regularly, this by no means suggests continuous progress towards some ideal of efficiency. Every update has the potential to introduce new frictions with other elements of the network, as the case of a faulty software patch that made whole generations of Roombas behave like "drunkards" (Clark 2021) illustrates.

S.'s family's complex cleaning routine depends on a number of interlocking practices to be carried out in the right order. Some of these practices (preparing a continuous workspace, vacating the area, relaying a starting signal, commanding the robot via the app) happen within, some outside of the home space; some have to be carried out in the physical environment, others in the two-dimensional model produced by the robot's mapping feature and accessed through the app. These outside connections seem to follow the logic of destabilising the notion of the home already discussed in the context of mobile media. Nevertheless, both the motile medium's sensory relation to its domestic surroundings, as well as the production of and interaction with its map of the home constitute acts of reterritorialisation in which the home space is rendered perceivable and actionable.

---

18 See https://www.irobot.com/en_US/pet-promise.html [last accessed June 22, 2022].

Work

As service robots promise the automation of household chores, their domestication process is marked by a re-distribution of tasks between robot and user. Whether an actual reduction in the time spent for cleaning is achieved, often remains questionable. This is evidenced by the vignettes in which we have encountered various forms of work related to the adaption and operation of robotic vacuum cleaners: the preliminary "infrastructure work" (Schabacher 2022) of setting up and maintaining the various hardware and software components, as well as preparing the robot's workspace; the work of cleaning alongside it during its operation; and finally, the work of trouble-shooting and smoothing out the cleaning process by looking up information online, performing basic maintenance and carrying out modifications on both the robot and the environment. As Jackman and Brickell (2022) note in their study on the automation of household tasks, these observations seem to be congruent with established feminist work that has "[...] long unravelled the commonly-held view of labour-saving technologies as 'freeing' women from domestic work, for other non-housework tasks, including leisure and paid work (Bose at al., 1984; Cox and Federici, 1975)." While Sung's and colleagues' (2008) research suggests that domestic robot ownership is almost evenly distributed across genders, the point stands that the time freed up by not having to vacuum the floor immediately gets absorbed by other tasks connected to cleaning or maintenance. According to Bose et al. (1984: 57),

"[...] some "costs" associated with household technology changes have been accommodated by individual families or housewives under the assumption that they are individual – if not unique – burdens. An example is the new stresses associated with selecting specific equipment from a large marketplace array, learning to use it, storing it, cleaning it, and repairing it."

As outlined in the preceding vignettes, these burdens nowadays include engaging with the online discourse surrounding the robots, like product reviews, testing videos and top lists showcasing the different models' supposed advantages and disadvantages.[19]

Accountability

In order to live up to the expectations evoked by the 'smart' descriptor, domestic robots need to structure their cleaning in a way that is well-planned or at least can be perceived as such. Here, the way in which the robot's pathfinding unfolds not

---

19 E.g. iRobot's own overview table https://www.irobot.com/en_US/comparison-chart.html [last accessed June 22, 2022].

only underpins its actual efficiency in cleaning its work area, but also shapes how it is evaluated by the other inhabitants of the home. According to Vaussard et al. (2013: 13) "planning transparency", that is, the robot's ability "[...] to trace a smart, smooth, and efficient path that is comprehensible to some extent to humans" (ibid) is paramount, if a robot is to be accepted into the household. Rendering the robot's path understandable not only makes it seem less unpredictable and, by extension, less stupid, but also provides the user with a sense of control over the machine. As Sung et al. (2007: 159) note with respect to earlier works, "[r]esearchers like Bell, Norman, and others argue that technologies should make their actions accountable. In other words, people should be able to see into a technology's process to understand how a system got from start to finish." In the case of the Roomba, "how the system got from start to finish", that is, which path the robot took and whether its movement was as smooth and efficient as promised, is not always readily perceived.

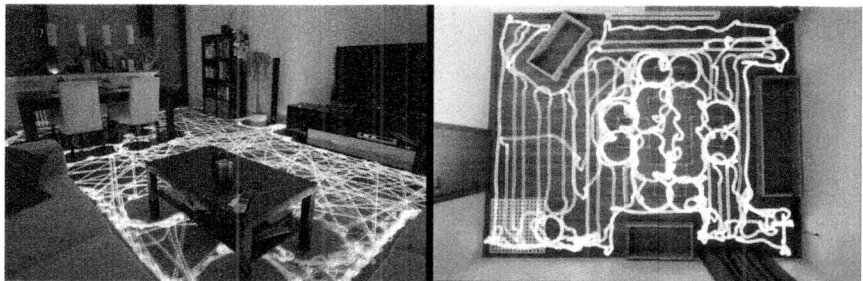

Fig. 1: Left: Long exposure photography of a Roomba's path. (Source: Andreas Dantz, https://www.flickr.com/photos/szene/8649326807/in/pool-roomba/) Right: Long exposure testing carried out in a standardised testing room. (Source: Gianmarco Chumbe/CNET, https://www.cnet.com/home/kitchen-and-household/this-is-why-your-roombas-random-patterns-actually-make-perfect-sense/)

To address this need for accountability, users and journalists have developed testing practices like 'pickup tests',[20] in which large amounts of dust or grains are purposefully distributed on the floor to challenge the robot's capabilities, and 'long exposure tests' (Fig. 1), in which the Robot's path – and by extension its cleaning pattern – are rendered visible as trails of light in photo or video footage. (cf. Bennett 2021) The results of these tests are usually documented in the form of review articles or YouTube videos and serve a twofold purpose in the domestication process: before the initial adoption, they act as a tool for comparison and decision-making, afterwards they provide a yardstick against which the user's robot and its cleaning behaviour can be measured. Newer models also feature built-in accountability tools like Roomba's 'Clean Map Report' which provide detailed

---

20   E.g. https://youtu.be/GfLUQuYekIo. [last accessed June 22, 2022].

information on the cleaned area and the time the robot took for the job. But as these are supplied by the manufacturer and rely on the robot's own sensors, they are naturally treated as less reliable than the efficiency maps produced by long exposure testing within the community.

The platformisation of home space

A. works in the field of computer science and prioritises her protection of privacy, she deliberately decided against a robot with advanced mapping and object recognition capabilities, especially after reading of iRobot's cooperation with Google on the net. She explains that in the time following the initial purchase, her family used "Alf", their older model Roomba, to vacuum the whole house. Having come to the conclusion that "carrying the robot from one floor to another and preparing each room in advance is too tedious" they have now limited the robot's area of operation to the family's bedrooms, because it "fits well under the beds".

As noted above, domestication scholars understand media as being doubly articulated: as physical objects that one 'needs to make room for' and as providers of symbolic content that have to be integrated into household activities.[21] Non-representational media like robots seemingly call the original double articulation into question, seeing that they neither deliver 'content' into the home (like the TV) nor provide a telecommunication channel (like the phone). Nevertheless, another kind of double articulation, whose two sides are comprised of "hard- and software, object and algorithms", replaces the former one, as geographers Del Casino Jr. et al. (2016: 3) point out. They stress that "[t]his is not to suggest an either/or ontology of robots but a both/and whereby geographers must take up the theoretical and political implications of the hardware/software matrix and what it means for human and more-than-human bodies and relations" (ibid). It is precisely this double articulation, in which the complex learning routines outlined above and – in a more general sense – the robot's agentic "capacities that extend their technicity and enable them to do additional work in the world" (Dodge and Kitchin, 2009: 1352) are rooted.

While domestication, understood as "a process of bringing things home" (Silverstone 2006: 233) has always involved crossing the boundary between inside and outside, between public and private (cf. ibid), two distinct streams of information come to the fore in the context of motile media: an inbound stream of

---

21   The concept is sometimes also enlarged to a triple articulation including the technological object, the symbolic environment it grants access to and the individual text or message (cf. Hartmann: 2006). In the case of ICTs, the individual text could come to mean a singular software update or an individual act of accessing the app to control the robot.

software updates, which can prompt drastic changes in the medium's capabilities, and an outbound stream of sensory data gathered inside the home space. The first stream can simply be understood as expanding the commodification process, allowing the technology to have a software career (signified by increasing version numbers) in addition to the already established succession of ever-new and improved models on the hardware side. The theoretical and political implications of the second stream need some more contextualizing.

Cleaning robots are positioned as a stepping stone towards more intricate ways of home automation, making it a timely endeavour to study them from a domestication perspective. This is hardly a novel thought: During Roomba's initial rise to popularity, Sung et al. (2008: 1) noted, that the robotic vacuum cleaner is "[...] an exemplary case for understanding how householders respond to robotic products that replace blue-collar work in the home, which some researchers believe to be the future of home robotic products". Today, robots like the Roomba act as surveyors, fuelling the further proliferation of IoT technologies by providing manufacturers with spatial data about the home space. Accordingly, iRobot CEO Colin Angle emphasised Roomba's role in laying the foundations for future smart homes during the announcement of iRobot's cooperation with Google in 2018: "Robots with mapping and spatial awareness capabilities will play an important role in allowing other smart devices in the home to more seamlessly work together", ultimately creating what the two companies call a "more thoughtful home".[22] In eschewing the usual attribution of 'smartness' and substituting it for 'thoughtfulness', Angle deliberately evokes the imaginary of a home that adapts itself to the needs of its inhabitants – a home in which a continual process of domestication runs itself.

Automation being driven by maps with ever-higher granularity is a motive also commonly found in the realm of autonomous driving, where mapping and modelling efforts are increasingly carried out by specialised companies trying to establish themselves as platforms. (Kanderske 2021). It comes as no surprise then, that iRobot has been cooperating with Google, the company who initially "popularized a model of cartography as platform" (Plantin 2018: 1) with their *Maps* application. More recently, Amazon announced its intentions to acquire iRobot, supposedly to supplement the data generated by their Echo Dot smart speakers – the 'ears' of their smart home ecosystem, so to speak – with visual data gathered by Roombas inside the home. Amazon, who actively work to position Alexa as the centrepiece through which other IoT technologies are accessed (cf. Strüver in this volume), seems to pursue a similar strategy in securing access to mapping and object recognition technologies already employed in their customers' homes.

---

22 https://media.irobot.com/2018-10-31-iRobot-and-Google-Collaborate-to-Advance-the-Next-Generation-Smart-Home [last accessed 06.07.2022].

As A. understands these dynamics, her conscious decision to forego the advantages of a model with heightened sensing capabilities is grounded in anxieties about data security and privacy. Indeed, her fear that sensory data gathered within her home could become available to an outside public – whether by accident or via a platformised business model – seems to be justified, as both the connected devices themselves and the expanding data supply chains fuelled by them provide ample opportunities for personal information to leak out or to be outright stolen (cf. Guo 2022). As data increasingly flows out of the home, it generates the possibility for extractive practices that have been variously theorised as 'surveillance capitalism' (Zuboff 2019) or 'drone capitalism' (Richardson 2008) which "operates within the wider transformation of labour by robotics and automation" (ibid.: 86).

Conclusion

Adapting domestication theory's categories of objectification and incorporation for the study of motile media necessitated attending to movement patterns, conceptualised as routes, and recurring adaptive practices, conceptualised as routines. As we move from focusing on positionality to the orchestration of moving bodies in space, time geography's notion of the path as both spatial route and temporal routine has suggested itself as an adequate analytical tool for studying motile media. Taking cues from Hägerstrand's (1970) chronogeographic visualisations, it seems worthwhile to map these paths to understand the intricate ways in which the various human and non-human members of the household interact with and adapt their quotidian activities to each other and to the micro geographies of the home (Fig. 2). Going beyond the exploratory scope of this article, the visualisation could be extended to the micro level of individual cleaning patterns and cleaning interactions as well as to the macro level of outside connections and global data flows. For now, it shows a typical cleaning routine: the robot is scheduled to vacuum a set of rooms while the user works at an external location and sporadically checks the progress at home via her smartphone. Notably, Hägerstrand's notion of a recalcitrant material home base constituting the start and end point of all quotidian movement resonates well with domestic robots: on one hand, they exhibit the same movement pattern on a smaller scale, as they usually depart from and return to a charging station – a home base nested into the bigger home that surrounds it, so to speak. On a more fundamental level, the robots' domain of operation is the physical domestic space – which they reterritorialise by constantly mapping and re-mapping it.

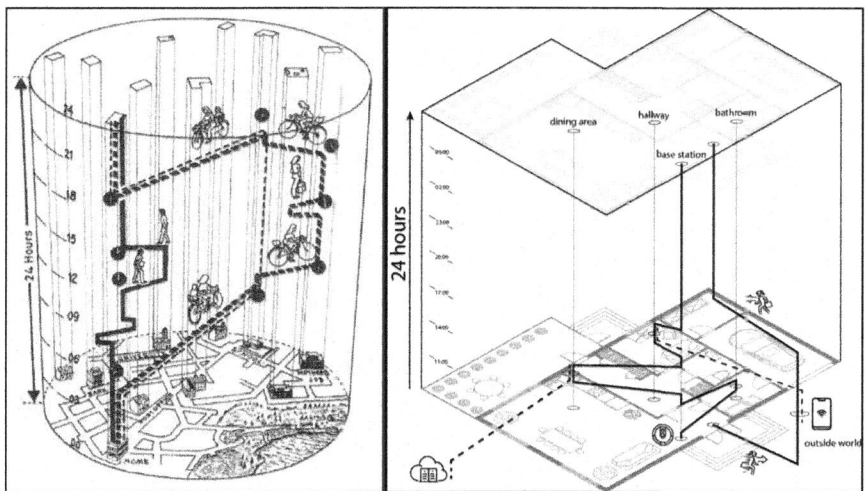

Fig. 2: Left: Chronogeographic representation of the activity programmes of the members of a Swedish family during a single day (reproduced from Parkes & Thrift 1980: 252).
Right: Simplified chronogeographic representation of the routes and routines of a motile vacuum robot during a single day.

The vignettes have shown that new forms of domestic work *and* domestication work connected to vacuum robots' adaption to the home space have emerged. Here, the work carried out before acquisition mainly takes place in the web, where potential users can sift through immense quantities of information about different models to inform their decision; after the initial acquisition, the work shifts towards the domestic micro-geographies of the home and to the surface of the robot itself, where both preparatory infrastructure work and continuous roombarisation work have to be enacted to facilitate the robot's smooth operation. Notably, commodification has turned into an ongoing process that demands frequent attention from both the manufacturers and the users, as a) continuous software updates change the robot's behaviour and b) newer models actively push for further adaption by prompting the user for directions on how to handle certain situations and objects encountered on their ways through the home.

In her book "The New Breed", Kate Darling (2021) argues that thinking through robots by likening them to animals might prove more productive than simply conceptualizing them as a form of automation bound to eventually replace human labour and – in some cases – humans themselves. After all, animals, understood as "autonomous, sometimes unpredictable agents" (Darling 2021: xiv) have existed, and indeed worked, alongside humans in much the same fashion that robots do now for long stretches of history, be it as tools, products, or companions (ibid: xv). The domestication approach might be uniquely suited for this task, as it has always situated technology within the semantic field of 'wildness' and 'tameness' to understand how it finds its place within the home. But it is only with the advent of motile media whose agency is rooted in their capability to sense and move through their surroundings, that the practices of domesticating media can be mapped onto those of domesticating animals in a way that moves beyond mere metaphor. Over the course of writing this article, a series of similarities between the domestication of media and animals already suggested itself, e.g., modifying the robot's behaviour by limiting its sensory input via 'blinders', and the use of increasingly virtualised fences to influence the robot's movement patterns. In future work on the domestication of motile media, it could be worthwhile to intentionally elicit these similarities.

Finally, with the implementation of more and more IoT technologies into ever-'smarter' homes, the domestication approach has to shift its view towards networks, media ecologies and platforms. As robots "connect to our homes" and "sync with our lives"[23], objectification now also comprises the connections that networked IoT devices establish between themselves. Likewise, incorporation may unfold semi-autonomously, as routines are adjusted based on data gleaned from the domestic environment and other devices within the network. These developments raise questions of privacy, data security and – ultimately – dangerous concentrations of economic power. That Amazon's plan to acquire iRobot for $1,7 billion has recently come under scrutiny by the US Federal Trade Commission – the fear being that Amazon could near-monopolise the smart home market – emphasises the vital strategic importance ascribed to motile media's data gathering capabilities. Paying close attention to the way in which the domestication of one media technology paves the way for and synergises with the domestication of further IoT technologies will only become more urgent, as robots capable of navigating and mapping their surroundings drive the platformisation of domestic space.

Acknowledgements

Diese Arbeit wurde gefördert durch die Deutsche Forschungsgemeinschaft (DFG) – Projektnummer 262513311 – SFB 1187. Funded by the Deutsche Forschungsgemeinschaft (DFG, German Research Foundation) – Project-ID 262513311 – SFB 1187.

---

23 If we are to believe the website for iRobot's 'Genius' app which has since been rebranded into the 'iRobot Home App': https://about.irobot.com/iRobot-Genius [last accessed July 06.07.2022].

References

Allen, Robert D. (1981): "Motility." In: The Journal of Cell Biology 91/3, pp. 148–155.

Baym, Nancy K. (2010): Personal Connections in the Digital Age, Cambridge: Polity Press.

Bender, Hendrik (2018): "The New Aerial Age: Die wechselseitige Verfertigung gemeinsamer Raum-und Medienpraktiken am Beispiel von Drohnen-Communities." In: Otto, Isabell/Schramm, Samantha/Thielmann, Tristan/Ghanbari, Nacim (eds.), Kollaboration, Leiden: Brill Fink, pp. 121–146.

Bennett, Brian (2021): "This is Why Your Roomba's Random Patterns Actually Make Perfect Sense." In: CNET, https://www.cnet.com/home/kitchen-and-household/this-is-why-your-roombas-random-patterns-actually-make-perfect-sense/ [last accessed June 24, 2022].

Berker, Thomas (2011): "Domesticating Spaces: Sociotechnical Studies and the Built Environment." In: Space and Culture 14/3, 259-268.

Bose, Christine E./Bereano, Philip L./Malloy, Mary (1984): "Household Technology and the Social Construction of Housework." In: Technology and Culture 25/1, pp. 53–82.

Clark, Mitchell (2021): "iRobot Says It'll Be a Few Weeks Until It Can Clean Up Its Latest Roomba Software Update Mess." In: The Verge, https://www.theverge.com/2021/2/24/22299346/irobot-roomba-update-issues-vacuums-fix-several-weeks?scrolla=5eb6d68b7fedc32c19ef33b4 [last accessed June 24, 2022].

Darling, Kate (2021): The New Breed: What Our History With Animals Reveals About Our Future With Robots, New York, NY: Henry Holt and Company.

Dodge, Martin/Kitchin, Rob (2009): "Software, Objects, and Home Space." In: Environment and Planning A 41/6, pp. 1344–1365.

Elden, Stuart (2013): "Secure the Volume: Vertical Geopolitics and the Depth of Power." In: Political Geography 34, pp. 35–51.

Federici, Silvia/Cox, Nicole (1975): Counter-planning From the Kitchen, New York, NY: Falling Wall Press.

Friedrich, Kathrin (2020): "Im virtuellen Zaun. Umgebungen adaptiver Medien." In: Ladewig, Rebekka/Sepp, Angelika (eds.), Milieu-Fragmente. Technologische und ästhetische Perspektiven, Leipzig: Spector Books, pp. 243–249.

Forlizzi, Jodi. (2007): "How Robotic Products Become Social Products: an Ethnographic Study of Cleaning in the Home." In: 2007 2nd ACM/IEEE International Conference on Human-Robot Interaction (HRI), pp. 129–136.

Forlizzi, Jodi/DiSalvo, Carl (2006): "Service Robots in the Domestic Environment: a Study of the Roomba Vacuum in the Home." In: Proceedings of the 1st ACM SIGCHI/SIGART Conference on Human-Robot Interaction, pp. 258–265.

Graham, Stephen (2016): Vertical: The City From Satellites to Bunkers, London: Verso Books.

Guo, Eileen (2022): "A Roomba Recorded a Woman on the Toilet. How Did Screenshots End Up on Facebook?" In: MIT Technology Review, https://www.

technologyreview.com/2022/12/19/1065306/roomba-irobot-robot-vacuums-artificial-intelligence-training-data-privacy/ [last accessed June 24, 2022].

Hackenschmidt, Sebastian/Engelhorn, Klaus (eds.) (2014): Möbel als Medien: Beiträge zu einer Kulturgeschichte der Dinge, Bielefeld: transcript Verlag.

Hägerstrand, Torsten (1970): "What About People in Regional Science?" In: Papers of the Regional Science Association 24, pp. 6–21. https://doi.org/10.1007/BF01936872

Haddon, Leslie (2003): *"Domestication and Mobile Telephony."* In: Katz, James (ed.), Machines that Become Us: The Social Context of Personal Communication Technology, New Brunswick: Transaction Publishers, pp. 43–56.

Haddon, Leslie (2006): "The Contribution of Domestication Research to in-home Computing and Media Consumption." In: The Information Society 22/4, pp. 195–203.

Hannam, Kevin/Sheller, Mimi Sheller/Urry, John (2006): "Mobilities, Immobilities and Moorings." In: Mobilities 1/1, pp. 1–22.

Hartmann, Maren (2020): "(The Domestication of) Nordic Domestication?" In: Nordic Journal of Media Studies 2/1, pp. 47-57.

Hartmann, Maren (2006): "The Triple Articulation of Icts. Media as Technological Objects, Symbolic Environments and Individual Texts." In: Berker, Thomas/Hartmann, Maren/Punie, Yves/Ward, Katie J. (eds.), Domestication of Media and Technolog, Berkshire: Open University Press, pp. 80–102.

Høyer Leivestad, Hege (2016): "Motility." In: Salazar, Noel B./Jayaram, Kiran (eds.): Keywords of Mobility: Critical Engagements, New York: Berghahn Books, pp. 133–151.

Ingold, Tim (2000): The Perception of the Environment: Essays on Livelihood, Dwelling and Skill, London: Routledge.

Jackman, Anna/Katherine Brickell (2022): "'Everyday Droning': Towards a Feminist Geopolitics of the Drone-home." In: Progress in Human Geography 46/1: 156–178.

Kaerlein, Timo (2018): Smartphones als digitale Nahkörpertechnologien: Zur Kybernetisierung des Alltags, Bielefeld: transcript Verlag. https://doi.org/10.1515/9783839442722

Kennedy, Jenny/Arnold, Michael/Gibbs, Martin/Nansen, Bjorn/Wilken, Rowan (2020): Digital Domesticity: Media, Materiality, and Home Life. New York, NY: Oxford University Press.

Kozinets, Robert V. (2020 [2009]): Netnography: the Essential Guide to Qualitative Social Media Research, London/ Thousand Oaks, CA: SAGE Publications.

Kozinets, Robert V. (2015): Netnography: Redefined, London/Thousand Oaks, CA: SAGE Publications.

Laurent-Simpson, Andrea (2021): Just Like Family: How Companion Animals Joined the Household. New York, NY: NYU Press.

McCosker, Anthony (2015): "Drone Media: Unruly Systems, Radical Empiricism and Camera Consciousness." In: *Culture Machine 16*, Online: https://culturemachine.net/vol-16-drone-cultures/drone-media/.

Miggelbrink, Monique (2018): Fernsehen und Wohnkultur: Zur Vermöbelung von Fernsehgeräten in der BRD der 1950er- und 1960er-Jahre, Bielefeld: transcript Verlag. https://doi.org/10.1515/9783839442531.

Morley, David (2007 [2006]): Media, Modernity and Technology: The Geography of the New, London: Routledge.

Morley, David (2006 [2003]): "What's "home" Got to Do With it? Contradictory Dynamics in the Domestication of Technology and the Dislocation of Domesticity." In: Berker, Thomas/Hartmann, Maren/Punie, Yves/Ward, Katie J. (eds.), Domestication of Media and Technolog, Berkshire: Open University Press, pp. 21–39.

Morley, David (1995): "Television: Not So Much a Visual Medium, More a Visible Object." In: Jenks, Chris (ed.), Visual Culture, London: Routledge, pp. 170–189.

Parkes, Don/Thrift, Nigel J. (1980): Times, Spaces, and Places: A Chronogeographic Perspective. New York, NY: Wiley.

Pentenrieder, Annelie (2018): "'Nach Zuhause'. Dynamische Reflexionen zwischen verkörperten und materialisierten Navigationsroutinen im Taxi." In: von Bose, Käthe/Bublitz, Hannelore/ Fuchs, Matthias a.o. (eds.): Körper, Materialitäten, Technologien, Paderborn: Fink, pp. 119–135. DOI: https://doi.org/10.25969/mediarep/13050.

Pink, Sarah/Leder Mackley, Kerstin (2016): "Moving, Making and Atmosphere: Routines of Home as Sites for Mundane Improvisation." In: Mobilities 11/2, pp. 171–187.

Plantin, Jean-Christophe (2018): "Google Maps as Cartographic Infrastructure: From Participatory Mapmaking to Database Maintenance." In: International Journal of Communication 12, pp. 489–506.

Richardson, Michael (2018): "Drone Capitalism." In: Transformations 31, pp. 79-97.

Scholz, Sebastian. (2022): "Sensormedien-Milieus und Technikökologien der Wahrnehmung. Navigieren in/mit> more-than-human Infrastrukturen" In: Navigationen - Zeitschrift für Medien-und Kulturwissenschaften 22/1, pp. 199–218.

Sheller, Mimi/Urry, John (2006): "The New Mobilities Paradigm." In: Environment and Planning A 38/2, pp. 207–226.

Silverstone, Roger/Haddon, Leslie (1996): "*Design and the Domestication of Information and Communication Technologies: Technical Change and Everyday Life.*" In: Mansell, Robin/Silverstone, Roger, (eds.), Communication by Design: The Politics of Information and Communication Technologies, Oxford: Oxford University Press, pp. 44–74.

Spigel, L. (1992): Make Room for TV: Television and the Family Ideal in Postwar America, Chicago, IL: University of Chicago Press.

Sprenger, Florian (2022): "Navigationen und Relationen. Eine medientheoretische Skizze und ein interplanetarisches Beispiel." In: Navigationen – Zeitschrift für Medien- und Kulturwissenschaften 22/1, pp. 243–254.

Sprenger, Florian (2019): Epistemologien des Umgebens: zur Geschichte, Ökologie und Biopolitik künstlicher environments, Bielefeld: transcript Verlag.

Star, Susan Leigh/Ruhleder, Karen (1994): "Steps Towards an Ecology of Infrastructure: Complex Problems in Design and Access for Large-scale Collaborative Systems." In: Proceedings of the 1994 ACM conference on Computer supported cooperative work.

Turkle, Sherry (2008): "Always-On/Always-On-You: The Tethered Self." In: Katz, James E. (ed.), Handbook of Mobile Communication Studies, Cambridge, MA: MIT Press. https://doi.org/10.7551/mitpress/9780262113120.003.0010 [last accessed November 4, 2022].

Vaussard, Florian/Fink, Julia/Bauwens, Valérie/Rétornaz, Philippe/Hamel, D., Dillenbourg, Pierre/Mondada, Francesco (2014): "Lessons Learned From Robotic Vacuum Cleaners Entering the Home Ecosystem" In: Robotics and Autonomous Systems 62/3, pp. 376–391.

White, Steven (2009): "Companion Animals: Members of the Family or Legally Discarded Objects?" In: The University of New South Wales Law Journal 32/3, pp. 852–878.

Zuboff, Shoshana (2019): The Age of Surveillance Capitalism: the Fight for a Human Future at the New Frontier of Power, New York, NY: PublicAffairs.

Frustration Free: How Alexa Orchestrates the Development of the Smart Home

Niklas Strüver

Abstract

This article examines the role of the Alexa voice assistant in shaping the development of smart home technologies. The investigation is based on an analysis of blog posts by Amazon's Alexa Team, which provide guidance to third-party developers on technological changes and possibilities. The concept of "orchestration" as a form of managed domestication initiated by a single party is utilised to understand how Amazon attempts to leverage platforms, standards and infrastructures surrounding Alexa to influence the development of smart home technologies. As more households are being equipped with supposedly home and life augmenting smart technologies, smart speakers and Alexa are marketed as the central connecting device between the different smart home technologies that helps users avoid compatibility problems. The study finds that companies wishing to build smart home technologies are encouraged to follow certain paths of development endorsed by Amazon, which is a crucial aspect of Alexa's role in coordinating the smart home. Throughout the analysis connections between managed domestication at the organizational level and the domestication of smart home devices by users are explored. Finally, a conceptualisation of technology development in the smart home ecosystem from an orchestration perspective is provided.

Keywords

Alexa, Amazon, Voice Assistants, Smart Home, Third-Party, Developers, Platform, Infrastructure

1. Introduction

More and more households are being equipped with smart technologies that are supposed to augment the home and the life within it. Voice assistants[1] (VA) or intelligent personal assistants (IPA) like Alexa or Google Home are on the forefront of this product group often referred to as Internet of Things (IoT). These devices afford a lot of possibilities for users ranging from simple tasks like setting a timer to more complicated tasks such as coordinating light and music volumes or scheduling meetings and reminders (Phan 2019). Many of the actions, however, are not intrinsic to the assistant itself. A big part of the advertised benefits is enabled by a connection with *Smart Home Technologies* (SHTs). All devices need to be integrated into a smart home and its daily routines by users – which reportedly can be difficult to coordinate (Strengers/Nicholls 2017: 88). Smart speakers are increasingly marketed as the central connecting device between the different technologies of the smart home that helps users avoid *compatibility problems* (Phan/Kim 2020).

This integration will be studied under the overarching term of *domestication* (Silverstone et al. 1992). In the case of VAs in conjunction with SHTs the domestication process of all these technologies is interrelated: The domestication of IoT devices might influence the domestication of IPAs and vice versa. Since these devices are connected to vast networks and rely on each other for their functioning, their domestication processes have to be interrelated. Brause and Blank (2020: 759) call "the impact of networked devices in each other's domestication" *externalisation*. Thinking outside of the household, this means that devices from different manufacturers become dependent on one another. Considering domestication as the *wider construction of institutions* that come with technologies (Sørensen 2006), the nature of the relationship between these companies can be analysed on a business-to-business (B2B) level. In the following, Alexa will be conceptualised as a *platform technology* (van Dijck et al. 2018) that attempts to shape its own surroundings according to Amazon's business goals of a *frustration free smart home*. The reduction of *friction* is a central goal for the domestic IoT and "requires standardisation across domain boundaries" (Goulden 2021: 235). Since standards are often shaped by powerful actors (Bowker/Star 2000), the focus will be on how Amazon – as a powerful actor in the smart home market (European Commission 2022: 13) – conducts an "orchestration of multiple partial views" (Suboticki/Sørensen 2021: 1242) to control the SHTs that are built by *Original Equipment Manufacturers*

---

1   The terms IPA, Voice Assistant, Alexa, Echo or smart speaker will be used synonymously throughout this article for better readability. However, it is important to differentiate between these initially: In the case of Amazon, the voice assistant software *Alexa* runs on the *Echo* hardware devices (e.g. speakers, cameras, appliances). The combination of software and hardware eventually forms the smart speaker.

(OEMs). This idea of orchestration will therefore be explored as an act of *taming* OEMs' building practices by qualitatively analysing blog posts on Amazon's *Alexa Device Makers Blog*[2] and investigating the question "what techniques of orchestration does Amazon employ to tame building practices of OEMs?". Conceptualising the idea of orchestration for the smart home market on a B2B level will illuminate the workings of the smart home sector as well as contribute to the sociotechnical understanding of IPAs and how they interact with SHTs. To understand how Amazon tames OEM's building practices, the body of research on device interconnections will be summarised.

2. Characteristics and functions of IPAs in the IoT

The general function of VAs consists of performing tasks that users ask of them in the form of questions and voice commands. For example, IPAs can provide information about products, plan navigation routes and times, locate restaurants, places of interest or supermarkets, and perform simple tasks such as setting a timer, retrieve information and creating calendar entries (Phan 2019). Hence, VAs unite various activities that would usually require several separate technologies in a single device[3] that is operable through voice control and is always on. Alexa can execute the mentioned functions based on its own device but a lot of the advertised benefits of a VA stem from a connection to other devices. This is where IoT devices produced by other companies come in. If Alexa is supposed to control the living room light, the assistant will need to be connected to a smart light bulb inside the living room – often by means of a third bridging device. The same goes for other smart devices that can be controlled by a VA. These SHTs could, and have for the longest time and still do function(ed) without a VA through smartphone apps, interface panels or remote controls. These control interfaces (especially in a multi-manufacturer device scenario) can complicate and impede daily practices in a smart home (Strengers/Nichols 2017; Strengers et al. 2019; Dahlgren et al. 2021; Humphry/Chesher 2021). Various attempts to solve this problem exist. These include control hubs that serve as a bridge and have their own app to control all other devices. However, differing software and hardware standards that are used complicate interaction immensely (Phan/Kim 2020). The European Commission (2021) aptly summarises the market situation: "Lack of interoperability due to technology fragmentation, lack of common standards and the prevalence of proprietary technology." Due to the complicated operation (Hargreaves et al. 2018)

---

2   https://developer.amazon.com/en-US/blogs/alexa/device-makers
3   Technically speaking, Alexa is the interface for Amazon's cloud services *Alexa Voice Service* (AVS) and *Amazon Web Services* (AWS), where all requests are processed by various machine learning algorithms (Crawford and Joler 2018), which are constantly optimised based on the incoming usage data.

and interoperability issues, the smart home has had the status of an imaginary more than an actual technology for a long time (Darby 2018). It is at this junction where IPAs come in: They are marketed as a central interface enabling interoperability and accessibility by streamlining any usage through voice interaction (Dahlgren et al. 2021), supposedly eradicating the clutter of different apps and remote controls. Voice assistants can then become important in establishing comfortable smart home settings that create *pleasance* (Strengers et al. 2020) for their users. In their roles as platforms (Goulden 2019) IPAs serve as interfaces that can set a variety of devices and services in motion creating (economical) dependencies between companies (European Commission 2022: 55–56). How technologies can be built when they are supposed to interact with Alexa is to a large degree decided by Amazon (Natale/Cooke 2021: 1007). This *political economy of the domestic IoT* (Goulden 2021) can express itself in the standards that are required to enable an interoperable and frictionless domestic IoT. How these standards are set to enable a reduction of friction is, however, largely unexplored. In the next chapter a conceptualisation for this will be offered by outlining a specific form of domestication theory and exploring theoretical ideas to apply them to IPAs and orchestration.

3. Domestication of company practices: Techniques of orchestration

Domestication can be described as a process of adopting new technologies by users. Technologies have "to be 'housetrained'; they have to be integrated into the structures, daily routines and values of users and their environments" (Berker et al. 2006: 2). The emphasis lies on social processes triggered by bringing a new technology (or media object) into "accordance with the household's own values and interests" (Silverstone et al. 1992: 14) as well as practices. This process is reciprocal and relational and includes various actors, institutions, and other entities (Silverstone 2006: 233) in a coproduced sociotechnical process, transcending a mere socialisation of technology (Sørensen 2006: 46). Domestication is a continued process of making links between people, artefacts, practices, interpretations, and organisational efforts. More generally, it is about making material connections and the practices surrounding them stable for everyday life (Klocke/Hartmann in this issue). These technologies should not be understood in isolation (Goulden 2021: 221). This multi sided process is complicated by interconnected, spatially distributed devices that interact in a VA-controlled smart home. In a networked home, device interconnections mean that the domestication of one device is affected by the other's and vice versa: "the impact of networked devices in each other's domestication" (Brause/Blank 2020: 759), a process called *externalisation*. This aspect of interdependencies of devices in the homes of users alludes to the underlying social, political, and technical structures and institutions that shape how users are able to domesticate their VA and IoT devices. Therefore, departing from the locus of the household, domestication will be viewed from a perspective of institutions like governments or corporations, as it is common in the *Nordic stream* of domestication research (Hartmann 2020). This version of domestication theory is dedicated to the construction of a wider everyday life and its institutions (Sørensen 2006: 46) and is closely related to *Science and Technology Studies* (STS). It is concerned with socio-technical relations that go beyond the household and include technologies and domestication areas beyond media objects that are domesticated by individuals or a small group of people (Hartmann 2020: 48). This is mainly because technologies require "construction of social institutions of infrastructure and regulation" (Sørensen 2006: 40) that become part of the domestication process. Just like in the household, these types of domestication are not free from conflicts and power struggles (Sørensen et al. 2000: 173). This is why this view on domestication is especially instructive. "When people need to be aligned in their use of a technology, domestication may require orchestration [...]. When goals and preferences differ, managerial interventions of some sort may be required, such as instigating negotiations and command and control efforts." (Suboticki/Sørensen 2021: 1234) This form of *managed domestication* is a negotiated and organised process that allows for coordination enables compatibility and the establishment of limitations. Suboticki and Sørensen use the metaphor of *orchestration* for this type of managed domestication. In this sense, orchestration shall be viewed as a form of "control without the tried-and-tested coordination mechanisms of ownership and authority" (Tiwana 2014: 52), as a more subtle and softer mode of managerial control that affords influence over the domestication process for powerful actors. This concept is an important link between researching the "construction of a wider everyday life" (Sørensen 2006: 46) through the lens of domestication research and the production of IPAs and SHTs since it addresses the B2B side of technology domestication: The social institutions, infrastructures, regulations, protocols, and ultimately power relations encompassed in developing SHTs and IPAs are central to users as well as companies, as they shape the whole smart home ecosystem. Through domestication efforts, a powerful actor in this process can influence all involved entities. In the sense of the title of this special issue "taming digital practices" (Waldecker/Hector in this issue) Amazon's attempts to domesticate or *tame* the development practices and devices of OEMs will be viewed through this idea of orchestration. The act of taming is an active organised process reducing complexity (Hacking 1990; Silvast/Virtanen 2019) by employing different methods of organising the development process. With these techniques, Amazon can attempt to tame the variety in technology development and control "what can and cannot be built, sustained, or thrive in the ecosystem" (van der Vlist, 2022: 91). These attempts will be scrutinised under the question "*What techniques of orchestration does Amazon employ to tame building practices of OEMs?*" Three further, interlocking theoretical ideas are necessary to analyse Amazon's domestication of OEMs:

A. One method of orchestration appropriated for the research on domesticating technologies between companies by Sørensen et al. (2000: 173-175) consists of the idea of configuring the user (Woolgar 1990; Grint/Woolgar 1997). Generally, configuring the user means to establish a certain way that a technology is supposed to be used and domesticated. In this case, OEMs will be considered as users (on a B2B level) that are being configured by Amazon in a social and in a technical way. On the one hand, OEMs can be swayed by a portrayal of expectations and desires of the smart home end-users led by the desire to produce popular devices. On the other hand, concepts and expectations of comfort, that smart home users supposedly have, can be transformed into technological standards that smaller manufacturers routinely adopt "in order to protect themselves from claims of professional negligence [...]" (Shove 2003: 199). By those means, OEMs can be *enrolled* into Amazon's visions (Grint/Woolgar 1997: 28, 78). In sum, this concept of configuring the user will be applied to OEMs that are configured by a portrayal of smart home end-users.

B. By setting standards and developing technologies for SHTs and offering these through Alexa as infrastructure (Bowker/Star 2000: 37) to help satisfy quality controls, Amazon establishes a deep technological integration into the SHT ecosystem. This integration is established by developing and providing infrastructural tools "such as software and communications devices; checklists and protocols; and styles of reasoning [...]" (Silvast/Virtanen 2019: 465). These may range from actual hardware and software provided by Amazon to standards and certificates offered by Amazon, that OEMs can achieve. By these means, Amazon guides OEMs in their development process for SHT and simultaneously limits design options for devices. The creation of these sociotechnical tools that become an infrastructural part in the SHT development process is another technique of taming and reducing the complexity that OEMs' development practices can bring into the ecosystem.

These domestication mechanisms highlight how Amazon as a powerful market entity can attempt to orchestrate the domestication process by influencing the way that OEMs build their devices. In this way, Amazon can leverage different means to orchestrate the larger ecosystem around Alexa and ensure that OEMs build their devices in ways that suit Amazon's goals, or at the very least assure that IoT devices are built with Alexa in mind[4].

Lastly, to contextualise these two techniques of taming, it is important to frame Alexa as a platform. Most platforms share similar attributes and mecha-

---

[4] It is essential to remember that a domestication process means that both sides change in non-linear ways (Sørensen et al. 2000) and will result in changes on both sides that accommodate for each other's devices. However, it is important to be sensitive to power imbalances in these negotiation processes.

nisms which allow them to structure their surroundings (Dolata 2019: 184–185). Understanding some of the core tenants of platforms – and the platform companies behind them – helps understand the mechanisms of orchestration deployed by Amazon. In its unifying role for the smart home, the IPA needs to be the connecting point for many different actors and technologies. Platforms are technologies that offer integrations for different complementary attachments to it and facilitate additions (e.g., content, apps, services, devices) to the platform ecosystem (Baldwin/Woodard 2008; Srnicek 2017: 96), while controlling how these additions interact with the platform (van Dijck et al. 2018: 38). The establishment and harnessing of *network effects* that create increasing marginal benefits is central to the functioning of most platforms: The more numerous the users who use a platform, the more valuable that platform becomes for everyone else. "But this generates a cycle whereby more users beget more users, which leads to platforms having a natural tendency towards monopolisation." (Srnicek 2017: 45) For the IPA-controlled smart home market this means that the IPA that is compatible with more SHTs offers more choice to prospective new smart home users, which in turn creates incentives for OEMs to build their devices to be compatible with it, thus reinforcing this process[5] and possibly creating a monopoly. This process interacts with the aspect of configuring the user **(A)**. Network effects can similarly be harnessed through the concentration of resources enabling platform companies to utilise their technical and logistical infrastructures as well as their research and development (R&D) capacities efficiently across platforms (Dolata 2019: 190). Especially these last effects can be leveraged to offer OEMs an infrastructure, as it was described above **(B)**. Lastly, this offering of infrastructure to OEMs is meant to ensure that their innovative products will benefit the platform ecosystem: "Instead of itself attempting to innovate in diverse markets and domains [...], the platform owner can massively distribute innovation work to large numbers of [...] developers" (Tiwana 2014: 62). Involving OEMs as providers of innovation enables Amazon to focus on the development of Alexa, while OEMs provide knowledge in their specific domains, which is essential to system designers like Amazon (Sørensen et al. 2000: 174). Analysing the Alexa Device Makers Blog can illustrate these techniques of orchestration that Amazon uses to tame OEMs' building practices.

---

5   Other crucial network effects for platforms come in terms of information about customers and the development of algorithms through the collection, analysis, and reappropriation of data (Srnicek 2017: 50–60). These effects have significance with IPA, too (see e.g. Natale/Cooke 2021: 1005), they are, however, not the focus of this article.

4. Method

A qualitative document analysis (Bowen 2009; Kuckartz 2014) was performed to study the Alexa Device Makers Blog. Amazon's Alexa Team uses this blog to announce new developments for Alexa and to promote the possibilities for OEMs. These texts provide a kind of technological diary reporting Amazon's development and visions for Alexa and the smart home ecosystem. They document technological development that Amazon achieves and plans when it comes to the domestic IoT and gives information about Alexa's (imagined) role and capabilities for OEMs and end-users alike. The contents of the posts range from technological reports, or descriptions of new tools and in-depth tutorials to stories of companies that work with Alexa and news stories that address current events. Although OEMs are likely the intended audience, this wide range of topics and the somewhat repetitive and erratic style of writing make it unclear what type of technological proficiency the recipients are supposed to have. They were therefore not analysed as journalistic documents, but as a documentation of technological and narrative development. Data was selected according to the question of whether the contents describe the interconnection between IPA and IoT devices. This means that posts focussing more on marketing events (e.g. "Register Now for Alexa Live 2021"), advertising (e.g. "3 Tips on how to think about robotics"), or news stories (e.g. "Alexa leader offers career tips to women") were not taken into consideration, since they were not expected to contribute much to conceptualising orchestration effects between Amazon and OEMs. Because technologies used in the market are likely to change and be reiterated upon quickly, a three-year time frame was chosen. Relevant posts published between January 17th, 2019 and March 15th, 2022 (n=51)[6] that target the domestic IoT were selected and collected (using MaxQDA Web Collector). This method of data collection produced text documents of every analysed blog post in a MaxQDA-proprietary data format. This format prohibited certain text editing (such as line numbering) and made the line references of coded segments unusable. This decreases the accuracy of quotations in the analysis section. However, since most documents are relatively short and clear in their messages, this caveat weighs less heavily. Posts were analysed using thematic qualitative text analysis (Kuckartz 2014: 69–80). This analysis was guided by deductive categories derived from the established theory, as well as from inductive categories that evolved during the first rounds of coding (Kuckartz 2014: 55, 63). Main categories were constructed around the theory, relevant text segments were coded and analysed in-depth in MaxQDA. The analysis of texts was derived from comparing coded segments of the subcodes to each other. The concept of orchestration as an act of taming is

---

6   The blog posts (BP) have been given an abbreviation according to their number in the data set (BP#). The data and documentation can be accessed here: https://fodasi.e-science-service.uni-siegen.de/handle/fodasi/38.

thus conceptualised by illustrating reoccurring topics in the analysed blog posts and enriching the material with theory elements. Finally, limitations of this study need to be acknowledged. Selection bias and the lack of triangulation with other research materials (Bowen 2009: 32) need to be accounted for: This study mainly aims to conceptualise the idea of orchestration for domestication research on a B2B level and is more interested in establishing the sociotechnical importance of this process than pursuing conclusive results about the IoT sector.

5. Orchestrating the Smart Home

The following analysis connects developed theoretical arguments to empirical data in order to portray Amazon's orchestration attempts in the IoT market from the position of a market leader. It is important to keep in mind that Amazon's statements on these blog posts construct a social reality most likely benefiting their company's goals and their accuracy in depicting reality should therefore be questioned (Jasanoff 2015). This does not lessen the impact that statements can have on OEMs who are dependent on Alexa to gain access to a market, which helps to make the consequences of Amazon's proclamations real. The following section is structured around the two analytical main topics of configuring the user (5.1) and providing infrastructure and standards (5.2) as means of orchestration. The separation of these two concepts is more of an analytical one. Both concepts will be used to complement each other when necessary, while the impact of platform logics is pervasive throughout.

5.1 Configuring the user through Alexa

Amazon's taming aspirations towards OEMs start with a portrayal of smart home end-users. By portraying its customers in a certain way, Amazon sets expectations for OEMs and users alike of how exactly an interaction with a smart home should be. After all, "[c]onvenience is a complex concept but one that is used to sell any number of appliances and devices." (Shove 2003: 195) This is a powerful reason to construct a notion of comfort that can (only) be achieved by the use of certain technologies. By producing this narrative, end-users might expect said comfort and, more importantly, OEMs might want to deliver technologies that enable that comfort in order to be successful on the market. Staple Amazon sentences such as "[w]ith connected devices becoming increasingly ubiquitous around the world, customers have come to expect a struggle-free, tinker-free, and stress-free experience when setting up their devices" (BP 41) are frequently reiterated (e.g. BP17, 43). These emphasise that users wish to live in a world of ubiquitous smart technology that gives *delightful experiences* through frictionless functionality (BP17). Amazon sees itself as a service brand with an "obsession with providing premium customer experiences" (BP51). This *customer obsession* serves as a guiding philosophy across all endeavours (BP7) and applies to Alexa and the (extended) services it offers. Customers demanding frictionless service and a desire to serve this customer is therefore a narrative OEMs will be constantly confronted with, nudging them to share these goals. To ensure this level of service, the smart home ecosystem Amazon intends to build in cooperation with OEMs becomes ubiquitous. Since constructing a "'360 degree' service experience" (West 2022: 117) can hardly be achieved by a single company, Amazon has subscribed to the idea that the smart home necessarily consists of devices and services produced by multiple companies. This somewhat intertwines the success of Alexa and the SHT built by OEMs. Implicitly assuming that this will cause frictions, Amazon therefore portrays itself as the mediating platform that assures customer's comfort (BP7). As frictionless systems recede into the background of practice and become visible only upon breakdown (Bowker/Star 2000: 33–34), smart home users should not – according to Amazon – experience connectivity issues with their devices (BP34), or need to do device maintenance (e.g., updating software, or replacing batteries) in general (BP35). Therefore, all of these problems are supposed to be solved on the device maker's side, giving users "more time to enjoy the convenience of Smart Home technology." (BP34) These expectancies portrayed in the blog posts are in line with what West calls a *served self*, which is a consumer that has their needs and preferences attended to by Amazon and is a motif for the whole company and Alexa (2022: 135). This construction of a normality that users and other companies are organised around (Shove 2003: 203) can put OEMs under pressure to cater to the needs of customers depicted by Amazon – as it is a powerful "circulation of stories and tales about the experiences of users" (Grint/Woolgar 1997: 75); a configuration of OEMs.

In a heterogenous smart home managing all the devices might become tedious. Amazon cites *device setup complexity* (BP41) and problems as one of the biggest sources "of Amazon customer service contacts and returns for smart home devices" (BP35) and thus suggests a minimisation of these problems through Alexa. To facilitate a frictionless infrastructure for customers and OEMs alike, Alexa handles these tasks in the background (BP7). If this were a reality, Alexa would serve as a *frictionless interface* (Sadowski 2020: 47) standardising different domains. Reducing complications seems to be a central goal of the domestic IoT and Amazon is poising Alexa as a key component to minimise friction in the act of consumption (Hill 2020: 225; West 2022: 142) and IoT interaction. OEMs can choose to establish their own Alexa smart home skill linking devices with Alexa, or directly link their services to the AVS cloud so that customers do not have to enable a skill, and use devices with even less effort to setup the system (BP2, 3). This integration process often happens in iterations of increasing reliance on Amazon's services, as can be seen in this description of a cooperation with the OEM Kasa:

"While Kasa smart home devices were originally controlled only via the Kasa mobile app, with the popularity of Alexa, the obvious solution was to add Alexa voice control to the smart plug. TP-Link first built a custom Alexa skill to control their devices, then eventually created an Alexa Smart Home skill. However, the company knew there was still room for improvement, especially with the initial setup. [...] 'The user had to download the Kasa app and perform a dozen taps to make the device controllable. That's too many.' For example, with the Kasa app alone, it took a customer 10 to 15 taps to configure a Kasa smart plug on their phone before they could control it with Alexa. [...] Today, when a customer buys a Kasa smart plug, they simply take the device out of the box, plug it in, and within seconds, the device is connected and ready to be controlled using Alexa smart home voice commands." (BP20)

Here the rising expectations propagated by Amazon are directly linked to how OEMs perceive their own products and then rely on Amazon to enhance them. This is exemplary for the orchestration ideas of configuring OEMs and providing infrastructures to aid them as a technique of taming. Alexa seemingly eliminates the need for OEMs to develop and maintain their own apps to setup and control devices and reduces the amount of Alexa apps consumers need to remember and interact with (BP27, 41, 44). Amazon aspires to erase the need for cumbersome bridge technologies – like apps, hubs, or remote controls (Stengers/Nicholls 2017: 88) – in a smart home with Alexa. According to Amazon, this easy to integrate *off-the-shelf voice interaction* (BP24) becomes a necessary inclusion for SHTs (e.g., BP50, 51), putting pressure on OEMs to develop with a deep Alexa integration in mind, which seemingly is the customer's wish:

"Alexa provides the familiar experiences they [customers] already know and love." (BP4)

"Customers love their ACK [Alexa Connect Kit] devices; every ACK device to date has a 4-star rating or higher on Amazon.com." (BP32)

"Many customers now see Alexa integration as a 'minimum requirement' for smart home products [...]." (BP50)

To further create the image of an inevitable Alexa integration into all SHTs, Amazon advertises a wide range of device types that already feature Alexa integrations[7] stating that an Alexa integration boosts consumers' confidence in brands (BP28, 29), lowers development costs (e.g., BP33, 50) and enhances device security (BP40, 50). Between extensive development tools offered by Amazon and VA becoming the access point to the smart home, Alexa as a platform gradually

---

7   For example, Wi-Fi routers (BP15, 27, 35), ovens, pressure cookers, grills, and other kitchen appliances (BP 18, 31, 46, 48), vacuum cleaners (BP3, 16, 24) or door locks and cameras (BP12 51).

becomes *infrastructuralised* (Plantin et al. 2018) for OEMs. In this role, the IPA eventually could replace the need for smart home users to interact with the actors in the OEM ecosystem and vice versa. In short, Amazon leverages computational power, a global infrastructure (Crawford/Joler 2019), R&D resources (Dolata 2019: 189) and a rhetoric that constructs user expectancies that are not fulfillable without Alexa in order to configure OEMs to develop their products to be compatible with Alexa. Reconsidering the definition of orchestration as a form of taming that uses negotiations and control efforts that don't rely on direct authority (Tiwana 2014: 53; Suboticki/Sørensen 2021: 1234), the idea of configuring users has shown how Amazon orchestrates OEMs' practices by painting the picture of an expectant smart home-user. The next chapter will explore how Amazon establishes optional device standards that are de-facto industry standards; control without authority.

5.2 Infrastructures to build a dream on

To guarantee a frictionless entrance of SHTs into the Alexa ecosystem, Amazon establishes standards and infrastructures that OEMs can utilise when building/developing their devices. The certificates *Works With Alexa* (WWA), *Frustration Free Setup* (FFS) and *Certified for Humans* (CFH) are prevalent in the dataset and marketing. In order to achieve the desired interoperability with VAs like Alexa, OEMs might feel the "need to follow certification processes to gain approval for their customised integrations and abide to the, mostly non-negotiable, terms and conditions of these platforms." (European Commission 2022: 56) Therefore, standards set by Amazon, (similar to Google and Apple, which offer comparable certificates) are important to the industry and can be analysed as another tool for orchestrating the smart home ecosystem. All three standards share a similar purpose and frequently occur in the same documents and coded segments.

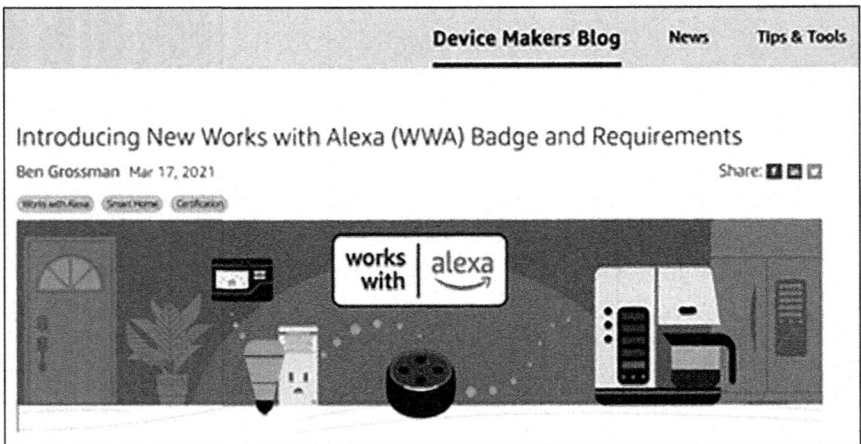

Fig. 1: *Works With Alexa (BP28)*

Fig. 2: Frustration-Fee Setup (BP22)

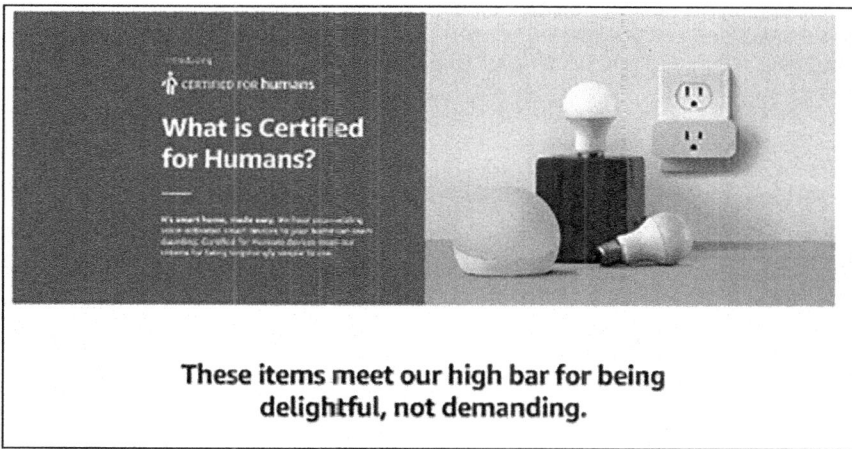

Fig. 3: Certified For Humans https://www.amazon.com/b?node=19982322011

Before discussing what these badges mean for OEMs, it is necessary to understand why they should be desirable – in Amazon's eyes. Launched in 2016, WWA (Fig. 1) is supposed to signal to customers that OEMs' "products integrate seamlessly with Alexa" (BP51). Similarly, the FFS (Fig. 2) standard was initiated in 2018 and is "aimed at making setting up a smart home absolutely simple" (BP35) by enabling customers to "plug the device right out of the box and get connected in as little as under a minute." (BP20) This is supposed to simplify the setup process (BP16, 17) and offer a "struggle-free, tinker-free, and stress-free experience." (BP41) Lastly, CFH (Fig. 3) can be described as a combination of the other two standards, as a CFH certified product also needs to hold the WWA and FFS badge (BP35). In essence, all three certificates boil down to a badge that OEMs can display on their product pages and device boxes that are supposed to increase customer engagement because of suspected higher degrees of functionality, compatibility, and safety (BP5, 20, 23, 28, 35, 51). Amazon emphasises that certified devices are also displayed in special categories on Amazon.com, which increases visibility (BP14, 32, 33, 50). Stated in simple terms, certified devices are the answer to the demanding customer profile painted by Amazon (as seen previously), while also benefiting OEMs. Again, Amazon is establishing their picture of a consumer that desires a frictionless and frustration free smart home, while leveraging their own commercial platform market space in order to create incentives for OEMs to develop Amazon certified devices. This positions their platforms (namely Amazon.com and Alexa) as a gravitational point for OEMs in the name of customer obsession. As is customary with platforms, access to these benefits is granted generously and at a low entrance barrier in order to increase market capture (van Dijck et al. 2018: 38) and certify as many products as possible:

"'Integrating Frustration Free Setup with our Alexa-enabled devices was a very simple process,' says Zhang. 'We had great support from Amazon throughout the entire journey.' Frustration Free Setup's developer portal is a one stop shop for developers to access instructions, technical documentation, software, and data specifications." (BP16)

Seen from an infrastructural point of view, this quote alludes to an attempt at orchestration through standards that is seated at a deep technological level. In order to be eligible for all three badges certain technological requirements set by Amazon need to be fulfilled. Most frequently, standards are reflections of values, opinions, rhetoric and organisational policies stabilised by the establishment of an infrastructure (Bowker/Star 2000: 135). Considering that the reduction of friction is a proclaimed aim for the IoT sector and that this "requires standardisation across domain boundaries" (Goulden 2021: 235), these badges are an example for an attempt at setting standards for the reduction of friction. The practices of a field can be strongly shaped by its infrastructures, standards and values that go into forming them, which will be explored next.

The FFS badge offers a great example for this because the term *frustration free* is also a standard for packages that get sent via Amazon.com. Frustration free packaging is supposed to reduce frictions in the logistics of delivery while simultaneously addressing consumer comfort and concerns about wasteful packaging. Sellers wanting to access Amazon's market need to adapt to the packaging specifications set by Amazon (West 2022: 56–57). This standard gives Amazon the power to influence businesses all across the world. With packaging, it is the famous brown box. For SHTs, having a badge on the packaging is one important factor (BP14). Less like in packaging, however, Amazon heavily influences the products inside the boxes carrying badges: OEMs need to have a constant monitoring of server and device statuses with inbuilt alarms that "automatically notify your dev team about anomalous activity when critical incidents happened (e.g. customer-impacting issue [...] which may require interaction with Alexa team and/or fixes on developer side)." (BP12) Tracking coincides with Amazon's compulsory troubleshooting and traffic-tracking tools that ensure device and service availability and reliability. OEMs also need to update their devices when Amazon makes changes to the specifications of their standards (BP28) so that devices satisfy "connectivity, service reliability, and feature standards for quality and integration with Alexa." (BP29) These changes, however, should not be implemented in times when Amazon engineers might not be available for support (BP12). This aligns OEMs' *development and maintenance practices* (Bowker/Star 2000: 49) with Amazon's and puts them in a reactive role needing to respond to changes in infrastructures or standards made by Amazon that *cascade* to their own devices (Slota/Bowker 2017: 540). Further, Amazon requires OEMs to first test their devices themselves (BP23, 26, 39) and then have them certified by authorised test laboratories[8], which "help developers streamline the path to certification and reduce time to market while assuring their product delivers the high quality and consistent experience that Alexa customers expect." (BP10) All of these requirements are guided by Amazon's desire to ensure quality, which might generally not be unusual in the industry. However, being the singular instance that sets and adjusts requirements for badges and assesses each product according to its own standards puts Amazon in a powerful position to orchestrate the way in which OEMs build products. This powerful influence is typical for platform companies that utilise their central position to shape the ecosystem in their interest (van der Vlist 2022: 91). For packaging, West (2022: 57) argues that the attention Amazon gives to *the Box* is justified because it is a significant touchpoint a customer will have with Amazon. This argument draws the connection between the domestication processes of externalisation on the micro level and orchestration on an institutional macro level. If translated to the smart home, this argument underlines the importance of externalisation and shows why Amazon attempts to ensure that devices adapt into the Alexa ecosystem as frictionless as possible. In a networked smart home operated by interaction with Alexa, the VA is the prime touchpoint between users, their smart home and Amazon. SHTs that are complicated to domesticate for users could shine a bad light on Amazon, since from a user's perspective, Alexa, as the platform of the smart home, does not enable the promised comfort. This effect of co-dependent domestication on the user level (externalisation) makes Amazon invest into taming OEMs' practices on a company level (orchestration), which will

---

8   As in the case of frustration free packaging, which requires certification from the *International Safe Transit Association* (West 2022: 57), these independent organisations are authorised by Amazon to specifically test devices on proprietary standards. Finding *suitable test subjects* (Grint/Woolgar 1997: 94) that might want to test OEMs devices is offloaded to Amazon and its contractors, giving Amazon another instance of power over the construction process.

in turn affect the micro level. Certificates offered by Amazon therefore affect users and OEMs alike as a form of taming.

This infrastructuralisation around Alexa and its badges becomes even more evident when considering the extensive offers of ready-made software packages called *software development kits* (SDK) and off-the-shelf hardware called *Alexa Connect Kits* (ACK). SDKs allow OEMs to use adaptable software packages to develop their product, offer Amazon's device management software and enable control through Alexa (BP25, 34, 36). By using these strictly Amazon-managed SDKs OEMs can "concentrate more on integrating more features instead of worrying how each would be supported with voice intent interpretation". (BP24) Coincidentally using some of the SDKs for Alexa control in a product makes it automatically qualify for Amazon's badges (BP33). Similarly, the ACK is advertised as a

"managed service from Amazon that makes it easy to connect your product to Alexa, and deliver voice-forward experiences for your customers. With ACK, you don't need to write an Alexa skill, manage a cloud service, or develop complex network and security firmware to connect your product to Alexa. Instead, you integrate an ACK hardware module into your product -- and presto!" (BP49)

ACKs are chipsets that OEMs can buy and incorporate into any IoT device during the manufacturing process. They afford Alexa connectivity, a development board, Wi-Fi access, network security, cloud access and make all devices accessible to Alexa (BP33, 35, 42). Lastly, devices with integrated ACK will automatically meet the requirements for WWA, FFS and CFH (BP32). By developing SDKs and ACKs that are ready to deploy for most imaginable IoT devices, Amazon again leverages its own R&D and platform power (Dolata 2019: 189) in order to create tools that, according to Amazon, are extremely cost-effective and adapted to the ecosystem (BP15, 43, 48) whichOEMs might find increasingly harder not to incorporate in their devices. This then reinforces the importance of Alexa and the badges for OEMs. This aspect of platform technologies reduces innovation cost and time for third-party contractors (Plantin et al. 2018: 296). It changes the type of development which smaller companies trying to enter the smart home sector need to do themselves in order to gain access to the *vast technological systems and platforms* (Crawford/Joler 2018) enabling voice control through Alexa. This way, OEMs are incentivised to develop with Alexa compatibility in mind by offering simple implementation into smart homes as well as an audience (end-users) for their products that comes with the large userbase of Alexa. Building, development, testing, certification, advertisement, packaging, shipping through Amazon.com and ultimately the purpose (comfort) of devices that OEMs might build for the smart home are deeply indebted to Alexa in so many ways. Amazon's technical, organisational, and logistical infrastructures become *platformised* (Plantin et al. 2018) as OEMs gain access to all of these services through the Alexa platform. The focus on the platform as an infrastructure for OEMs allows Amazon to set the institutional constraints for the interactions of SHTs and Alexa in the smart home. The practices of OEMs therefore are "[...] embedded in a larger social context where the methods and resources available impose important constraints on their practices." (Sørensen et al. 2000: 351–352). This roots Alexa at a *subtending* infrastructural level (Slota/Bowker 2017: 540) in the building of technology as well as the organisational practices of development and maintenance[9].

While the acts of orchestrations seem to relieve OEMs workload, the back-ends of SHTs become more homogenous in the sense that they are based on similar building blocks, achieve the same goals, by similar means; all provided by Amazon. Lastly, this is reminiscent of the influence Amazon has on the retail industry: "Given Amazon's control of the ecommerce market, its certification regimes for sellers amount to more than just the demand of one client, but rather a form of governance for packaging and manufacturing industries as a whole." (West 2022: 57) In this case however, Amazon is extending its role as an essential part of the internet economy to the smart home and the development of new technologies, effectively attempting to tame an entire branch of devices. This last aspect will be expanded upon next, since it allows for synthesis of the topics covered so far.

---

9 Defining notions of comfort, easy set-up, integration, and interconnection is of course not in Amazon's power alone but "depends upon a complex supply chain of interdependent institutions and interests (Shove 2003: 198–199). The companies producing VAs, however, are in a powerful position to define goals of technology solutions (European Commission 2022: 101–102). Their influence can be seen in interoperability initiatives like Matter or Zigbee that are joint endeavours including many SHT and VA companies (BP1). While, in theory, this could pose a threat to Amazon's market dominance by making SHT interoperable with different IPAs, the BPs show how Amazon counteracts this by taking a leading role in the development of these interoperability standards (BP5, 45) and also by embedding them into all Echo devices (BP7, 16). Consequently, the proprietary FFS standard is embedded into the specifications of the supposedly open Matter technology, which enables all of Alexa's benefits to Matter devices in order to increase relevancy despite the standard's inclusion of other VAs. Through infrastructuralised badge standards built into many SHTs, Amazon ensures that devices built based on Matter are easy to integrate with Alexa, while still advertising its commitment to interoperability, choice and an open smart home.

6. Understanding the frustration free ecosystem

After studying the Alexa Developer Blog through the lens of orchestration, answers to the research question have been given throughout multiple arguments. Forming a synthesis between theoretical arguments of orchestration and results of their application to the blog posts, a model of domestication processes for the smart home can be generated (Fig. 4)[10]. The following part attempts to describe the process of the taming of OEM's building practices by Amazon's orchestration techniques. However, given platforms' general necessity of drawing in users as well as Amazon's customer focus, it will begin by looking at some aspects of the users' domestication processes in the smart home to inform the orchestration effects on a B2B level.

Despite being an idea developed on the user level, the concept of externalisation in the domestication of IPAs and SHTs (Brause/Blank 2020), has an impact on the orchestration at the B2B level. **Users** start this process by selecting their preferred IPA and SHTs from the available devices in the smart home market for their home. Domesticated by users, IPAs and SHTs have an impact on each other's domestication (externalisation), e.g., effects of interoperability and shared functionalities. This in turn reflects on the success of these devices, since shortcomings of a product (like a complicated setup) might reflect badly on the others, while a frustration-free domestication of the smart home on a user level might promote general usage eventually; making devices interdependent on user- and business-levels. Devices are the boundary between companies and users after all (Sørensen et al. 2000: 173–175). These effects of the user-level can then be traced to the business entities involved, who ultimately want to sell and distribute their products. Thus, Amazon's style guide for Alexa developers "refers to the user as a 'customer' throughout: a clear indication of their intended role." (Natale/Cooke 2018: 1007) In its goal to maintain Alexa's leading position in the smart home market, **Amazon** develops Alexa as a central platform for the domestic IoT by enabling more interoperability and functions through the VA, offering more choice for OEMs and users. With the connection to SHTs becoming a core marketing feature of Alexa, the further development generates expectations towards OEMs, who find themselves pressured to fulfil the requirements and expectations that *Amazon* sets for SHTs working with Alexa. In order to control how SHTs can connect to Alexa, Amazon develops socio-technical standards, which become central certification points for SHTs. To simplify the connection between Alexa and SHTs further, Amazon offers off-the-shelf development

---

10 This representation necessarily is reductionistic. As previously mentioned, the impact of IPA-competitors like Google and Apple as well as regulatory institutions and other hybrid initiatives like Matter do play a role. However, by focussing on the Alexa-SHT-ecosystem, the orchestration processes can be analysed in greater detail.

software and technology. These infrastructures can be used to build SHTs with Alexa integration, reducing or eradicating all connection work. These processes loop recursively as Alexa and all technologies concerned with Alexa are innovated upon.

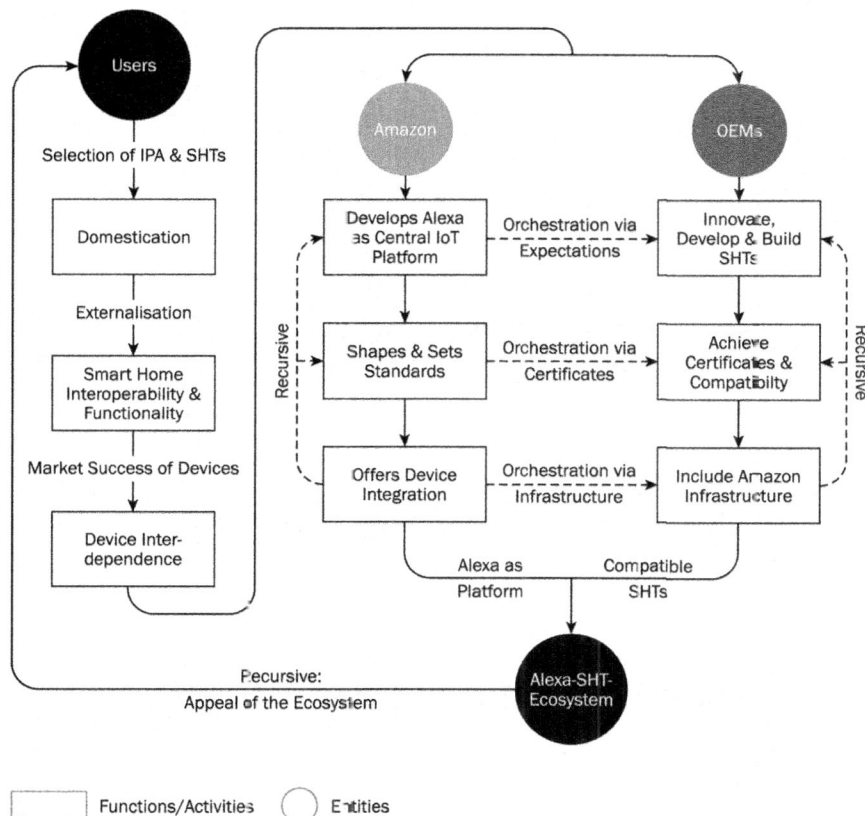

Fig. 4: *Orchestration in the Smart Home Ecosystem*

OEMs build and develop SHTs, which brings innovation of devices to the smart home market (Tiwana 2014: 62). However, they are heavily influenced by the imaginaries and expectations that Amazon proposes for a future of the smart home. Since IPAs are supposedly the central interface of the smart home, enabling a smooth connection with these is essential to OEMs. Therefore, achieving compatibility and relying on Alexa certification and services for their devices gives them access to a large user base and becomes a de-facto industry standard. To focus more on innovating and refining their products and improve their core services as a brand, OEMs can forgo spending time on connecting their devices with Alexa, by incorporating Amazon's infrastructures into their devices. These processes, too, occur recursively as devices are innovated and reiterated upon. However,

SHTs carry the influence of IPA in their design and become dependent on IPA as a subtending platform and infrastructure.

Combining Alexa as a platform and Alexa-compatible SHTs, both strings constitute the **Alexa-SHT-ecosystem** that users can chose from when building their smart homes, forming the last recursive loop before the whole process is repeated. Orchestration has an impact on compatibility and connectivity between devices and can affect the attractiveness of the Alexa-SHT-ecosystem for users, which – according to the logic of network effects – affects Alexa's appeal for OEMs. In this mechanism, Amazon's idea behind the frustration-free smart home achieved by orchestration through Alexa becomes evident: Alexa being attractive to end-users as a platform for a frictionless smart home, makes the IPA an appealing platform to OEMs. This in turn increases Alexa's presence on the VA market and stabilises Amazon's market position on the VA market. In this position, Amazon as a service provider with its self-declared customer obsession aims to enrol OEMs into their created infrastructure to ensure that the smart home is as frictionless as possible. Recalling Suboticki and Sørensen's (2021) definition of orchestration, this aligns OEMs in their use of voice technology with Amazon's visions for the smart home through different orchestration techniques. By the means of orchestration, Amazon effectively tames OEMs and their devices to fit into the Alexa ecosystem in a similar way as users domesticate technologies into their homes.

This last recursive loop shows how actions on the user side (choosing devices under the influence of externalisation effects) can affect the institutions that shape and enable these interactions (IPA's and SHT's interactions and functions shaped by orchestration techniques) and be influenced by them at the same time: Activities on the micro level shape macro-level institutions, while these institutions structure the interaction on the micro level (Giddens 1984: 141)[11]. This perpetual reciprocity shows how both externalisation and orchestration are complementary analytical points when studying networked devices in the home as they influence each other.

7. Conclusion

This study illuminates the workings of IPAs in the smart home sector and contributes to the sociotechnical understanding of IPAs and how they interact with SHTs. To facilitate this, an STS-influenced idea of domestication research (Sørensen et al. 2000; Sørensen 2006) was used to explore the techniques of orchestration (Tiwana 2015; Suboticki/Sørensen 2021) that Amazon employs to tame OEMs'

---

11 The processes described here and in Fig. 4 necessarily have different temporalities since the development, reception, reiteration, domestication, and orchestration of technologies are very different processes with varying velocity-dynamics.

building practices for SHTs. Analysing the Alexa Device Makers Blog as a diary of technology development and imaginaries for Alexa gives an insight on Amazon's perspective on this process. The theories of user configuration (Woolgar 1990), infrastructure (Bowker/Star 2000), and platform studies (Plantin et al. 2018) that were used to conceptualise Amazon's orchestration help frame the development of technologies to reduce frustration for end-users as an act of sublty influencing OEMs' development practices. In this way, the political economy of the domestic IoT (Goulden 2021) can be seen under sociotechnical aspects of the work of standardisation that is required to make the smart home work. By analysing the certificates and technologies that Amazon continually develops to drive standardisation, Amazon's attempt at becoming a subtending infrastructure for SHTs could be seen as acts of orchestrating and influencing OEMs. The analysis of blog posts shows how the infrastructuralisation of Alexa as a platform positions Alexa at the centre of development processes and ensures that OEMs build their devices in ways that suit Amazon's goals or, at the very least, assure that SHTs are built with Alexa in mind. It therefore qualifies as an act of taming OEMs in the sense that a conscious, organised, and technological process is employed by Amazon to tame the complexities (Silvast/Virtanen 2019: 465) that come with a technology which interfaces with multiple manufacturers. The idea of the frustration-free smart home is mainly driven by the attempt to reduce the variety of building practices in the name of interoperability and efficiency while effectively securing Amazon's market position in the IoT sector. These B2B processes were put into perspective by considering "the impact of networked devices in each other's domestication" (Brause/Blank 2020: 759) on a micro level. The eventual necessity of IPAs and SHTs to be bought and domesticated by users highlights the importance of a smooth device interaction on a micro level: Shortcomings of one device could reflect badly on others, while frictionless connections might promote the use of IPAs and SHTs alike, connecting the manufacturers technologically and economically.

Adding the user level to the analysis finally enables the development of a graphic model of the linkages between micro and macro processes in the domestic IoT. This model puts the actors in the smart home sector into relation with each other and emphasises the effects of orchestration while also incorporating the influence of the user level. Viewing the construction of institutions, infrastructures, and standards (Sørensen 2006: 40–41) of technologies like IPAs and SHTs from this perspective reveals the pervasive acts of influence that a company like Amazon has over the smart home. This figure shows how Alexa as a platform controls expectations and innovation in the ecosystem (van der Vlist 2022: 203). This is especially important to analyse critically if seen in context of Amazon's constant pursuit to *essentialise convenience* and *normalise monopoly*, for which Alexa is a crucial asset (West 2022: 117, 128–133). Making Alexa a seemingly indispensable part for users and OEMs showcases the power that Amazon holds over the domestic IoT. The contribution of this article to analysing orchestration attempts on a sociotechnical level allows a perspective on IPAs and SHTs and the power hierarchies that are built into technologies. This perspective expands the body of research on device interconnection in the smart home as it addresses the role of VA for the smart home. It focuses neither on the economic and regulatory aspects of the IoT (European Commission 2021; 2022), nor on the direct domestication at the user level (Brause/Blank 2020). It further contributes to understanding the narrative of the reduction of friction as a work of "standardisation across domain boundaries" (Goulden 2021: 235) and a central driver for the IoT sector (Darby 2018). Future research could expand on this work by contrasting the orchestration attempts analysed here with the evaluation and practices of OEMs. A qualitative study of development practices could show how the effects of orchestration affect the actual development process and would give a new perspective on the field of the smart home and voice assistants. This would give voice to a vital entity of the smart home ecosystem and could emphasise that orchestration and taming are non-linear processes that change all involved parties (Sørensen et al. 2000), as "imposed standards will produce work-arounds" (Bowker/Star 2000: 159). The orchestration model developed in this article can be applied to study the impact of other IPAs like Google Assistant and Siri in their ecosystems as they share a large sum of similarities. In conclusion, the concept of orchestration has proven to be a fruitful way of questioning the wider sociotechnical construction of the smart home as it has shown how Alexa tames the development of the smart home.

Acknowledgements

I have no conflict of interest to declare. I want to thank Tim Hector, David Waldecker, Dagmar Hoffmann and various discussants for providing helpful comments at different stages of this article. I further want to thank the anonymous reviewers for their thorough work and valuable suggestions. Finally, I would like to thank Roete Design for the graphic design of the central figure of this piece.

Gefördert durch die Deutsche Forschungsgemeinschaft (DFG) – Projektnummer 262513311 – SFB 1187. Funded by the Deutsche Forschungsgemeinschaft (DFG, German Research Foundation) – Project-ID 262513311 – SFB 1187.

References

Baldwin, Carliss Y./C. Jason Woodard (2008): The Architecture of Platforms: A Unified View.
Berker, Thomas/Hartmann, Maren/Punie, Yves/Ward, Katie J. (2006): „Introduction". In: Thomas Berker/Maren Hartmann/Yves Punie/Katie J. Ward (eds.), Domestication of Media and Technology, Maidenhead: Open University Press, pp. 1–17.

Bowen, Glenn A. (2009): "Document Analysis as a Qualitative Research Method". In: Qualitative Research Journal, 9/2, pp. 27–40.

Bowker, Geoffrey C./Star Susan Leigh (2000): Sorting Things Out: Classification and its Consequences, Cambridge/Massachusetts: MIT Press.

Brause, Saba Rebecca/Blank, Grant (2020): "Externalized Domestication: Smart Speaker Assistants, Networks and Domestication Theory". In: Information, Communication & Society, 32/4, pp. 751–763.

Crawford, Kate/Joler, Vladan (2018): Anatomy of an AI System. http://www.anatomyof.ai. (accessed 13.12.2019).

Dahlgren, Kari/Pink Sarah/Strengers, Yolande/Nicholls, Larissa/Sadowski, Jathan (2021): "Personalization and the Smart Home: Questioning Techno-Hedonist Imaginaries". In: Convergence: The International Journal of Research into New Media Technologies, pp. 1–15.

Darby, Sarah J. (2018): "Smart Technology in the Home: Time for More Clarity". In: Building Research & Information, 46/1, pp. 140–147

Dolata, Ulrich (2019): "Privatization, Curation, Commodification: Commercial Platforms on the Internet". In: Österreichische Zeitschrift für Soziologie, 44/1, pp. 181–197.

European Commission (2021) Preliminary Report on Consumer IoT Sector Inquiry. European Commission. https://ec.europa eu/commission/press corner/detail/en/qanda_21_2908. (accessed 12.01.2022).

European Commission (2022): Commission Staff Working Document Accompanying the Document: Final Report on Consumer Internet of Things Sector Inquiry, Brussels.

Giddens, Anthony (1984): The Constitution of Society: Outline of the Theory of Structuration, Cambridge: Polity Press.

Goulden, Murray (2019): "Delete the Family: Platform Families and the Colonisation of the Smart Home". In: Information, Communication & Society, pp. 1–18.

Goulden, Murray (2021): "Folding and Friction: The Internet of Things and Everyday Life". In: Deana A. Rohlinger/Sarah Sobieraj (eds.), The Oxford Handbook of Sociology and Digital Media, Oxford University Press, pp. 219–240.

Grint, Keith/Steve Woolgar (1997): The Machine at Work: Technology, Work, and Organization, Malden, Massachusetts: Blackwell: Polity Press.

Hacking, Ian (1990): The Taming of Chance, New York: Cambridge University Press.

Hargreaves, Tom, Wilson, Charlie/Hauxwell-Baldwin, Richard (2018): "Learning to Live in a Smart Home". In: Building Research & Information, 46/1, pp. 127–139.

Hartmann, Maren (2020): "(The Domestication of) Nordic Domestication?" In: Nordic Journal of Media Studies, 2/1, pp. 47–57.

Hill, David W. (2020) "The Injuries of Platform Logistics". In: Media. Culture & Society, 42/4, pp. 521–536.

Humphry, Justine/Chesher, Chris (2021): "Visibility and Security in the Smart Home". In: Convergence: The International Journal of Research into New Media Technologies, pp. 1–19.

Jasanoff, Sheila (2015): "Future Imperfect Science, Technology, and the Imaginations of Modernity". In: Sheila Jasanoff/Sang-Hyun Kim (eds.), Dreamscapes of Modernity: Sociotechnical Imaginaries and the Fabrication of Power, Chicago/London: University of Chicago Press, pp. 1–33.

Kuckartz, Udo (2014): Qualitative Text Analysis: A Guide to Methods, Practice & Using Software, Los Angeles: SAGE.

Natale, Simone/Cooke, Henry (2021): "Browsing with Alexa: Interrogating the Impact of Voice Assistants as Web Interfaces". In: Media, Culture & Society, 43/6, pp. 1000–1016.

Phan, Linh-An/Kim Taehong (2020): Breaking Down the Compatibility Problem in Smart Homes: A Dynamically Updatable Gateway Platform. Sensors, 20/10, pp. 1–19.

Phan, Thao (2019): "Amazon Echo and the Aesthetics of Whiteness". In: Catalyst: Feminism, Theory, Technoscience, 5/1, pp. 1–38.

Plantin, Jean-Christophe/Lagoze, Carl/Edwards, Paul N./Sandvig, Christian (2018): "Infrastructure Studies Meet Platform Studies in the Age of Google and Facebook". In: New Media & Society, 20/1, pp. 293–310.

Sadowski, Jathan (2020): Too Smart: How Digital Capitalism is Extracting Data, Controlling Our Lives, and Taking Over the World, Cambridge, Massachusetts: MIT Press.

Shove, Elizabeth (2003): "Users, Technologies and Expectations of Comfort, Cleanliness and Convenience". In: Innovation: The European Journal of Social Science Research, 16/2, pp. 193–206.

Silvast, Antti/Virtanen, Mikko J. (2019): "An Assemblage of Framings and Tamings: Multi-Sited Analysis of Infrastructures as a Methodology". In: Journal of Cultural Economy, 12/6, pp. 461–477.

Silverstone, Roger (2006): "Domesticating Domestication. Reflections on the Life of a Concept". In: Thomas Berker/Maren Hartmann/Yves Punie/Katie J. Ward (eds.), Domestication of Media and Technology, Maidenhead: Open University Press, pp. 229–248.

Silverstone, Roger/Hirsch, Eric/Morley, David (1992): "Information and Communication Technologies and the Moral Economy of the Household". In: Roger Silverstone/Eric Hirsch (eds.), Consuming Technologies: Media and Information in Domestic Spaces, pp. 9–17.

Slota, Steven C./Bowker, Geoffrey C. (2017): "How Infrastructures Matter". In: Ulrike Felt/Rayvon Fouché/Clark A. Miller/Laurel Smith-Doerr (eds.), The Handbook of Science and Technology Studies, Cambridge, Massachusetts: MIT Press, pp. 529–554.

Sørensen, Knut H. (2006): Domestication: "The Enactment of Technology". In: Thomas Berker/Maren Hartmann/Yves Punie/Katie J. Ward (eds.), Domestication of Media and Technology, Maidenhead: Open University Press, pp. 40–61.

Sørensen, Knut H./Aune, Margarethe/Morten, Hatling (2000): "Against Linearity – On the Cultural Appropriation of Science and Technology". In: Meinolf Dierkes/Claudia von Grote (eds.), Between Understanding and Trust: The Public, Science and Technology, Amsterdam: Harwood Academic, pp. 165–178.

Srnicek, Nick, (2017): Platform Capitalism, Cambridge/Malden, Massachusetts: Polity Press.

Strengers, Yolande/Hazas, Mike/Nicholls, Larissa/Kjeldskov, Jesper/Skov, Mikael B. (2020): "Pursuing Pleasance: Interrogating Energy-Intensive Visions for the Smart Home". In: International Journal of Human-Computer Studies, 136.

Strengers, Yolande/Kennedy, Jenny/Arcari, Paula/Nicholls, Larissa/Gregg, Melissa (2019): "Protection, Productivity and Pleasure in the Smart Home: Emerging Expectations and Gendered Insights from Australian Early Adopters". In: Proceedings of the 2019 CHI Conference on Human Factors in Computing Systems, Presented at CHI '19: CHI Conference on Human Factors in Computing Systems, Glasgow Scotland UK: ACM, pp. 1–13.

Strengers, Yolande/Nicholls, Larissa (2017): "Convenience and Energy Consumption in the Smart Home of the Future: Industry Visions from Australia and Beyond". In: Energy Research & Social Science, 32, pp. 86–93.

Strengers, Yolande/Nicholls, Larissa (2018): "Aesthetic Pleasures and Gendered Tech-Work in the 21st-Century Smart Home". In: Media International Australia, 166/1, pp. 70–80.

Suboticki, Ivana/Sørensen, Knut H. (2021): "Designing and Domesticating an Interstructure: Exploring the Practices and the Politics of an Elevator for Cyclists". In: Urban Studies, 58/6, pp. 1229–1244.

Tiwana, Amrit (2014): Platform Ecosystems: Aligning Architecture, Governance, and Strategy, Waltham, Massachusetts: Morgan Kaufmann (Elsevier).

Van Dijck, José/Poell, Thomas/de Waal Martijn (2018): The Platform Society, New York: Oxford University Press.

Van der Vlist, Fernando Nathaniël (2022): The Platform as Ecosystem: Configurations and Dynamics of Governance and Power, Utrecht University.

West, Emily (2022): Buy Now: How Amazon Branded Convenience and Normalized Monopoly, Cambridge Massachusetts: MIT Press.

Woolgar, Steve (1990): "Configuring the User: The Case of Usability Trials". In: The Sociological Review, 38/1, pp. 58–99.

Reinventing Drones: From DIY Experimentation to Professionalisation

Hendrik Bender and Marcus Burkhardt

Abstract

Driven by do-it-yourself communities, drones were reinvented in the early 2000s as non-military, civil technologies. This paper traces the history and genealogy of civil drones in the past two decades as ongoing becoming-media. Building on domestication theory we analyse the emergence of "wild" drone practices by attending to the public engineering of drones in DIY publics as well as to the exploration of potential drone uses, e.g. as toys, flying waiters, pizza deliverers, programming platforms, or simply as airborne cameras. The possible uses of these unmanned aerial vehicles seemed unlimited in the beginning. Against this background the paper discusses the socio-technical stabilisation of drones. We show how drones have come and are still coming together as a heterogenous socio-technological ensemble through cooperative negotiation of different actors. The increasing taming or "closure" of drones is analysed as a mode of domestication on three different levels: featurisation, professionalisation and regulation.

Keywords

drone, UAV, DIY, taming, professionalisation, featurisation, regulation, stabilisation of practices, social construction of technology, cooperation

This article is concerned with the development of non-military drones in the past 15 years and their ongoing becoming-agentic-media. As agentic media, drones today appear and operate as partially autonomous technologies that are imagined as innovating various fields of practice. When the first drones for recreational use came onto the market in the early 2010s, they opened up a space for experimentation. Whether as toys, flying waiters, pizza deliverers, robotics or programming platforms, or simply as airborne cameras, the possible uses of these unmanned aerial vehicles (UAVs) seemed unlimited at first. As opposed to expensive high-tech UAVs that were used by military forces at that time for reconnaissance, intelligence, and surveillance as well as in remote warfare, consumer drones were relatively cheap and consisted largely of technologies that were readily available on the market due to their use in the automotive and smartphone industries. Civil or recreational UAVs consequently did not originate in the development departments of the military-industrial-complex, but were designed, engineered and developed at the dining room tables and in the workshops of hobbyists who shared their ideas, "blueprints", and source codes online and cooperatively re-invented drones.[1] Hobbyist developers, entrepreneurs and other technology enthusiasts praised this development as a way to "demilitarize and democratize" (Anderson 2012b) drones. At the same time, critics warned about the risks of these "new" technologies as their inbuilt cameras and sensors pose potential threats to privacy and allow for new forms of surveillance. From a legal point of view, civil drones operated in a grey area between airspace regulation and privacy law. Throughout the past decade the DIY character of early drone practices was increasingly supplanted by imaginaries of drones as disruptive technologies with large scale economic as well as social impact in areas like logistics, agriculture, and disaster response. In the course of this development the experimental practices of developing and using drones with their seemingly open-ended possibilities were tamed through featurisation, professionalisation and regulation that shape present drone practices and influence their future.

For engaging with the recent history and ongoing development of civil drones, we draw on Joseph Vogl who argued that one needed to pay special attention to the "scenes or situations where media [...] come into existence in a coming together of heterogeneous elements – apparatuses, codes, symbolic systems, forms of knowledge, specific practices, and aesthetic experiences" (Vogl 2007: 16). In the case of civil drones, this coming together of heterogeneous elements rests on the appropriation of and tinkering with existing technologies in online publics as much as the appropriation of and experimentation with ready-to-fly consumer drones. The appropriation of media technologies has long been discussed in domestication theory (see e.g. Silverstone/Hirsch 1992; Berker et al. 2006). At the centre of this body of research is the assumption that user practices take part in shaping media technologies beyond their designed purposes by integrating them into everyday routines:

At a metaphorical level we can observe a domestication process when users, in a variety of environments, are confronted with new technologies. These 'strange' and 'wild' technologies have to be 'house-trained'; they have to be integrated into structures, daily routines and values of users and their environments (Berker et al. 2006: 2).

---

1   Even though military drones had existed earlier and hobbyists were inspired by and somewhat competed with military UAVs, the drones they engineered neither directly used nor misused military equipment as Kittler (Kittler 2014) discussed with regard to Rock Music.

Domestication theory itself is based on the metaphorical appropriation of the concept of the domestication of species for analysing the integration of new media and technologies into everyday domestic contexts. The wildness Berker et al. refer to results from the novelty of technologies that are considered to be relatively stable artifacts ready for consumption by "active users" (Suboticki et al. 2021). As Bakardjieva (2006) points out, the focus on practices of use in different contexts extends studies on the social construction of technology (SCOT) that put creators of technologies at the centre of their studies and asked for how technologies are developed and become stabilised over time (see Bijker et al. 1987).

Since the late 1980s and early 1990s, the distinction between creators and users of technologies has become ever more fluid. Platforms, social media as well as open-source software and hardware put the user as creator at the centre. In addition, many digital media technologies are subject to continuous updates, redesigns and changes. Contemporary cloud-based software services are characterised by "a kind of hyper-instability [...]: instead of a stable program nothing but a temporary relationship of queries across interfaces and devices, rendering something that was immaterial even more airy and vaporous" (Erickson/Kelty 2015: 41).

Similar to smartphones, civil drones are situated on the edge of this unstable technological assemblage. They are material objects, whose capacity to fly "unmanned" and more importantly autonomously has become a core characteristic that distinguishes these UAVs from radio-controlled model airplanes. However, it remains controversial what exactly drones are, how they are to be used and what purposes they can and should serve. In this paper, we aim to provide some insights into how civil drones *have come* and are *still coming together* as a heterogeneous technological ensemble. We borrow the notion of taming from domestication theory in order to analyse ongoing processes of stabilisation and specification of civil drones on three levels: the integration of user practices into drones as features, the exploration and consolidation of professional uses of drones and the adaptation of existing legal frameworks to provide civil drones both with legal spaces for operating in public and to make their operations accountable. Yet, if drones are evolving technologies that are increasingly tamed on multiple levels, we need to address what constitutes civil drones as "'wild' technologies" (Berker et al. 2006: 2). To approach this, we focus on the reinvention of drones by DIY hobbyists. Incidentally the development of civil drones started out in the households of tinkerers before civil drones became consumer goods that afforded open experimentation in the beginning rather than instrumental uses. We contend that the specificity of civil drones as agentic media technology is not to be found at a single scene or situation that we will describe. Only in synopsis does the plot thicken and do civil drones gain specificity through inventive uses.

1. Drone Experimentation

1.1 DIY-Engineering of civilian Drones

Unmanned Aerial Vehicles (UAVs) – commonly referred to as drones – have a relatively long history that reaches back to the early 1900s. Their development is closely intertwined with their military uses for target practice, reconnaissance and even combat. Yet, UAVs gained strategic importance as remote weapons only at the turn of the millennium with the decision to arm Predator drones and their rapidly growing deployment during the Obama administration (2009–2017) in the wake of the "war on terror" that was declared by George W. Bush following the 9/11 attacks in 2001 (cf. Hashim/Patte 2022). While the use of UAVs in combat started to fuel controversies about killer drones (Sauer/Schörnig 2012), hobbyists began to reimagine and reinvent drones by experimentally combining conventional remote-controlled model aircraft, computing platforms, and sensors in order to build a do-it-yourself autopilot. These activities were documented, discussed and coordinated online. The first weblogs and forums specifically dedicated to building autonomously flying r/c models were founded as early as 2003.[2] DIYDrones, a forum that quickly became a centre of hobbyist drone development, was created and promoted by Chris Anderson in May 2007, who at the time was editor-in-chief of WIRED, a technology magazine.

DIYDrones, based on the Ning platform, was intended as a social network that would allow UAV enthusiasts to exchange their ideas. In July 2012 in an issue of WIRED dedicated to the topic of drones, Anderson claimed retrospectively that he kickstarted the "Domestic Drone Boom" (Anderson 2012b) with DIYDrones. Having been fascinated with radio-controlled model airplanes since he was a teenager, Anderson picked this hobby up again in early 2007 as a pastime with his children (cf. Anderson 2007d). Over the course of a month, the joy of flying model airplanes turned into a project of creating an "aerial robot" (Anderson 2007e). The first autopilot created by Anderson was based on the Lego Mindstorm NXT.[3] [Figure 1]

At first, Anderson documented his experiments on his blog longtail.com, which was originally dedicated to his book "The Long Tail" that appeared in 2006. However, as his writings on r/c airplanes and UAVs were largely off-topic to the themes typically covered on longtail.com, Anderson launched the GeekDad blog as part of WIRED as well as DIYDrones. While intended as a social network for drone enthusiasts, DIYDrones resembled a personal blog at first. At the beginning, almost all posts in the blog section were published by Anderson himself. And even

---

2   See for example the blog of the Paparazzi UAV, https://blog.paparazziuav.org/.
3   The Lego Mindstorm Set is a product of the Lego company that includes a computable Lego brick that controls a set of modular sensors and motors and allows to build small programmable robots.

today, Anderson remains the single largest contributor to the community having authored almost 20 percent of all blog posts on DIYDrones.[4]

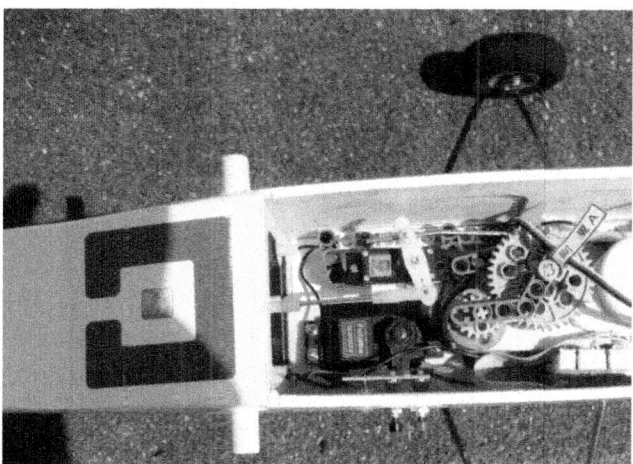

Fig. 1: Lego Mindstorm as autopilot in a model airplane (https://diydrones.com/profiles/blogs/705844-BlogPost-25).

As a journalist, book author and editor-in-chief of an influential technology magazine, Anderson knew how to attract public attention and to gain reach. Therefore, Anderson's writings on DIYDrones cannot only be understood as public documentation of development work, but must also be read as public staging. In a post detailing instruction on how to build a Lego autopilot published on June 12, 2007, Anderson describes his motivation as follows: "The main aim of this project is to both make the world's cheapest full-featured UAV and the first one designed to be within the reach of high school and below kids, as a platform for an aerial robotics contest" (Anderson 2007a). By early 2008, this motivation was formalised in a full-fledged mission statement that rests on five principles or rules: UAVs should be *simple*, *cheap*, *safe* and their development should be *participatory*, with members of DIYDrones interacting with each other in a *civil* manner (cf. Anderson 2008a). The declared goal of Anderson and DIYDrones was to develop a safe UAV platform that would cost less than $1000 and could serve as an experimental robotics platform for technology enthusiasts, students and kids alike. While this goal presented a common motivation to the community, the question of what purpose such a low-cost autopilot and thus a UAV platform would serve remained largely unaddressed. The focus was on tinkering and experimentation itself.

---

4   On March 3, 2022, 13,914 blog entries were published on DIYDrones 2,718 of which have been authored by Anderson since May 2007.

It is important to note that neither Anderson nor the members of DIYDrones did in any respect invent autopilots for UAVs. In 2007, autopilot modules that could easily be installed into model aircraft were commercially available on the market, thus turning these aircraft into autonomous vehicles. However, such autopilots were very costly, similar in price to custom-made drones that some companies offered for purchase as well. The expensiveness of autopilots was what bothered Anderson and others in the DIYDrone community most because the individual components required for building an autopilot, such as microcontroller units, sensors, GPS, radio receivers, servo and motor controllers could be purchased relatively cheaply.

The goal of building not just an autopilot, but an inexpensive one, is also reflected in the explorative approach Anderson took. Almost from the beginning Anderson worked on different autopilot projects which he compared to the U-NAV Picopilot, an off-the-shelf autopilot that served as "the reference platform against which we benchmark the more innovative (and cheaper) custom UAV" (Anderson 2007f). In addition to the Lego Mindstorms autopilot, Anderson experimented with using a cell phone (cf. Anderson 2007b) as well as the BASIC Stamp (cf. Anderson 2007c), a small inexpensive microcontroller manufactured by Parallax Inc., as autopilot platforms. While using a cell phone had the benefit that it came equipped with inbuilt sensors, GPS, camera and considerable computing power, the BASIC Stamp could be more easily programmed in PBASIC and was equipped with a serial bus that allowed for connecting it to technical components like servos.

In early 2008, Anderson brought Jordi Muñoz, a 21-year-old amateur, who was developing an autopilot for r/c helicopters based on the Arduino microcontroller, to the attention of the community. The Arduino had several advantages over the BASIC Stamp. On the one hand, it was more powerful and at the same time cheaper, on the other hand, a developer community had already formed around the controller. Muñoz, who originally presented his autopilot in the Ardurino community forum, then joined DIYDrones as well. In addition to the technical advantages, the open license of the Arduino board manufactured in Italy allowed the microcontroller to be modified, rebuilt, and sold without paying licensing fees. In March 2008, Anderson proposed to the DIYDrones community to end the comparative exploration of different hardware platforms for creating an UAV autopilot and to shift the sole focus of future development work on Arduino. As a consequence, BASIC Stamp was abandoned as the – up to then – most promising hardware platform, and porting work of the existing source code to the new platform started.

Following Wiebe E. Bijker, the commitment to the Arduino board can be understood as a new "technological framework" that provided common "problem-solving strategies and practices of use" (Bjiker 2012: 167) for the community. The switch to Arduino resulted not only in the replacement of a single hardware component, but also in the necessity to learn a new programming language and new electrical engineering skills. In this context, the Arduino platform became a condition of cooperation for the further development of the DIYDrones autopilot. At the same time building upon the Arduino enabled the DIYDrones community to draw on the existing knowledge and technical resources of the Arduino communities.

Besides the microcontroller sensors like gyroscopes, accelerometers and GPS receivers for registering flight statuses such as altitude, speed, direction, and location constituted core components of the autopilot to be developed. Even though retailers for electronics components already offered sensors and measurement units for hobbyist projects, these components were still relatively expensive. To get around this issue, community members explored repurposing these elements from existing products. For example, the accelerometer built into the so-called Nunchuk controller of the Nintendo Wii – a game console that had enjoyed great popularity since 2006 due to its motion control – was used to detect altitude. Descriptions and circuit diagrams on how to take apart the inexpensive Wii controller and connect its sensor to the Arduino board were shared in online forums (cf. Chad 2007). [Figure 2]

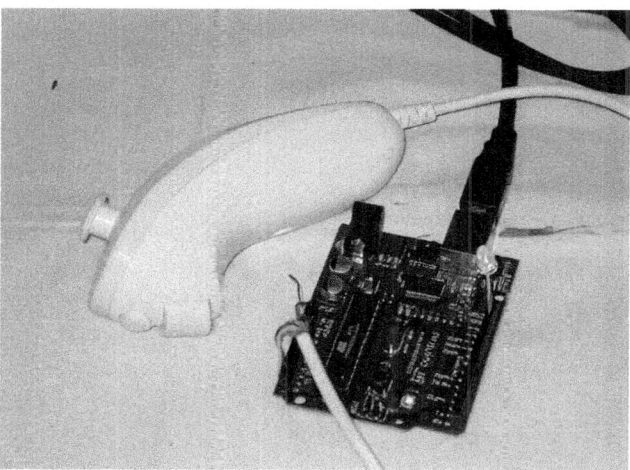

Fig. 2: *Wii Nunchuk Controller connected to an Arduino Board (Chad 2007).*

The innovativeness of the DIY maker community in general and DIYDrones in particular rests, to a certain extent, on this creative appropriation of existing technologies that often transgresses the legal boundaries set by intellectual property rights, terms of use, and end-user licenses. For example, while app developers for the iPhone are prohibited to use its location services to control an autonomous vehicle, members of DIYDrones nevertheless experimented with their iPhone's technological possibility to program flight-routes of UAVs (cf. Anderson 2008c). Such practices of appropriation, tinkering and wild experimentation along with the forum discussions surrounding them contributed to the specification of the required components for realising a low-cost UAV autopilot. At this early stage, a shared understanding of drones as autonomous sensor platforms was incrementally formed.

1.2 Drones Enter the Consumer Market

The effort by Anderson, Muñoz, and the DIYDrones community to create an affordable autopilot was not void of commercial aspirations. Anderson was driven, at least in part, by "an unfortunate tendency to 'industrialize [his] hobbies'" (Anderson 2012a, 102) as he confessed in his 2012 book *Makers*. In 2008, he started selling construction kits for autonomous blimps that he compiled at his dining room table (Anderson 2012a: 103; Anderson 2008b). The following year Anderson and Muñoz founded *3D Robotics*, a company that initially manufactured and sold UAV components and later ready-to-fly UAVs as well as analytic software for aerial images (Anderson 2012a: 103f.; van Wegen et al. 2017).[5] The market outlook for non-military drones was, however, very limited according to a report published by the Federal Aviation Administration in 2010. The Forecast for the Fiscal Years 2010–2030 projected that only about 15,000 commercial and recreational drones would be in active use in the U.S. by 2020 (FAA 2010) – an estimation that proved to be wrong after just a few years. Yet indeed, the DIY community's approach to equipping r/c aircraft with low-cost autopilot modules continued to be demanding in terms of both technical and piloting skills. This started to change with the launch of low-cost ready-to-fly drones in early 2010. New commercial actors such as the French manufacturer Parrot and the Chinese manufacturer DJI – short for Da-Jiang Innovations Science and Technology – entered the stage. They would go on to dominate the consumer drone market and play a major role in shaping today's image of drones. In some respects, this marketisation of drones can be understood as closure and stabilisation of the drone as a technological entity. As we will show, this closure also constituted an opening that allowed for the creative exploration of ways of using or utilising drones.

In 2010, Parrot launched its first mass-produced "ready-to-fly" drone called AR.Drone. The drone, which consisted largely of a Styrofoam body and was propelled by four separate motors, could be flown via an iPhone app without any major assembly. It was advertised as a toy for augmented reality games and cost less than $300. In spite the relative low price the drone was equipped with a wide range of sensors: a two-axis gyroscope, a three-axis accelerometer, an ultrasonic sensor, and two digital cameras that were used for speed measurements, flight stabilisation and streaming live video sent to the controlling iPhone. The quadcopter design combined with the built-in sensors and a microcontroller computing unit made it possible to fly the AR.Drone with little to no piloting skills. Difficult

---

5   3D Robotics was acquired in 2021 by Kitty Hawk (GIM International 2021).

and accident-prone tasks like take-off and landing could now be accomplished at the push of a button. The first version of the AR.Drone, however, was not equipped with a GPS module, limiting its capabilities to perform complex flight manoeuvres autonomously.

The launch of the AR.Drone contributed to the stabilisation of non-military drones. To borrow a term from Bijker et al., the AR.Drone "reified" drones in that it shaped the image of drones "in the consciousness of the members of relevant social groups" (Bijker et al. 1984: 48) as quadcopters. On a second level, it also proved the economic "makeability" of quadcopter UAVs, demonstrating their increasing "economic stabilization" (Bijker et al. 1984: 48). This twofold stabilisation marks a certain closure in drone development while at the same time opening up drones for new 'lay' users beyond the already established DIY communities and r/c hobbyists, giving way to new experimental practices. On the technological level the AR.Drone invited this experimentation through its open Application Programming Interface (API), which allowed users to modify the drones software, in order to create new applications such as augmented reality games, a use case that was seen as a potential and promising area of future drone applications. As a robotic and programming platform, the drone was, however, used in areas of research and education as well.

Two years after its initial release, the AR.Drone 2.0 was launched. Parrot made version 2.0 of its toy drone available for iPhone and Android users alike and expanded it by including a three-axis magnetometer that could be used to determine the drone's direction of flight. This magnetic compass brought several new functions with it. On the one hand, it allowed simple flight routes to be programmed by setting the direction and duration of flight. On the other hand, the sensor enabled the drone to be set in relation to the controlling device, resolving the problem of inverted control known from r/c aircraft, which occurs when a drone flies towards the pilot. Additionally, flight data such as camera footage, altitude, direction and speed could now automatically be uploaded to the so-called AR.Drone Academy and shared from there with social media platforms. It is, however, noticeable that only few recordings of flights made with the onboard 1280x720 pixel camera are found on video platforms today. By contrast, videos of flights filmed from the ground are more common, which indicates that a main focus was on documenting flight behaviour and the modifications users made to their drones rather than using drones as devices for remote vision.

A shift of user practices toward the photographic capabilities of small UAVs can be observed after the launch of the Phantom 1 drone by DJI in 2013. While the Phantom 1 was also designed as a quadcopter it differed both conceptually and technically from the AR.Drones. The Phantom did not follow a lightweight construction method and consisted of a hard-plastic shell. As a consequence, the hardware could only be modified to a limited extent. The Phantom drone, however, had a very accurate control, high flight stability, and could be equipped with various high-resolution action cameras allowing the capture of high-quality aerial footage previously reserved to professional applications. In the months following the release of Phantom 1, DJI as well as third-party vendors released a broad range of accessories for enhancing the quality of images recorded using the drone. Overall, these developments focused primarily on a smooth and fluid camera image and movement, which in turn made the drone interesting for the potential user group of photography enthusiasts.

As the quality of the cameras attached to the drones increased, so did the distribution of the captured footage on video-sharing platforms and social media. Urban and rural landscape shots were particularly popular and circulated on Facebook, YouTube, Vimeo, Twitter and Instagram. Notwithstanding the variety of recorded sceneries, a certain "standard aesthetic" emerged: pictured objects – in many cases scenic or architectural landmarks – were shown from an oblique or orthogonal angle from above, with the drone performing a slow but steady movement (cf. Jablonowski 2022). In 2013, Dronestagr.am was launched as one of the first websites dedicated to sharing drone photographs, which further contributed to the growing popularity of this new kind of imagery. Through contests as well as a collaboration with the National Geographic, the website gained both contributors and public reach (cf. Hochmair/Zielstra 2014). The increasing circulation of drone photographs at that time attests to the stabilisation of recreational photographic practices with drones.

During that time, sales of drones began to increase rapidly. Contrary to the FAA estimate, Parrot and DJI are believed to have sold over 250,000 UAVs worldwide in 2013 alone (cf. Phillips 2015). And in the years that followed, numerous other manufacturers such as 3D Robotics and Yuneec as well as a number of crowdfunding projects released their own ready-to-fly UAVs. With the introduction of ready-to-fly drones the experimental practices shifted from drone development to exploring their uses in practice. At that time, the potential areas of application seemed almost unlimited. Reports about sometimes bizarre imaginaries and new uses of drones appeared frequently: whether as a tacocopter, for delivering food (cf. Bonnington 2012), as a chococopter built from food (cf. Chocolate Copter 2014; Jablonowski 2015), or even as a sex toy (cf. Dildoeverything 2016).

2. Taming the Drone

The early phase of non-military DIY and commercial drone development was characterised by experimentation, tinkering, and an openness in drawing together and appropriating technical elements in the technological ensemble of civil drones.[6] To the DIYDrones community, it was clear from the outset that the autopilot is the

---

6 The notions of technical elements and ensembles are borrowed from Simondon (2016: 27f.).

defining characteristic of UAVs. However, the conceptions of what an autopilot is and what it does were diverse and they have remained diverse to a certain extent. What all UAV autopilots have in common is that they significantly reduce the skills required for a successful flight, even though some demand a higher skill set than others. Getting drones to fly autonomously to a certain extent was only the first step in drone experimentation. Putting the flight capabilities to the test and exhibiting them in online publics became popular once the first ready-to-fly drones entered the market. Once the spectacle of successful flights faded, the focus shifted more and more to the exploration of potential uses of drones. While the market introduction of ready-to-fly shaped the public imaginary of drones as quadcopters, their "coming together" did not end there. In this section we use the term taming to describe the gradual specification and socio-technical stabilisation of drones on three distinct levels: featurisation, professionalisation and regulation. This distinction, however, is purely analytical. None of the levels is disconnected from the others; rather, they are mutually dependent.

2.1 Featurisation

One line of development that has significantly contributed to the stabilisation of drones as technical objects and to their becoming-agentic-media can be conceptualised as featurisation. We understand featurisation as the translation or inscription of emergent practices into technological features. Following Madeleine Akrich, these features can be understood as scripts that (re)define what is "delegated to a machine" and what is "left to the initiative of human actors" (Akrich 1992: 216). Due to the openness of DIY autopilot projects and many ready-to-fly consumer drones, users could and were in fact encouraged to, develop new features, either by contributing code to the core software or by using the software development kits (SDKs) released by manufacturers to develop standalone drone applications. In addition, developer communities and manufacturers closely observed how their devices were used and added new features to their software accordingly. The transcription of practices into technical features is a process in which competencies between technical objects and users are constantly redistributed.

The deskilling of users mentioned earlier has been an important factor in the rapid proliferation of ready-to-fly consumer drones since 2012. The first ready-to-fly drones were designed for their *controllability* in particular. Functions such as *autonomous take-off* and *landing*, which have become common features today, automated risky flight manoeuvres that require a certain experience and skill when manually piloting r/c aircraft. Expensive accidents are not uncommon when beginners learn to control a model aircraft remotely – a process which typically requires an experienced teacher. With drones, these competencies were now redistributed between autopilot and user. *Learnability* and *useability* represent important factors in technology adaptation (cf. Carroll et al. 2003). Other features such as the *return home* function or *obstacle avoidance* further facilitated the controllability.

However, one feature in particular has shaped today's image of drones: the automation of standstill flight. The design of UAVs as quad- or multicopters in combination with the built-in sensors, microcontroller and flight control software allow these drones to hover relatively steadily on a spot without the input of a control signal. An increase in learnability and usability was also achieved by improvements to the user interface. Whereas status messages could initially only be read from light or sound signals, manufacturers now rely on detailed messages that appear on a display. The promise of simplicity, ease of use, and controllability was paradigmatically illustrated by 3DR in an advertisement for its Solo drone which, in reference to *2001: A Space Odyssey*, depicted a monkey flying the drone. [Figure 3]

Fig. 3: Excerpt from a promotional film by 3D Robotics for the Solo drone (https://www.youtube.com/watch?v=PfN9lTp8mao).

The standardisation of flight support features increased accessibility for a larger and more heterogeneous group of users. At the same time, it contributed to a conceptual closure of drones. Flight turned from a skilful accomplishment to a usable feature that could be explored in various areas of application. Recreational uses of drones particularly focused on practices that exhausted their capacities as a flying camera. Here, the processual nature of featurisation takes shape as the technical implementation of user practices. Around 2015, more and more drone models appeared with so-called "smart" features that automate certain flight patterns that first appeared as popular manual practices in footage recorded by users. One example of a technical implementation of user practices is the dronie, i.e., a selfie taken by a drone, which became very popular on social media in 2014 (cf. Bender 2018; Jablonowski 2022). In most cases, the "dronie" consists of a short video recording in which users first film themselves up close and then let the drone ascend at an oblique angle until the surrounding landscape unfolds around them. [Figure 4] A manually created "dronie" requires a certain level of piloting skills, because an aesthetically pleasing angle of flight and rate of climb must be achieved. Once turned into a pre-programmed feature, only the start and end points of the "dronie" have to be set. Through this technical inscription, skills and competencies of using the drone for a specific purpose are redistributed (cf. Akrich 1992). This can also be observed in the automation of other flight patterns, such as Zipline or Orbit mode. These modes are designed to allow users to implement

Hollywood-like camera movements that would otherwise require complex manual flight manoeuvres.

Fig 4: Typical example of a "dronie" (https://www.youtube.com/watch?v=dMoP_N3mvHI).

Taken together the examples of featurisation of recording functions show that design and appropriation processes are increasingly interwoven not only in DIY but also in the commercial sectors. Although featurisation is based on a certain technical framework, i.e., on equipping the drone with certain sensors, computing units and control options, the technical object remains open to some extent, as it can be used for new purposes and enhanced by new technical possibilities on the basis of its programmability. This openness is also evident in the data practices enabled by drones. The various recombinations of the collected sensor data allow to implement new features without changing the technical framework. For example, one further development of the 'dronie" is the Follow-Me mode, which is designed to enable the drone to follow its user automatically. For this purpose, the drone's position, determined via GPS, is set in relation to the coordinates of the controller carried by the user. In addition a computational object recognition procedure is used to keep the user at the centre of the shot – a function that has proven to be relatively error-prone. In this case, the drone accesses the same position data needed for autonomous "dronie". However, by combining this with image recognition software, new features can be realised. At the same time, image recognition enables the implementation of features like gesture control or face recognition. In this process, user practices stabilise through a slowly differentiating spectrum of possible actions.

In recent years, it has become apparent that the mutability of drones or digital technical objects in general can not only be used to expand the possibilities for action, but also to limit the scope of action at a regulatory level. Legal provisions, which will be discussed in more detail below, are increasingly being implemented at a technical level. For example, position data collected can be used to prevent users from flying drones within no-fly zones, such as those around airports or hospitals. In this context, users are increasingly required to create a user account on first commissioning the drones, specifying their region. The map data downloaded on the basis of the region is then permanently aligned with the drone's GPS data during the flight. If a drone enters a no-fly zone, the continuation of the flight is interrupted. This form of geo-fencing can be extended to include country-specific regulations such as flight altitude and speed. Drones are metaphorically speaking put on an invisible leash.

In summary, featurisation can be described as a process of technical implementation of patterns of practice into routine technical actions or scripts that afford and stabilise specific user practices without determining them. At the same time, the process remains open to change, so that a gradual redistribution of competence and agency between technical object and user can occur over time.

2.2 Professionalisation

The eagerness to experiment, the combinability and the seemingly unlimited areas of application are also reflected in the early ideas about potential commercial uses of drones. In December 2013, Jeff Bezos announced that his company Amazon was pursuing a project for the use of delivery drones, which led to a veritable drone-euphoria (cf. Rose 2013). Amazon was, however, not alone in fuelling the logistical imaginary of drone use. German parcel service DHL also worked on developing drones that would deliver packages to remote and difficult-to-reach locations such as islands (cf. Welch 2014). Together with the "Deutsche Gesellschaft für Internationale Zusammenarbeit", a German development agency focusing on international development cooperation, and the drone developer Wingcopter, they tested the use of drones for delivering pharmaceuticals in Tanzania (cf. DHL 2019). Numerous prototypes developed by other companies followed. Although the individual projects differed in scale, they nevertheless had one thing in common: a logistical imaginary of drones as an innovative and integral part of everyday public life. However, the development of such logistics drones presented the companies with numerous technical, infrastructural and legal challenges. Unmanned flight over long distances not only requires internal, redundant control systems and an area-wide infrastructure, but also a dedicated traffic management system that coordinates the anticipated number of actors in the air. Despite numerous investments and registered patents, Amazon has not yet been able to realise its project. DHL also stopped all projects in August 2021 due to regulatory requirements and high costs (cf. Landmesser 2021).

Nonetheless, the logistical vision of drones has largely remained one still lacking widespread practical application today. It has significantly contributed to shifting the image of drones as a toy to the notion of a technology with serious practical applications. As "hypothetical object" (Akrich 1992) or "performative artifacts" (Suchman et al. 2002; Ernst/Schröter 2020), delivery drones demonstrated the anticipated possibilities of the new emerging technology. The idea of a sky populated by drones inspired both utopian and dystopian notions of a high-tech and largely automated digital society. Such notions must always be thought of in sociotechnical terms. They are "collectively held, institutionally stabilized, and publicly performed visions of desirable futures" (Jasanoff 2015: 4), which shape the social and economic acceptance of new technologies. While drones in some areas have never left the realm of the imaginary, they nevertheless stimulated broader public and political discussions of their use.

In other areas, however, which could rely on existing infrastructures and familiar practices, the integration of drones into already established professional settings proved more successful. One of the first industries to make commercial use of drones was the US film industry. Since the non-amateur, professional uses of drones were largely prohibited within the U.S. and Europe at first, film productions using drones initially took place in countries with less strict regulations (cf. Fung 2013). In 2014, the FAA gave in to the increasing pressure from seven different production companies and the Motion Picture Association of America (MPAA) and approved the commercial use of drones for film and television productions (cf. Barnes 2014). At that time, the MPAA argued that the use of drones as a new tool for storytelling would enable producers to realise aerial shots that would otherwise require the use of helicopters. It was also claimed that replacing helicopters by drones would be more cost-effective and lead to an increase in security (cf. MPAA 2014). Even though reports of drone accidents rendered such safety claims doubtful (cf. BBC News 2014), the FAA granted six of the seven production companies permission to use drones in their productions. Conditions included that drone operators obtain a private pilot's license, fly their drones in line of sight at all times, and limit its use to "sterile areas", i.e. clearly secured and demarcated areas of the film set (cf. Barnes 2014). In particular, the requirement for a pilot's license meant that drones were mainly used by production companies that already had expertise in aerial photography and accordingly had trained airplane and helicopter pilots. This development can be understood as a first form of institutional professionalisation of drones. The distinction between recreational and commercial – nonwork and work – use is being supplemented by the distinction between amateur and professional, i.e. recreational pilot and trained pilot (cf. LaFlamme 2018).

In film production, drones not only served as cheaper replacement for helicopter flights. The fluid transitions between close-up and long shots enabled by drones also led to the formation of a new cinematic language that simultaneously impacted recreational drone practices as well as the features of newer drone models. Despite the relatively strict limitations, the FAA's decision was widely welcomed by business enterprises. For example, an article published in reaction to the FAA decision by the US business magazine Forbes stated, "Drones for commercial use are here to stay. Businesses and individuals are increasingly embracing and deploying them for the benefits they can bring to everyday life" (Varah 2014).

The use of drones by major Hollywood studios was all but a first step in professionalisation of drone cinematography and photography. In the US, the new regulations led to the creation of specialised companies that offered a wide range of services from aerial recordings for smaller television productions to filming real estate and wedding photography. Unlike large production firms, many of the smaller companies did not rely on the use of especially developed camera drones, but instead largely used conventional ready-to-fly consumer drones. Here the boundaries between recreational and commercial uses of drones remained fluid. As LaFlamme (2018) points out, the distinction between work and hobby was less obvious in the context of ready-to-fly consumer drones than in the large ventures of logistics and film companies. This "grey area" was exploited by entrepreneurs and service providers in the beginning to circumvent regulatory requirements in order to make commercial use of drones. Nevertheless, the specialisation in the photographic and videographic uses of drones led to a differentiation of practices and thus a stabilisation emerged.

Another field of application, in which drones were used relatively early, is remote sensing. In diverse areas such as archaeology (cf. Reinhard 2013), geology (cf. García-Selles et al. 2014), geography (cf. Pin Koh/Wich 2012) and even agriculture (cf. Tripicchio et al. 2015), drones were explored as an experimental alternative to existing remote sensing platforms like satellites and airplanes. The drones not only proved to be particularly cost-effective, but their low flying altitude enabled aerial images to be captured at a higher resolution than was possible using conventional methods. The flight data (e.g., GPS and flight altitude) of the small UAVs linked to the aerial images also made them easily usable for photogrammetric techniques. In this context, drones have stabilised as motile sensor platforms. Arthur P. Cracknell, who has served as editor-in-chief of the International Journal for Remote Sensing for 25 years, described the role of drones in a historical review as follows:

It is probably no exaggeration to say that the next revolution in the acquisition of remote sensing data has been the arrival of the UAV (Unmanned Aerial Vehicle, drone, or whatever else we choose to call them) on the scene. Of the three needs of spatial, spectral and temporal resolution the UAV particularly addresses the questions of spatial and temporal acquisition. Once you have a UAV you can acquire data where and when you want it, and reasonably cheaply. (Cracknell 2018: 8422)

Especially in scientific contexts, DIY and ready-to-fly multicopters were used for surveying and mapping tasks, as they "require less flight training", "hold their position even in strong winds", "can take off and land within a small area with the ability to rotate and move in all directions" (Smith et al. 2014: 176). Before the programming of fixed routes became a common feature, the open-source software solutions of the drone communities like QGroundControl or ArduPilot Mission Planner had been used widely. Starting around 2014, numerous scientific publications and journals focused on evaluating which drones, equipment and methods were best suited for specific remote sensing procedures. Drones increasingly become knowledge objects according to Charles Goodwin (1994) that bundle theories, artifacts, and expertise. Negotiated and shaped in discursive practices such knowledge objects characterise a profession and distinguish it from other professions according to Goodwin (1994). In the case of remote sensing, the use of drones represents a similar change as the harnessing of satellite imagery once did. As a result, previously fixed practices were replaced or extended and new workflows established. At the same time, the scientific sector, like other early professional drone applications faced an uncertain legal framework, as scientific use did not necessarily equate to commercial use. In addition to the stabilisation of drones as knowledge objects in remote sensing, specialised products, platforms, and services emerge that provide commercial software and hardware solutions, training programs, data acquisition and analysis. Especially in the context of precision agriculture, these services and platforms are built on a logic of value partaking attesting to yet another level in the professionalisation of drone practices (cf. Chesbrough et al. 2018: 934).

From the prototypes of logistics companies through their use as artistic means in the film industry to their firm integration into workflows in the field of remote sensing, drones oscillate between being a "hypothetical object" with all its imaginaries to a "piece of equipment integrated into the various sectors of economic life" (Akrich 1992: 221). In this process of professionalisation, practices and routines stabilise, while drones were placed in ever new commercial contexts of sensory application based on their interpretative openness and technical flexibility. Therefore, professionalisation can be characterised by the inclusion of drones as a tool and knowledge object in established professions or the formation of new professions on the one hand, and on the other hand it refers to the institutionalisation and monetisation of drone practices. It is striking that professional and commercial use is often described in public and political discourse as a technical and social innovation or "key technology", while recreational use is increasingly marginalised as an unnecessary nuisance and risk of potential misuse. This phenomenon is reinforced by the demands of professional sectors for clearer legal regulations.

2.3 Regulation

As the example of the US film industry shows, professional users pushed for clearer regulation of drones early on. In both North America and much of Europe, commercial use of drones was largely prohibited or complicated by complex regulatory requirements. The use of drones for recreational purposes, on the other hand, was mostly regulated by a number of drone-unspecific laws, such as peeping tom laws and regulations pertaining to the use of model aircraft. Because of their similarity to r/c aircrafts, drones initially fell under what LaFlamme calls the "hobbyist exception, a disturbance of the boundaries between work and nonwork that arose from a loophole in a key piece of drone legislation" (2018: 122). Around 2015 as the sales of hobby drones soared, not only the vague demarcation between recreational and commercial uses was increasingly put to the test, but also incidents, malfunctions and crashes became more frequent, prompting calls for tighter regulations in the recreational sector as well (cf. Whitlock 2015). In the context of these ongoing legal negotiations, the possibilities and limits of drone use are being defined. This contributes also to a conceptual stabilisation of what UAVs and drones legally are as well as what distinguishes them from model aircraft, and in what spaces drones act.

In August 2016, the European Aviation Safety Agency (EASA) published a first draft of the "Prototype' Commission Regulation on Unmanned Aircraft Operation", which represents an attempt at common regulation of drones in the European Union. The draft proposed that recreational uses of UAVs, as opposed to their commercial applications, should be significantly restricted. The understanding of "unmanned aircraft", on which the EASA draft was based, was very broad, "'UA' (unmanned aircraft) means any aircraft operated or designed to be operated without a pilot on board" (EASA 2016: 5).

This definition has provoked criticism especially among stakeholders of the r/c model aviation community, as it implies that all r/c model aircraft – with or without autopilot, sensors and cameras – should legally be considered as drones. Restrictions on recreational use of drones would therefore also affect the legal uses of r/c model aircraft. In response, the German Model Aviation Association (DMFV 2016) has released a statement calling for a more differentiated understanding of drones and UAVs:

[D]rones – "unmanned aircraft" as defined by EASA – are designed so that they can be sold anywhere and flown without special knowledge or training. They are usually not about flying alone, but are platforms for tasks such as collecting data through photography and filming, or transporting goods. (DMFV 2016)

In contrast to EASA, the DMFV foregrounds user practices and required piloting skills to draw a distinction between drones and r/c aircraft. As reflected in the current FAQ published on the EASA website the agency still insists on the similarities between the two: "both have a flying part and a remote control. In addition, both may be used for recreational purposes" (EASA 2021a). Interestingly, both EASA and DMFV disregard the fact that, unlike drones, there is little to no commercial use of model aircrafts:

Prior to the advent of unmanned aviation, aircraft modelers were not regarded as amateur [or professional] pilots because the devices that they operated were not aircraft: they were model aircraft, an ontological distinction rooted less in the size of the device than in its marginal, autotelic nature. (LaFlamme 2018: 145)

In 2019, the European Commission adopted regulation 2019/947 "on the rules and procedures for the operation of unmanned aircraft" which addresses both drone use and r/c model aviation. Yet, it includes passages that specify conditions of accepted hobby uses. As a result, the EU regulation closes the grey area between model flight and drone use.

To a certain extent, this stricter regulation of hobbyist uses of unmanned aircraft is at odds with the innovativeness attributed to hobbyists. An action plan for unmanned aerial systems and innovative aviation concepts by the German government for example states, "Sports and recreational activities often give rise to ideas and technologies that can be helpful in the professional use of UAS" (BMVI 2020: 28, author's transl.). Recreational uses are seen as potential drivers of innovation that could be beneficial for professional uses as well. In consequence, the complete taming of the hobby sector through rigid restrictions is seen as a threat to future innovation.

With the European Drone Regulation coming into force in 2020, the direct distinction between recreational and commercial use was largely eliminated. Instead, different risk levels are specified which are translated into a classification scheme that distinguishes drones by take-off weight and use cases by the flight proximity to uninvolved persons. These factors determine whether a certificate of competence or a remote pilot certificate is mandatory for an unmanned aircraft's operation. Here, a further form of professionalisation and institutionalisation of drone practices is observed. While the certificate of competence can be acquired via an online course with a final multiple-choice test on the EASA homepage for a processing fee, separate state-certified flight schools have been created for the remote pilot license. These fee-based courses, which are held over several days, are designed to train prospective drone pilots not only in the theoretical and practical handling of drones, but also in general aviation law. Legal provisions are thus no longer directly oriented to user practices but define a space of action in which usage is considered safe. Depending on these spaces different competencies are required. For the recreational sector, this means that the increased cost of a pilot certificate will either make a large proportion of practices impossible or shift them from urban areas to less populated rural areas. The drone community dronestagr.am even went so far as to briefly announce the death of recreational use:

[A]fter a great period of freedom during which you could fly your drone just about anywhere and film anything you wanted, rules and restrictions proliferated in all countries, whistling the end of the recreation and killing an outstanding hobby, a source of escape and unprecedented beauty. (Dronestagram 2022)

These new drone regulations also have a direct impact on aspects of featurisation. Manufacturers are obliged to indicate a categorisation of the drones, which means that older models must either be rechecked or fall into a more restrictive category. In order to make drones accessible, especially for recreational use, i.e., to fall into a category where a pilot's certificate is not required, appropriate weight limits must be observed. At the same time, the regulations represent a redistribution of certain competencies between human actors and technical artifacts. Whereas previously pilots had to ensure themselves that they maintained a legally defined flight altitude and avoided no-fly zones, this has now largely been delegated to the drone's mandatory geo-awareness system which automatically restricts the drone's radius of action.

While the current European regulation that will take full effect only in 2024 aims, in part, at defining spaces of accepted action, i.e., it specifies where, how and under what conditions drones are allowed to fly, another part of the regulation aims at creating means for making and holding drones and their operators accountable.

A main motivation for this is to allow for the identification of drones as well as for the potential prosecution of responsible drone operators, which is of particular importance in situations in which neither the drones' purpose nor their operator can be obviously identified. In a first attempt to ensure accountability, a registration and labelling requirement was introduced (cf. BMVI 2017). Operators were required to register the drone with the competent authority and to provide it with a fireproof badge that should contain the name and address of its owner. In the event of a crash or accident, it should thus be possible to retrospectively identify the pilot. However, it turned out to be problematic that in the case of violations, the pilot could only be located via the badge attached to the drone. For example, the sighting of two drones in December 2018 paralysed operations at London's Gatwick Airport for 33 hours, with more than 1,000 flights cancelled (cf. Shackle 2020). Although a large contingent of police and security personnel were involved in the search for the pilots responsible, they could not be identified despite several suspects and a false arrest. The incident made it clear that purely physical identification was not sufficient in many cases. In order to prevent this, the new European provisions require the equipment of an electronic remote identification system which is referred to as "e-identification". In practice, this means that drones weighing more than 250g must permanently transmit a signal containing the position of the drone and the operator ID of the pilots. The 'e-registration', i.e. the entry of operator and drone into a digital central register, and the 'e-identification' aim to ensure that pilots can be remotely identified in the event of an incident. However, the problem of accountability manifests itself not only at the level of legal provisions, but also at the level of public acceptance. A 2018 study by the German Aerospace Centre (DLR) shows that drones for recreational purposes, in contrast to their professional use (especially in the field of disaster control), are accepted by the public only to a very limited extent (cf. DLR 2018). In this context, the term 'drones' is often negatively associated and connected to safety and privacy concerns. A study by the University of Southern Denmark (Bajde et al. 2017a; 2017b) came to a similar conclusion. The study shows that uninvolved people are particularly disturbed by the fact that they do not know why the drone is in the air. "Not knowing who is operating a drone, and for what purpose, significantly exacerbates feelings of privacy violation" (Bajde et al. 2017a: 23). Also, in this study it becomes apparent that professional uses are by far more accepted than recreational ones. In most cases, however, it is not obvious to bystanders what purpose the drone serves. The e-Identification system is intended to be used for this purpose as well. In the future, bystanders should be able to read the remote identification signal with the help of a smartphone application and thus identify whether the drone in the vicinity is being used for recreational or professional purposes. In this way e-registration, e-identification and geofencing are fundamental services for the complete integration of drones into the controlled airspace.

To ensure this integration, several international research programs are working to develop an unmanned aerial systems traffic management (UTM). At the European level, the *Single European Sky ATM Research Programme* (SESAR) is working on the expansion of a system called U-Space. The U-space is defined as "a set of new services relying on a high level of digitalisation and automation of functions and specific procedures designed to support safe, efficient and secure access to airspace for large numbers of drones" (SESAR 2022). In the United States the FAA and NASA, too, have been working together on the development of an UTM since 2018 (cf. FAA 2020). In both cases, the focus is on promoting the commercial exploitation of drones, "thereby harnessing potential for jobs and growth creation in this new sector of the economy" (SESAR 2022). Current political and regulatory efforts therefore seem to focus in particular on the development of a large-scale infrastructure to ensure social and, above all, commercial use of drones. The recreational use however is increasingly considered as an unnecessary nuisance that needs to be tamed.

3. Conclusion

While the origins of drones as military technologies reach back to the early 20th century, this paper traced the history and genealogy of non-military drone development and use in the past two decades as an ongoing becoming-media of drones. During this time, drones were reengineered and at least in part reinvented as semi-autonomous unmanned aerial vehicles by do-it-yourself enthusiasts who made it a community effort to create a more affordable auto-pilot for piloting small aircraft. The innovations brought about by this community stemmed from the creative appropriation of existing technologies. These practices of tinkering and wild experimentation, as well as the discussions of the members, contributed to an incremental specification and becoming of UAVs as media equipped with agentic capacities, e.g., the common understanding of drones as autonomous sensing platforms. With the launch of the first ready-to-fly drones the focus of experimentation and tinkering shifted from the DIY engineering of UAV autopilots to exploring potential uses of drones. Consequently, drones underwent a twofold process of taming and stabilisation. On the one hand, the market introduction "reified" (Bijker et al. 1984) drones in that it shaped the image of drones as a quad- and multicopter "in the consciousness of the members of relevant social groups" (Bijker et al. 1984: 48). On the other hand, it proved the drones economic "makeability" (ibid.). While this can be understood as a form of closure, it also created an opening for new users beyond established DIY communities to experiment with drones. Unlike r/c aircraft, ready-to-fly drones can be operated without much prior knowledge or flying experience due to their increasingly autonomous functions. As we have shown, this was an important factor for the popularisation of drones as well as for the exploration of use cases for drones such as their use as airborne photographic platforms by hobbyist users.

Against the background of these experimental practices, this paper unpacked three dimensions of the ongoing taming of drones. First, the growing proliferation of ready-to-fly drones led to an increasing stabilisation of drone-specific practices. This was gradually reinforced by an incremental process of featurisation, i.e., the translation or inscription of emergent practices into technological features. Taking Madeleine Akrichs "de-scription of technical objects" into account, features can be understood as scripts that (re)define what is "delegated to a machine" and what is "left to the initiative of human actors" (Akrich 1992: 216). While the integration of autonomous features led to increased "learnability" and "usability" of drones, skills that were still on the pilot's side in r/c flight became progressively implemented into the drones' technological framework. Firmly integrated features can themselves become the starting point for new practices, which in turn can be technologically implemented.

As the second level of taming drone practices, we analysed their incorporation into commercial practices, a process we described as increasing professionalisation. Despite wide-spread logistical imaginaries, today's commercial uses of drones largely rely on UAVs as sensor platforms in such diverse areas as film production, agriculture, surveying, archaeology, geography, etc. Here, drone-specific industries of software and hardware manufacturers and specialised service sectors emerge that give way to specialised professional practices and routines which in turn contribute to the ongoing specification of drones which are increasingly being designed with their economic benefits in mind.

However, commercial uses of drones also require a reliable legal framework. In recent years, one could observe how such provisions have shifted in favour of professional use, while recreational practices have been increasingly delegitimised. This process of regulation was analysed as the third stabilising factor in the taming of drone practices. We argued that regulation contributes to conceptual closure of what constitutes a drone, even if this definition differs from that of other relevant groups. Additionally, legal regulations determine the spaces of action of the various actors and directly affect their practices. In this regard, current regulations lead to a redistribution of competencies between human actors and drones as semi-autonomous agents, e.g., in the case of geo-awareness systems. The integration of drones into traffic management systems is supposed to lead to a higher level of accountability of drones and pilots by entangling them into the pre-existing logics of civil aviation.

In describing the coming together of drones as media technologies equipped with agentic capacities through the opposing conceptual lenses of experimentation and taming, our aim was to unpack the complex becoming-media of non-military drones in the past two decades. At various levels, featurisation, professionalisation, and regulation are drivers of a gradual socio-technical closure of drones. These closures, however, create new openings for the ongoing becoming of drones.

Acknowledgements

Gefördert durch die Deutsche Forschungsgemeinschaft (DFG) – Projektnummer 262513311 – SFB 1187. Funded by the Deutsche Forschungsgemeinschaft (DFG, German Research Foundation) – Project-ID 262513311 – SFB 1187.

References

Anderson, Chris (2012a): Makers. The New Industrial Revolution, New York: Crown Business.
Anderson, Chris (2012b): "How I accidentally Kickstarted the Domestic Drone Boom." In: Wired Magazine, June 22, 2012 (http://www.wired.com/2012/06/ff_drones/).
Anderson, Chris (2008a): "The DIY Drones Mission (aka The Five Rules)." DIY Drones Blog Post, January 4, 2008 (https://diydrones.com/profiles/blogs/the-diy-drones-mission-aka-the).
Anderson, Chris (2008b): "BlimpDuino home page." DIY Drones Blog Post, June 23, 2008 (https://diydrones.com/profiles/blogs/blimpduino-home-page).
Anderson, Chris (2008c): "So much for the iPhone Autopilot." DIY Drones Blog Post, June 12, 2008 (https://diydrones.com/profiles/blogs/705844-BlogPost-38819).
Anderson, Chris (2007a): "GeoCrawler 1 (Lego Autopilot) Instructions." DIY Drones Blog Post, June 12, 2007 (https://diydrones.com/profiles/blogs/705844-BlogPost-728).

Anderson, Chris (2007b): "GeoCrawler 2 (Cellphone autopilot)." DIY Drones Blog Post, June 12, 2007 (https://diydrones.com/profiles/blogs/geocrawler-2-cellphone).

Anderson, Chris (2007c): "GeoCrawler 3 (BASIC Stamp autopilot)." DIY Drones Blog Post, June 12, 2007 (https://diydrones.com/profiles/blogs/705844-BlogPost-731).

Anderson, Chris (2007d): "Friday Fanboy returns: RC electric planes." The Long Tail Blog Post, February 03, 2007 (https://web.archive.org/web/20070227001725/http://www.longtail.com/the_long_tail/2007/02/friday_fanboy_r.html).

Anderson, Chris (2007e): "The sub-$1,000 UAV project." The Long Tail Blog Post, March 12, 2007 (https://web.archive.org/web/20070315210320/http://www.longtail.com/the_long_tail/2007/03/the_sub1000_uav.html).

Anderson, Chris (2007f): "GeoCrawler 4 (Picopilot off-the-shelf autopilot)." The Long Tail Blog Post, May 12, 2007 (https://diydrones.com/profiles/blogs/705844-BlogPost-727).

Akrich, Madeleine (1992): "The De-Scription of Technical Objects." In: Bijker Wiebe E./Law John (eds.): Shaping Technology|Building Society. Studies in Sociotechnical Change, Cambridge: MIT Press, pp. 205-224.

Bajde, Domen. et al. (2017a): "Public reactions to drone use in residential and public areas", (https://pure.au.dk/portal/files/142682693/Report_Public_reactionsto_drone_use_in_residential_and_public_areas_1_.pdf).

Bajde, Domen. et al. (2017b): "General public's privacy concerns regarding drone use in residential and public areas", (https://www.sdu.dk/-/media/files/om_sdu/institutter/marketing/imm/general+publics+privacy+concerns+(full+report)+2.pdf).

Bakardjieva, Maria (2006): "Domestication Running Wild. From the Moral Economy of the Household to the Mores of a Culture." In: Berker, Thomas/Hartmann, Maren/Punie/Yves/Ward, Katie J. (eds.) (2006): Domestication of Media and Technology, New York: Open University Press, pp. 62-79.

Barnes, Brooks (2014): "Drone Exemptions for Hollywood Pave the Way for Widespread Use." In: The New York Times, September 25, 2014 (https://www.nytimes.com/2014/09/26/business/media/drone-exemptions-for-hollywood-pave-the-way-for-widespread-use.html).

BBC News (2014): "Australian triathlete injured after drone crash." In: BBC News, April 7, 2014 (https://www.bbc.com/news/technology-26921504).

Bender, Hendrik (2018): "The New Aerial Age: Die wechselseitige Verfertigung gemeinsamer Raum- und Medienpraktiken am Beispiel von Drohnen-Communities." In: Otto, Isabell/Schramm, Samantha/Thielmann, Tristan/ Ghanbari, Nacim. (eds.): Kollaboration. Beiträge zur Medientheorie und Kulturgeschichte der Zusammenarbeit, Paderborn: Fink, pp. 121-146.

Berker, Thomas/Hartmann, Maren/Punie/Yves/Ward, Katie J. (eds.) (2006): Domestication of Media and Technology, New York: Open University Press.

Bjiker, Wiebe E. (2012): "The Social Construction of Bakelite: Toward a Theory of Invention." In: Bjiker, Wiebe E./Hughes Thomas P./Pinch, Trevor (eds.): The Social Construction of Technological Systems. New Directions in the Sociology and History of Technology, Cambridge: MIT Press, pp. 155-182.

Bijker Wiebe E./Law John (eds.) (1987): Shaping Technology|Building Society. Studies in Sociotechnical Change, Cambridge: MIT Press.

Bijker, Wiebe E./Bönig, Jürgen/van Oost, Ellen (1984): "The Social Construction of Technological Artefacts: Problems and Perspectives of the Study of Science and Technology in Europe." In: Journal for Science Research 3, pp. 39-51.

BMVI (2020): "Unterrichtung durch die Bundesregierung: Aktionsplan der Bundesregierung über unbemannte Luftfahrtsysteme und innovative Luftfahrtkonzepte", Drucksache 19/18800, (https://www.bmvi.de/SharedDocs/DE/Anlage/DG/aktionsplan-drohnen.pdf?__blob=publicationFile).

BMVI (2017): "Verordnung zur Regelung des Betriebs von unbemannten Fluggeräten", Drucksache 39/17, (https://dserver.bundestag.de/brd/2017/0039-17.pdf).

Bonnington, Christina (2012): "Tacocopter: The Coolest Airborne Taco Delivery System That's Completely Fake." In: WIRED, March 23, 2012 (https://www.wired.com/2012/03/qa-with-tacocopter/).

Carroll, Jennie/Howard, Steve/Peck, Jane/Murphy, John (2003): "From Adoption to Use: The Process of Appropriating a Mobile Phone." In: Australasian Journal of Information Systems 10/2, pp. 38-48.

Chad (2007): "Read wii nunchuck data into Arduino." Windmeadow Labs Blog Post, June 5, 2007 (https://web.archive.org/web/20080902193151/http://www.windmeadow.com/node/42).

Chesbrough, Henry/Lettl, Christopher/Ritter, Thomas (2018): "Value Creation and Value Capture in Open Innovation." In: Journal of Product Innovation Management 35/6, pp. 930-938.

Chocolate Copter (2014): "First Chocolate Quadcopter – delicious!!!", June 1, 2014 (https://www.youtube.com/watch?v=e6lRbiHswho).

Cracknell, Arthur P. (2018): "The Development of Remote Sensing in the Last 40 years." In: International Journal of Remote Sensing 39/23, pp. 8387-8427.

DHL (2019): "How medical drones help save lives in Tanzania", June, 2019 (https://www.dhl.com/global-en/delivered/insights/medical-drones-save-lives-tanzania.html).

Dildoeverything (2016): "Dildo Drone", April 18, 2016 (https://www.youtube.com/watch?v=pZCVG7zUaRA).

DLR (2018): "Einsatz ziviler Drohnen in Deutschland: DLR-Studie zeigt Zustimmung für Rettungs- und Forschungseinsätze sowie bestehende Vorbehalte", December 18, 2018 (https://www.dlr.de/content/de/artikel/news/2018/4/20181218_einsatz-ziviler-drohnen-deutschland.html).

DMFV (2016): "EASA-Regelung für Drohnen soll auch Modellflug regeln", (https://www.dmfv.aero/rechtundwissen/easa-regelung-fuer-drohnen-soll-auch-modellflug-regeln/).

Dronestagram (2022): "Our manifesto", July 30, 2022 (https://www.dronestagr.am/our-manifesto/).

EASA (2021a): "FAQ n.132025: What distinguishes a model aircraft from a drone?", (https://www.easa.europa.eu/faq/132025).

EASA (2021b): "FAQ n.132023: Does the new EU Regulation on drones also apply to model aircraft?", (https://www.easa.europa.eu/faq/132023).

EASA (2016): "'Prototype' Commission Regulation on Unmanned Aircraft Operations", (https://www.easa.europa.eu/sites/default/files/dfu/UAS%20Prototype%20Regulation%20final.pdf).

Erickson, Seth/Kelty, Christopher M. (2015): "The Durability of Software." In: Kaldrack, Irina/Leeker, Martina (eds.): There Is No Software, There Are Just Services, Lüneburg: meson press, pp. 39-55.

Ernst, Christoph/Schröter, Jens (2020): Zukünftige Medien. Eine Einführung, Wiesbaden: Springer VS.

FAA (2020): "Concept of Operations v2.0. Unmanned Aircraft System (UAS) Traffic Management (UTM)", March 2, 2020 (https://www.faa.gov/uas/research_development/traffic_management/media/UTM_ConOps_v2.pdf).

FAA (2010): FAA Aerospace Forecast Fiscal Years 2010–2030, (https://www.faa.gov/data_research/aviation/aerospace_forecasts/2010-2030/media/2010%20Forecast%20Doc.pdf).

Fung, Brian (2013): "It's a bird! It's a plane! It's a drone that makes movies!" In: The Washington post, August 15, 2013 (https://www.washingtonpost.com/news/the-switch/wp/2013/08/15/its-a-bird-its-a-plane-its-a-drone-that-makes-movies/).

GIM International. (2021): "Kitty Hawk Acquires 3D Robotics", June 17, 2021 (https://www.gim-international.com/content/news/kitty-hawk-acquires-3d-robotics?output=pdf).

García-Sellés, David/Pablo Granado, Pablo/Josep Antón Muñoz, Josep Antón/ Gratacos, Oscar / Carrera, Núria / Arbues, Pau (2014): "Capture and Geological Data Extraction: Tools for a Better Analysis and Digital Outcrop Modelling." In: Vertical Geology Conference 2014, February 5 – 7 2014, University of Lausanne, Switzerland.

Goodwin, Charles (1994): "Professional Vision." In: American Anthropologist 96/3, pp. 606-633.

Hashim, Ahmed S./Patte, Grégoire (2012): "'What Is That Buzz?' The Rise of Drone Warfare." In: Counter Terrorist Trends and Analyses 4/9, pp. 8-13.

Silverstone, Roger/Hirsch, Eric (1992): Consuming Technologies: Media and Information in Domestic Spaces, London: Routledge.

Hochmair, Hartwig/Zielstra, Dennis (2014): "Analysing User Contribution Patterns of Drone Pictures to the Dronestagram Photo Sharing Portal." In: Spatial Science 60/1, pp. 79-98.

Jablonowski, Maximilian (2022): Imagine Drones: Eine Kulturanalyse ziviler Drohnen, Berlin: Kadmos.

Jablonowski, Maximilian (2015): "Drone It Yourself! On The Decentring of 'Drone Stories'." In: Culture Machine 16, (http://www.culturemachine.net).

Jasanoff, Sheila (2015): "Future Imperfect: Science, Technology, and the Imaginations of Modernity." In: Jasanoff, Sheila/Kim, Sang-Hyun (eds): Dreamscapes of Modernity. Sociotechnical Imaginaries and the Fabrication of Power, Chicago: The University of Chicago Press, pp. 1-33.

Kittler, Friedrich A. (2014): The Truth of the Technological World. Essays on the Genealogy of Presence, Stanford: Stanford University Press.

LaFlamme, Marcel (2018): "Remaking the Pilot: Unmanned Aviation and the Transformation of Work in Postagrarian North Dakota", Diss., Rice University, (https://hdl.handle.net/1911/102256).

Landmesser, Detlev (2021): "DHL stellt Entwicklung ein Paketdrohren bleiben ein ferner Traum." In: Tagesschau, August 9, 2021 (https://www.tagesschau.de/wirtschaft/technologie/post-dhl-paketkopter-einstellung-101.html).

MPAA (2014): "Statement on Today's UAS Filing to the FAA", June 2, 2014, (https://www.motionpictures.org/press/statement-on-todays-uas-filing-to-the-faa/).

Phillips, Alan (2015): "Drone Sales Numbers: Nobody Knows, So We Venture A Guess." In: drone life, April 16, 2015 (https://dronelife.com/2015/04/16/drone-sales-numbers-nobody-knows-so-we-venture-a-guess/).

Pin Koh, Lian/Wich, Serge A. (2012): "Dawn of drone ecology: low-cost autonomous aerial vehicles for conservation." In: Tropical Conservation Science Vol.5/2, pp.121-132.

Reinhard, Jochen (2013): "Structure from Motion, Drohnen & Co. Neue Wege in der Dokumentation archäologischer Ausgrabungen". In: TUGIUM 29, pp. 177-188.

Rose, Charlie (2013): "Amazon's Jeff Bezos looks to the future." In: CBS News, December 1, 2013 (https://www.cbsnews.com/news/amazons-jeff-bezos-looks-to-the-future/)

Sauer, Frank/Schörnig, Niklas (2012): "Killer drones: The 'silver bullet' of democratic warfare?" In: Security Dialogue 43/4, pp. 363-380.

SESAR (2022): "Smart ATM U-space", (https://www.sesarju.eu/U-space).

Shackle, Samira (2020): "The Mystery of the Gatwick drone." In: The Guardian, December 1, 2020 (https://www.theguardian.com/uk-news/2020/dec/01/the-mystery-of-the-gatwick-drone).

Simondon, Gilbert (2016): On the Mode of Existence of Technical Objects, Minneapolis: Univocal.

Smith, Neil G./ Passone, Luca/al-Said, Said/ al-Farhan, Mohamed/Levy, Thomas E. (2014): "Drones in Archaeology: Integrated Data Capture, Processing, and

Dissemination in the al-Ula Valley, Saudi Arabia." In: Near Eastern Archaeology 77/3, pp. 176-181.

Suboticki, Ivana/ Sørensen, Knut H. (2021): "Designing and Domesticating an Interstructure: Exploring the Practices and the Politics of an Elevator for Cyclists." In: Urban Studies 58/6, pp. 1229-1244.

Suchman, Lucy/Trigg, Randal/Blomberg, Jeanette (2002): "Working Artefacts: Ethnomethods of the Prototype." In: British Journal of Sociology 53/2, pp. 163-179.

Tripicchio, Paolo/Satler, Massimo/Dabisias, Giacomo/Ruffaldi, Emanuele/Avizzano, Carlo. (2015): "Towards Smart Farming and Sustainable Agriculture with Drones." In: Conference: Intelligent Environments conference 2015 (IE 15), Prague, (https://www.researchgate.net/publication/280156490_Towards_Smart_Farming_and_Sustainable_Agriculture_with_Drones).

Varah, Sean (2014): "Drones in Hollywood: What Industry Is Next?" In: Forbes, October 10, 2014 (https://www.forbes.com/sites/forbesleadershipforum/2014/10/10/drones-in-hollywood-what-industry-is-next/).

Vogl, Joseph. (2007): "Becoming-Media: Galileo's Telescope." In: Grey Room 29, pp. 14-25.

Wegen, Wim van/Anderson, Chris/McKinnon, Daniel (2017): "The Revolution of Drone-Carried Sensors." In: GIM International, 2017 (https://www.gim-international.com/content/article/the-revolution-of-drone-carried-sensors).

Welch, Chris (2014): "DHL drone will make deliveries to German island starting Friday." In: The Verge, September 24, 2014 (https://www.theverge.com/2014/9/24/6838443/dhl-drone-making-deliveries-to-german-island-juist).

Whitlock, Craig (2015): "Rogue drones a growing nuisance across the U.S." In: The Washington Post, August 10, 2015 (https://www.washingtonpost.com/world/national-security/how-rogue-drones-are-rapidly-becoming-a-national-nuisance/2015/08/10/9c05d63c-3f61-11e5-8d45-d815146f81fa_story.html).

Media Use of Older Adults in Bangladesh: Religion, Perceived Sinfulness and the Taming of Media

Tanja Aal, Dennis Kirschsieper, Md Rashidul Hasan, Claudia Müller

Abstract

This paper presents the findings of an exploratory study of media use among six older adults living in urban areas in Bangladesh based on semi-structured interviews. The study explores in detail how the older adults use different media and how their media use is embedded in their everyday life and social practices. The research focus is on newer media, especially the smartphone, but traditional media such as television are also addressed. One finding is that newer media are used mainly for social purposes, especially communication with family members, and less for individual purposes such as entertainment. We also find that newer media are in tension with religious beliefs and practices, leading in some cases to limited media use and rejection of certain media content or ownership of technology. To interpret this second finding, we draw on the assumption of 'wild' media within the domestication approach. The paper thus makes two contributions: first, detailed empirical insights into older adults' media use in Bangladesh; second, a conceptual contribution to the fruitfulness of the domestication approach in addition to Human-Computer Interaction (HCI) and Computer Supported Cooperative Work (CSCW).

Keywords

Domestication, Appropriation, ICT, HCI, CSCW, Taming, Older Adults, Bangladesh, Religion

1. Introduction

The smartphone is a global phenomenon that is not limited to younger users (Miller et al. 2021). Nevertheless, previous research on new media has been less concerned with older adults in Asia. In particular, there are not many qualitative studies that focus on individual older adults and their concrete lifeworlds or social practices and explore in detail how they use and appropriate new media. Also, domestication research still primarily focuses on Western nations. If we want to gain insight into such research in the Asian region, the sources remain limited.

We contribute to closing these research gaps with an explorative study on media accessibility and use in the home setting and beyond by six older adults in Bangladesh, taking into account both, traditional (TV) and new media (smartphones). We aim at tracing media appropriation processes by older people, when, how and why they may adopt or reject digital media.

With that we adopt an Human-Computer Interaction (HCI) and Computer Supported Cooperative Work (CSCW) perspective, fundamentally assuming that it is human actors who give meaning to media and technologies as part of their social practices. Here we are following the concept of "cultural appropriation", which refers, "like technology appropriation, (…) to the ways that people adapt and 'make the technology their own'" (Lindtner et al. 2012), whereby these becomes a cultural object through socially embedded attribution of meaning and values (Lindtner et al. 2012; Müller et al. 2015).

Our results point to a partly limited accessibility and use, whereby cultural, structural, socio-economic, age-related and individual aspects emerge as backgrounds. Since one of our central findings is that the smartphone is seen by the older adults in our study as both sinful and seductive, resulting in limited or even restricted media use or its rejection of ownership, we also address the media studies concept of domestication. In many ways, the HCI perspective of appropriation and the domestication approach overlap. However, the latter is linked to a specific assumption, namely that media are initially 'wild' and need to be 'tamed' (Hartmann 2019; Silverstone 2003; Ward 2006). In this paper we raise the question: Does this assumption apply to our empirical material? Is the domestication concept helpful in interpreting our findings and can it be a useful complement for HCI and CSCW?

Before presenting and discussing the results of our empirical study, we will explain the research background. First, we will provide the relevant contextual information, especially on religion and media use in Bangladesh (2.1). Since five of our six interview partners are female, we will also deal with gender relations here. Second, we will present the domestication approach, in particular the assumption that media are first 'wild' and must be 'tamed' (Hartmann 2019; Silverstone 2003; Ward 2006) (2.2) so that we can finally address the question of whether the concept is fruitful for interpreting our findings and whether it is a useful addition to HCI and CSCW.

2. Research background

2.1 Religion and gender-related media use in Bangladesh

Bangladesh is the eighth-most populous country (Worldbank Data 2023a) in the world with around 158.90 million (as of 1st July 2015) inhabitants (Bangladesh Bureau of Statistics et al. 2017) and is currently considered one of the least developed countries in the world. But with its rapid development growth, it is expected to be among the developing countries within 2026 (Takashi & Noriyoshi 2021). The literacy rate of females aged between 15 and 24 has increased (around 95.9% in 2020 compared to around 79.5% in 2011) (Worldbank Data 2023b). The country has four major religions with a Muslim majority (Hinks et al. 2018), Islam being practiced by 90.4% of its inhabitants. The other major religions are Hinduism (8.5%), Buddhism (0.6%), and Christianity (0.4%) (Wikipedia 2023). Religion plays an important role in people's lives as "political, social and cultural landscape" (Islam & Islam 2018).

Especially in rural regions, there is a considerable lack of technical infrastructure. In addition, women experience the digital gap within the existing patriarchal society. This has various reasons. On the one hand the level of education is still low due to difficult access to it, on the other hand, the dependency structure between traditional gender roles plays a major role (Sultana et al. 2018). Women are usually married at a very early age and are thus subject to the decision-making power of their husbands and the "importance and legitimacy of the woman's needs" (Sultana et al. 2018) ascribed to them. This affects all areas of life, such as access to education, occupational self-determination and career options, management of finances, household decisions and social interactions. The maximum scope of women's decision-making, if any, relates to a minor say in "house-hold decision-making, ownership of properties, and financial planning" (Sultana et al. 2018). This contrasts with the immense household-oriented efforts associated with their husbands' decisions, which are "excessive, unpaid and unrecognised" (Sultana et al. 2018). These living conditions generally lead to low literacy, little knowledge and a corresponding lack of technical and media competence. The latter is also caused by the fact that women's access to technology is controlled in a masculine (direct) and hegemonic (indirect) way. Direct influence corresponds, for example, to the husband's decision, which is often tied to his own advantage, e.g. due to the desire for constant accessibility, although women's own devices, if available, are also used for other purposes, "including talking to friends and family, coordinating business activities (e.g., selling their families' crops), and for entertainment (e.g., listening to music or watching videos)" (Sultana et al. 2018). Indirect influence takes place at the societal level. Society approves of such paternalism and even promotes it due to traditional role models. However, media and technologies are often shared within the family (in terms of mobile phones, primarily basic phones instead of smartphones are used, which greatly reduces access to the internet). This is primarily for financial reasons, but here again the aspect of male control over the woman's use of technology (time, duration and content) comes into play and negates her privacy. This results in a lack of knowledge as well as insecurity in dealing with digital media and the constant need for support from external individuals (Sultana et al. 2018). On the other hand, people share devices not only out of economic necessity, but also because sharing is a social and cultural practice that is deeply embedded in Bangladeshi society, which may be surprising from a Western perspective, as the prevailing Western paradigm of personal computing assumes that a device is used by a single person (Ahmed et al. 2017). Such causes of limited accessibility and use of media and technologies will be highlighted in our findings, with a view to ageing generations, especially older women, whereby images of ageing may also differ culturally. Understanding illness and disability as a normal part of ageing and not emphasising its freedom as much as North Americans and US-focused discourses on successful ageing, is a societal trend in Bangladesh, for example. Further, dependence on family caregivers is seen as normal and appropriate (Amin 2017).

2.2 Domestication approach and the wild media thesis

The domestication approach comes mainly from two sources: (1) a British variant of 'media and cultural studies', first developed in the late 1980s, which focused on the use and appropriation of new media in household contexts, which at that time was mainly television, and (2) a Norwegian 'science-and-technology-studies' (STS) approach developed at the same time, which understands domestication more broadly as the appropriation of technologies in different settings (by the state, within a company, etc.) (Hartmann 2009).

The concept of domestication does not only look at media content and individual reception, but also at embeddedness in social contexts and practices. For example, the meaning of "watching television" only emerges in the context of everyday family practices, suggesting that meaning is not inherent in the media but is ascribed by users in everyday life. Domestication can be defined as a process in which media enter the domestic sphere and users appropriate them (Silverstone et al. 1991). The smartphone as a mobile artifact requires an expanded definition as proposed by the Norwegian approach, which includes media use and appropriation in public spaces.

The assumption that media are initially "wild" and need to be "tamed" means in a general sense that they can challenge, disrupt or even destroy previous social practices (Hartmann 2019; Ward 2006). Although this basic assumption applies to both the British and Norwegian variant, in more specific terms, it is again important to look at the domestic sphere, as this can be considered an area which should actually be strongly protected from external influences. In this perspective, media initially represent intruders who invade and disrupt the protected sphere of the home or family. A simple example would be the family sitting at the dinner table together, but suddenly the telephone rings and interrupts family life. Furthermore, media in the domestic sphere can influence thoughts and decisions that are actually private. One example of the intrusive role of media is demonstrated by studies that have shown that in Bangladesh the government has successfully used television, radio and print media to get women to have fewer children (Islam & Hasan 2000; Rabbi 2012). In order to protect themselves from such influences, be they internal or external, the Amish people have, for example, banned telephones in their homes since 1909, although this was viewed critically within the community. They have integrated them instead in public areas to enjoy their benefits nonetheless. Their basic cultural attitude and historic orientation set a barrier against digital communication technology within their private spaces and led to a negative attribution of meaning to further strengthen and maintain these social barriers. This serves to protect the household, its members and family structures and thus the community as a whole and its basic values and needs (Zimmerman Umble 1992). In their study of Muslim Indonesian mothers, Lim (2016) identified fear of negative effects of online content on their children. Here participants fear "moral degradation, spiritual corruption and self-destruction", whereby they counteract such a technically-mediated decline in values through supervision/control, which is guided by "faith" and "religious ideals" (Lim et al., 2016). The authors speak of an actual "taming of 'wild technologies'" (Lim et al. 2016). Campbell (2007) also refers to technology being "modified", "cultivated" or "tamed". With regard to mobile artefacts such as the smartphone, this can be claimed for both the private and communal level. In this regard Bell (2006) states that "[c]ultural logic necessarily impact[s] the very ways in which new technologies are created, consumed, and indeed rejected". In this the 'moral economy of the household' unfolds, where "symbolic meaning transactions occur" in "distinct spaces" (Campbell 2007). Disruptions come, according to Lim (2016), with asymmetries "enabling one member [of a household] to impose conditions on another" within domestication processes. From the authors' perspective there exist various asymmetries, such as of power, expectation, practice, access, competencies and values (Lim 2016). A qualitative study by Roy (2018), which examined mixed-age individuals in a total of 14 middle-class households in relation to media consumption in Bangladesh shows that the domestication of media and technologies contributes to the maintenance of social structures and positions of power, whereby values and practices are preserved or reproduced, which ultimately maintains class and class distinctions. This is particularly common in religious groups who "evaluate, monitor and control their members' use of technology" (Campbell 2007). Nevertheless, many (religious) communities from various cultures have integrated digital technologies into their daily lives and spiritual routines. Techno-spiritual practices, especially supported via cell phones, have become common by now but remain critical as well (Bell 2006; Campbell 2007), especially for the older generations (Campbell 2007).

From what has been said so far, it has become clear that societal, individual and local characteristics are important when it comes to what domestic life looks like and how new media and technologies are integrated and used in it. The same medium, however, can be used in very different ways within family contexts and be integrated into family life, with cultural differences being a major influencing factor.

3. Methods

The explorative study we conducted gives a first impression of socio-cultural media practices of older people in Bangladesh and their embeddedness in their everyday practices by means of semi-structured interviews following a qualitative approach (Flick 1995).

In order to achieve a corresponding depth in the data, we limited ourselves to a small number of participants of a total of six, who were recruited according to a snowball system. This resulted in a focus on female participants, whose daily lives, perspectives, and practices we considered interesting against the backdrop of the strongly dominated role of women in Bangladesh. The sample therefore consists of five women and one man (see Table 1) who live in the cities of Dhaka (P1, P2, P3) and Chittagong (P5). One participant (P4) was partly living in Jessore and Dhaka city and one (P6) in Savar, and Upazila (administrative region/sub-district) of Dhaka and the Dhaka city.

Two of the participants (P2, P3) are married to one another. Their interview took place together, contrary to the original plan, because P3 (female) wanted to attend the interview with P2, which ultimately led to an influence on the interview design, as she occasionally complemented her husband in some of his answers. A separate interview in succession was subsequently refused, despite good reasons given by the interviewer. According to the participants' own statement, she would feel the same way as her husband, which expressed love and attachment for her.

The youngest participant is 56 years old, whereas the oldest is already over 80. They all belong to the social middle class and are among those households that have the financial means to purchase technical devices. Five out of six had their own smartphones at the time of the interview as well as internet access. Only one mentioned having the ability to use a computer.

	Age	Sex	Living with	Current City	Marital Status	Living In	Financial Dependency	Education	Religion
P1	70	F	Youngest son's family	Dhaka	Widowed	Own house	Youngest Son	Class 8	Islam
P2	62	M	Wife and 2 sons	Dhaka	Married	Tenant	Own (retired but shared business)	Bachelor's	Islam
P3	56	F	Husband and 2 sons	Dhaka	Married	Tenant	Husband and Son	SSC	Islam
P4	57	F	Husband and sometimes with son's family	Jessore & Dhaka	Married	Own & Tenant	Husband	HSC	Hindu
P5	64	F	Husband and the youngest son	Chittagong	Married	Own house	Husband	Bachelor's	Islam
P6	~80	F	Different child's family in different times	Savar (Dhaka) & Dhaka	Widowed	Son's and Daughter's flat/house	Sons and daughters	Class 5	Islam

Table 1: Study participants

We decided to use a snowball system strategy due to easy access to the family network of one of the authors, who is from Bangladesh himself and has detailed cultural and contextual knowledge. As all the participants knew the researcher or his family, it was comparatively easy to get invited into the homes of the participants which is otherwise rather difficult, especially when interviewing women who can be identified as a vulnerable target group. Also talking about religious practice is not common, which is why trust is essential.

All interviews, except the interview with P5, were conducted face-to-face while the researcher visited the participant's own home or the home, the participant was visiting at that moment. P5 was interviewed through a call via Facebook messenger.

All the interviews lasted between 30 to 70 minutes and were audio-recorded, except the interview taken through messenger service. Here notes were taken during the interview session.

The interviews were conducted in the participants' mother tongue (Bengali) and analysed via content analysis. The latter was done in several steps. Transcripts were clustered according to identified themes and given codes accordingly, while translating its content into English to make it available to the other researchers. Similar codes were then brought together to form themes. There were multiple arrangement-rearrangements done in the whole process of analysis. After a first result extraction and according to the recommendations after a first review phase, one of the themes (religious faith and images of ageing) was further elaborated on by way of a new round of interviews with two of the participants (P1, P4). Due to technical problems, the others could not be interviewed at the time of the second survey, unfortunately.

4. Findings: everyday practices and media use or rejection

The findings presented in this paper follow the research question on the accessibility, use and appropriation of media and technologies in the domestic sphere by older people in Bangladesh's urban regions, taking into account new and traditional media and technologies. Against this background, the following main themes emerged: 1) Accessibility of technology and autonomy, 2) Technology usage: Main areas, as well as 3) Restricted media use and refraining from media ownership.

4.1 Accessibility of technology and autonomy

While older people living in cities have access to smartphones and broadband internet connections, the older adults in rural areas may not have such opportunities. P2 mentions that he moved from the village to the city when he was young while most of his friends stayed in the village. In the rural areas, there is not much use of technology among people and elders rarely use any digital devices even today. In urban areas, people can get a smartphone or other devices easily and they are readily available at any shopping mall ortech store, which are can be found almost anywhere. In some rural areas, there is no big shopping mall and the financial condition of the older adults living there may mean they cannot afford a smartphone. Sometimes, they have to rely on the breadwinner in the family to buy them a smartphone but then again, there is no one to teach them how to operate that smartphone, P2 explains.

There are different reasons for purchasing a smartphone. Most of the participants decided to buy one because they are simply the cheaper option if people want to use the internet. According to the participants, however, they do not update their devices too often. Others, like P4, received their smartphones as a gift from their sons/daughters. P4 explained that she did not want to have a smartphone but one of her sons gave her his, so she started using it. Although she recognizes it as a useful device, she does not like phones in general. In addition, her smartphone is replaced regularly. If there is even a small problem, her husband or son will buy her a new phone or give her theirs so they can buy a new one for themselves. While smartphones are very common among the participants (P1–P5), the use of computers remains very rare Only one person learned about its use during a visit abroad to her son and grandchildren in the USA (P4). During this visit, she learned some basics but after she came back to Bangladesh, she did not operate it much. Her grandson, who lives with her, sometimes teaches her new things. If she faces any problem, her grandson will solve that problem.

While most of the participants do not experience any extraordinary restrictions in their autonomy, P6 faces strong limitations that can be compared to such rural circumstances as described above, even though she lives in urban areas. She lives in the different families of her children at different times, as living alone is no longer possible. Under these circumstances, she is very much bound to the daily practices of her relatives. Since she is no longer mobile for safety reasons, she is dependent on the time and resources (e.g. car) of her children or their partners., These resources are rarely available, which is why she can only visit her hometown once a year, for example. In addition, little consideration is given to her interests in her view:

"I still cannot operate a television. I did not try too much, though, because they (referring to the grandchildren) watch cartoons on the television the whole day. They don't give me time to watch Waz (a popular type of religious event in Bangladesh), but I want to see that. They say those are not good and they will see cartoons. Children find joy in cartoons; I find joy in watching Waz where people talk about religion, and I can learn from that or follow those." (P6)

As she does not have her own smartphone at her own request and cannot operate the television that is available to her, her access to the world, the associated information flow and personal enjoyment for greater well-being in daily life are highly limited and depend on presence, personal time, availability of the devices, and the internet connection or data volume of others.

4.2 Technology usage: main areas

4.2.1 Communication and maintaining social bonds

Except for P6, all participants owned a personal smartphone using WhatsApp, Imo, Messenger, and Viber for communicating with family members, friends, business partners or members of certain groups they join (music academy/P4, social welfare club/P5). P2 explains that this has made communication easier:

"Everything is set up in different software. In Viber, WhatsApp, Imo, I have everything set up. You go to software and touch, people's names will come up, then you click on the name and the call happens. Now, this has become easy because of the smartphone. In the past, you had to remember or write down numbers somewhere and get those when you need to call, press on the buttons of the phone and check with the written numbers if you have pressed all the digits correctly. Now it has become easy." (P2)

Nevertheless, when problems occur, children and grandchildren help to solve them when living nearby. A problem all of them mentioned, though, was related to the internet connection. For some participants, the Wi-Fi router was simply located too far away, some complained about the overall mobile operator's service. They had different ways of handling this situation, e.g.:

"I live on the lower floor and the Wi-Fi router is on the upper floor. I sometimes face network disturbances in my room. So, I go to the upper floor and make calls. Sometimes I open my door and come to the balcony, then I can have good internet access from the router's network. My husband buys minutes or data (from the sim operators), he does not use Wi-Fi networks. The sim operator's network is accessible from everywhere. So when my husband is at home, we can make a call from the lower floor. But when he is not at home, I go to the upper floor or the balcony opening my door and make calls. Sometimes I call from my room if the connection is good." *(P4)*

Communicating with grandchildren who live abroadmay differ from communication with those living in the same household, neighbourhoodor at least in the same country. Many of the participants are affected by similar circumstances (P1, P2, P3, P6). The primary barrier here is language, as the mother tongue of the parents is usually not mastered by the grandchildren abroad and the participants speak little or no English. So, during a phone conversation, neither can express what is on their minds. P2 and his wife (P3) see their granddaughter, who lives in London, only durings video calls, and she is too young to communicate. Therefore, there is not much interaction. P3 comments, *"Who lives near, I have more connectedness towards them. The grandchildren who live far, yes, I talk with them, but there is less connectedness. They also feel less connected towards me."*

"This is normal. The face-to-face conversation, like you and I are having, has a certain kind of connectedness. Those who are living far away suddenly come for a day to visit, share greetings, and smile, whether that smile is artificial or real I don't know. We ask general questions to each other and that ends there. They again go far after that." (P2)

P5 interacts with her grandchildren through video and audio calls. She mentioned that she had a good bond with the grandchildren and that they responded to her queries over the phone "100%".

Compared to this, as already mentioned, P4 does not like to talk over the phone no matter that it is a video or audio call. She can talk a lot face-to-face but she can't find topics to talk about through the phone. Even when she talks to her sons, she often greets them, asks about how they are and that's all.

"I don't like to talk on the video call. Sometimes I want to see the young granddaughter, that is why I use video call, but I don't like it. [...] On mobile, I can speak for one or two minutes but I can't talk more than that. I generally share greetings and do just the necessary talking and after that, if someone starts to speak for long, I become stressed. Those who talk too much on the phone, I don't call them out of fear of talking for hours. Even when I talk to my sons over the phone, I speak for a maximum of two minutes, but not more than that. It is not like I worry about mobile recharge or other things; the problem is I don't like to talk over the phone." (P4)

Communication options for P6 are very limited compared to the other participants as she doesn't own a smartphone herself as already mentioned.

4.2.2 Information and entertainment

Although all participants have access to the internet on a personal or family level, their usage varies. While P6 is highly dependent on her family members and their consideration for her needs, others have accounts on Facebook (P1, P2, P4, P5), where they are primarily connected to their relatives, regularly getting informed about their updates from a passive consumer perspective. P2 mentions that she only got an account because her daughter pushed her to get one. She now uses it for checking the news regularly. P1 watches a cooking show additionally. P2 is aware that probably not everything on Facebook is true but it provides news faster than the local TV channels: *"Although not every piece of news is is correct, it is also not true that everything is made up."* On television the news is shown once every full hour but on Facebook, the news channel broadcasts can be accessed at any time from anywhere, which she sees as an advantage. She adds, '*Sometimes, the news on Facebook may not be broadcast on Television" (P2).* P5 quickly sensed the addictive potential of Facebook. After realizing that she was spending too much time on Facebook, she started controlling the situation, spending less time on it now, but still on a daily basis. She also thinks that less meaningful relationships are built on the platform than what is possible in a face-to-face situation.

P4 mentions that she likes to read books on her smartphone but cannot search for or download them online. Her son assists her in this case, then she stores and reads them.

All the participants mentioned that they watch YouTube videos related to their religion. Some mentioned that they also liked to watch Bengali and Hindi TV dramas on YouTube and television. They also like to listen to songs on YouTube.

4.3 Restricted media use and refraining from media ownership

4.3.1 Religious faith and technology usage

In principle, piety and media use are not necessarily mutually exclusive, as P1 describes, but the latter also bears the risk of neglecting the former:

"If they maintain the religious path even within that [it is okay]. If someone focuses more on media consumption and forgets about the prayer and avoids praying, then that person can't be religious. [...] that is not correct. Many people make this mistake which depends on their mentality."

P5 confirms the risk outlined here:

"Sometimes I feel addicted to the phone and spend maybe a lot of time using the phone and can't get up early for the prayer. Then it feels it would have been better to act differently and use less."

P1 also mentions that she likes to listen to old songs or to watch drama shows and then she realizes that she is old and near death, so she should keep away from these because according to the Hujurs and Islam, this is a sin:

"I like songs, I like old songs very much and listen to them. I also watch good dramas. [...] I like to watch Indian cinemas [...] too. Sometimes I am afraid that I am committing sins. I prefer to enjoy these but control myself. I am aged now and anytime I may die. Watching these is not good, these are sinful. But sometimes I enjoy these. I watch dramas on television and enjoy music on it and mobile, both."

Digital entertainment is a reduced aspect of technology usage by all of our religious participants as religion and a pious way of life play an important role for them. P1 defines being religious as follows: *"If someone truly gives God time, perform religious activity regularly."* P5 differentiates somewhat more strongly here:

"It differs from man to man. Someone who prays five times a day may think of himself as religious, someone may feel he needs to do more than that to be considered religious. Someone can also think they can only do good work and not pray and still go to heaven and consider himself/herself religious."

Against this backdrop, P6 mentions that this is the reason why she does not have her own smartphone. This points to a clear difference between the two solution strategies for an inner conflict: P1 exercises control in order to calm her conscience, P6 acts by not having her own smartphone in order to limit permanent access for herself. When talking about their thoughts about successful aging, all the participants mention that they want to be religiously more involved before they die, so they try to invest more time in prayers and other religious activities such as fasting, reading religious books, etc. For four of the Muslim participants, daily prayers are very present. The first prayer has to be done before sunrise, the second at noon, the third in the afternoon, the fourth during the evening, and the last prayer of the day is done at night. Some Muslim older adults also pray an additional time during midnight which is called 'Tahajjud salat'. P1 is one of those trying to pray at any time required by Islam, even trying to pray special prayers if she can get up in the middle of the night (at around 3/4 am). Sometimes she prays another prayer after getting up for the second time in the morning, but recently she is unable to do that. She also reads the holy Quran every day and fasts during Ramadan. All these prayers require some time for making sure to wear clean clothes, getting fresh and clean by washing different body parts, going to the mosque, or using a clean cloth for making the prayer spot wherever they are, doing the prayer after that, reciting some important line and spending some more time praying. P1 remarks, *"If you pray five times regularly, you don't have much leisure."*

P5 explains to us a different picture of religious practice in everyday life and points to the great discrepancy within society when it comes to media use. Regarding her religious practice she says:

"This is not something to share, or I think I don't think is something to tell others. Maybe one day I have time and do a lot of praying and another day I don't and I do less. It depends on the social and family environment a lot. There are a lot of things written in books, but the reality is different. For example, in different parts of our country, people think differently about religion. Like people in Dhaka and Chittagong do not think the same about being religious. People in Noyakhali are very stereotypical and they might think if someone using a mobile they may get distracted from the religion. We see technology in a positive way and many stereotypical people think of it as negative. [...] [They even] say that women should not go out of their houses. Whereas the prophet said that to have education, women can even travel to China in their proper dress."

P5 shares the same perspective on stereotypes and explains a positive use of modern technologies in more detail, P1 underlines the details described:

"Those who say they cannot be religious because of using technology are very stereotypical. Because of the availability of technology, people can practice religion more often now. People can save different verses of the Quran and the process of religion on their phones and those are always with them which impossible before. [...] The device actually gives freedom to the people to be more religious or not, to be good or bad. Anyone can be whatever they want using these." (P5)

"I think because of the abundance of technology, people are doing many religious practices. We should not only see the bad of these techs because there are many positive sides also. We can get news all over the country from Youtube. We can know about religion from many hujurs [experts in religion]. [...] They used to make things up and teach people those. But now they are more educated and we can learn from them [...]. I can't say because of the technologies now people are less religious, rather they pray more now. Because earlier we didn't get to know more about religion, but now we can and we can think more and reflect on our activities. Which makes us pray or be more religious." (P1)

Both participants outline the positive side effects of media and technology use with regard to spiritual practice. Not using them in the way described is judged by P5 as 'being bad'.

4.3.2 Images of ageing in the view of the participants

With regard to successful ageing, the aspect of a pious life seems to be particularly relevant. P1 (70 years) says that *"if the mind ages and people lose their hobbies, then people get old."* She does not want to be in a position where she is bedridden, and this becomes a burden on her family. Instead, she wants to die with pride. Every day she thinks about her death and prays even more. For P5 (64 years) ageing *"depends on the society and the family and personal mentality, too. [...] It can happen at 50 years or at 60 years or even at 70 years"*, she says, not feeling old at this time of her life. P2 (62 years) mentions that he sometimes reflects on his past life and the mistakes he made. He thinks it is a virtue of getting older to recognize and accept all the mistakes:

"You will think about it when you are old. You will become aware of the learning process then [...]. This is [...] the virtue of old age. [...] Not everyone has a good past and when they are old, they try to connect everything to make sense of their situation."

He also thinks that people in society no longer value each other. There is no one to listen to what he says, so he shares most of his thoughts with his wife (P3), and his wife does the same. He is a little annoyed that his sons have not taken his advice so much to heart. He wants them not to spend unnecessarily and to lead a good lifestyle, but they like to hang out with their friends and sometimes tell their father that he does not understand modern times and practices. This frustrates him because they do not value his words:

"When my son comes from the office in the evening, I tell him to get fresh and have some snacks. But he may not like that and wish to spend time with his friends or whatever way he likes. But as parents, we have to tell him that he had a hectic day and now he should take a rest. They don't take it well. They think they have friends, and they are everything to them. What we advise them to do is hard for them to follow. We used to obey our parents. It was a rule that when the call for Maghrib prayer happened, children had to come back home, say their prayer, read holy books and get back to study. Now they don't say prayers or read scriptures. When I tell them to say their prayer, they make excuses."

Younger people, as P1 outlines, may also focus more on technology than on religious paths, as P5 confirms, and they are more into enjoying life. This sometimes leads to family conflicts:

"[...] It is my duty to tell them to pray. Like my grandson, sometimes I ask him why he doesn't pray or pray on time and I advise him to do so. He often doesn't pay heed to this. There are sometimes even conflicts with my son, too. When I ask him if he prayed or not, he starts to give excuses to avoid praying but I am strict with my word and question him why he did not pray. He knows that I ask him to do the right task." (P1)

The conflict is a normal thing in our culture. Like the youngers gets scold and advised by the elder members for doing right things and praying, when they will become old, they will also do the same to the younger family members. (P5)

According to P1, old age and successful ageing entail turning towards an adequate religious life:

"The most important thing for me now is that I can die with a good amal (a way of expressing the Islamic way of life). I have most of my life behind me, and I am no longer seeking earthly values. Now my only goal is whether I can go to Allah with the right Amal. Maybe before my family, religion, and husband were more important, but now, with age, everything has become less important."

For P5, trust and time count as the most important facets in old age. Such time, she likes to invest in relationships instead of technology. In the case of online banking, she recognizes the benefits but directly refuses to use such options. She says that she likes to go to the bank and that the people working there know her well. If she used online banking, she would not get the chance to visit and meet them. They are very friendly and have good connections with her. If she makes a call and asks them for a favour, they will immediately help her. This kind of relationship would not be possible through online banking apps. Her sons and husband wanted her to open an account with such a financial app, but she refused to do so. P2 responds in this regard that as they are old, they have less need to use the internet and do these things online.

5. Discussion: taming of media in the domestic sphere

5.1 Digitally supported everyday practices of older adults in Bangladesh

In this study we found that digitally supported everyday practices span the areas of 'social relationships, communication, entertainment, autonomy, and religion'. Against this background, personal virtual spaces as well as new spheres of privacy have emerged for some of the participants (P1–P5), while P6 lacks such autonomy and privacy willingly due to devices shared with family members, which influences time, duration and content of use (Sultana et al. 2018). Digitally based activities of personal well-being include reading books on the smartphone, watching drama and other shows and religious programs on Youtube or Facebook (primarily via smartphone as only P4 can access and handle a computer rudimentarily) or on TV, listening to music on Youtube, following the news on Facebook or on TV, communicating with relatives and other people via audio or video call and smartphone). Uses correspond to those identified in previous studies (Sultana et al. 2018).

We find enrichment through digital practices especially in the communicative field for example with regard to audio or video calls with relatives abroad. Being socially embedded is enormously important for our older participants, which is in line with other studies on the ageing society (Busch et al. 2021). Contact – albeit loose – can thus be maintained with the grandchildren for instance (P1, P2, P3, P6) and also contributes to maintaining a link with one's own cultural roots on the part of the younger generation abroad (Cheong & Mitchell 2016; Kaur & Shruti 2016). The term 'home', which according to Hartmann (2019) is to be understood as a place of (close) social relationships that goes hand in hand with feelings of security and emotional intensity, is extended here with reference to the former through the use of technology and transferred to the virtual level, even outside of the traditional home setting. However, the loss of deeper communication, i.e. emotional intensity, is lamented by the participants. This has also been found in other studies with the same target group (Hope et al. 2014). The descriptions of affected participants (P1, P2, P3, P6) suggest that due to the lack of emotional intensity (P1, P2, P3), which is often accompanied by language barriers of the younger generation (overall four participants), no security can develop, exist or remain within these relationships and the term 'home' in this extended form thus no longer corresponds to its original meaning.

Another enrichment is described by P2: It consists of the simplification of telephone calls due to modern smartphone technology which comprises several steps, e.g. the external documentation of telephone numbers, the reminding or provision of these, as well as dialling at the appropriate moment from within the device.

However, digital access is challenging due to issues with the connection, which also seems to be a major problem of infrastructure in urban and rural areas alike (Sultana et al. 2018). In the case of P6 access is also challenging due to the lack of personal media and technologies which prevents independency (Foong 2016). Appropriation and use are also made difficult for her due to "digital literacy" (Cerna & Müller 2021; Sultana et al. 2018) and the lack of consideration by her social environment. Although we cannot say whether this is a matter of direct masculine control (Sultana et al. 2018), this example nevertheless shows the dimension of family control, e.g. through the grandchildren, who do not consider P6's needs as important as their own, or through her children and their partners, who only let her use the smartphone to a limited extent, namely when it suits themselves or is possible. Whether the lack of consideration by other family members is influenced by indirect patriarchal structures (Sultana et al. 2018), disrespect for her age or has an interpersonal background, cannot be answered. More research is needed to shed light on such intricacies. However, it is clear from our findings that P6's access, appropriation, and use depends on presence, personal time, availability of the devices, and the internet connection or data volume of the other family members. This example illustrates the asymmetries of power or external control cited by Lim (2016), which regulates access, practice – which in this case is tied to the former –, competencies that depend on the latter, and values, which are embedded in the power hierarchies in the family setting. For P1–P5, there was an external necessity to own a smartphone instead, as the prices for calls are better and consultations with the service provider are essential. P6 remains unconcerned about this because of her temporary living situation, moving around within the family.

Age-related, societal, digital or family structures and socio-economic aspects influence the individual level of action, as can be seen here. However, this is also culturally and religiously influenced, as will be shown further on.

5.2 Disruptions through media and technology

Influences on social practices through media and technology are found in the form of disruptions (Hartmann 2019; Ward 2006) especially in the areas of religion in connection with entertainment. The religious participants in our study describe that their desire for digitally based entertainment – be it the use of the internet or television – conflicts with their faith or the restrictions associated with it (with regard to the consumption of music and dramas). In several studies, we find religion-based concerns regarding the accessibility and use of technology (smartphones, internet) due to fear of immoral content, which could negatively affect faith and values (Ahad et al. 2017; Bell 2006; Campbell 2007; Lim et al. 2016; Zimmerman Umble 1992). Lim et al. (2016) refer to the fear of "moral degradation, spiritual corruption and self-destruction". The reaction to this fear is often connected to supervision/control or rejection of specific media content and technology (Campbell, 2007). The ageing process of participants in our study is linked to thoughts about approaching death, which is why people place more emphasis on living a pious life in the present. Although techno-spiritual practices have now generally found their way into everyday life, digital practice is becoming a challenge in daily life, as media are considered a sinful seduction, 'wild' and 'in need to be tamed' (Bell 2006; Campbell 2007). We find value-oriented asymmetries (Lim 2016), which often prevail in a conservative form for the older generations. This is why their view of technology against the specific background of religious practice often remains critical (Campbell 2007). Against this backdrop, our exploratory study differs from Roy (2018), who found no evidence of religion as a constraining factor for media and technology use in her study of 14 mixed-age households in Bangladesh. P1 and P5 paradoxically underline this conservatism by talking about stereotypes that have a negative attitude towards technology in relation to religion. They do not count themselves among them, although they, along with P3, resort to a controlled approach to media and technology. As can be seen here, technology is therefore indeed "laden with cultural values" (McDonald 2016), and thus more than a purely functional object (McDonald 2016), which as such could not question piety. In order to live this value, our religious participants seem not only to pay attention to themselves and their own spiritual practice, but also transfer this to their family members (children, grandchildren). Thus, according to their statements, P1, P3 and P5 have taken on a supervisory role towards them in which they act in a lecturing manner and thus try to socially consolidate these values, which promotes conflicts in everyday life – a normal social process, according P5, between the generations, which is maintained (successfully) with ageing, as P1 explains.

Against this backdrop, P6's severely restricted access to television and a smartphone can also be perceived as a disruption, as the lack of consideration regarding the use of such devices by family members leaves negative traces in interpersonal relationships, even if these restrictions correspond to the opposite desire to consume less digital entertainment out of piety and the participant herself restricts this access by voluntarily giving up her own smartphone.

With regard to both aspects outlined here, the question arises as to how media and technology can be tamed, i.e., how can they be used in the social structure of everyday life, in a more trouble-free way (Ward 2006). In the case of authentic religious practice, control in form of abstinence (P6) or reduction of the amount of consumption (P1, P3, P5) are individual solutions, although these do not resolve the disorder per se, as remorse as well as consumption-oriented desires (religious shows, dramas on YouTube, for example) remain. In our study, the taming and restricted or non-use of media (content) and technology in the domestic everyday setting compete endlessly without a 100% benefit. With regard to Lim (2016) even non-use can be seen as "taming of 'wild technologies'". Since the power to decide on access and the form of use is incumbent on the participants themselves, who exercise control on the basis of value preservation, one cannot, however, speak of power or practice asymmetries (Lim 2016).

A further disruption of everyday social life occurs where expected digital practices cannot be carried out due to non-functioning of media and technology.

This poses a challenge for all participants in the context of structurally-related poor network connections, obviously in urban areas of Bangladesh as well as in rural ones (Sultana et al. 2018).

Finally, derived from the findings presented in this paper, modern business relationships such as online banking also represent a possible challenge in the domestic sphere. P2 and P4 completely reject the possibility of digital use of these services in order to maintain the existing social interaction and communication between themselves and the bank employees. Digital media are not sinful in this case, but can be described as 'cold', as emotional attachment is prevented in this situation. The deliberate non-use of specific digital offerings counteracts the general technological change and the accompanying social changes (Lim 2016), which are attributed a lower value than the previous relationships, which in turn can be transferred to the digital offering itself.

5.3 Individual and communal attribution of meaning of media and technology as well as domesticity

As Röser (2007) states, meaning is not inherent in the media but is ascribed to it by users in everyday life. The participants use the smartphone less for individual purposes and more to maintain social relationships, whether it is through direct communication online or by following family news on social media (i.e. Facebook). In the lives of P4 and P5, online communication plays just as important a role in maintaining the connection to grandchildren living further away as it does for those with relatives abroad. In contrast to the relatively young age cohort in which the participants fall (4 people/56 to 64 years; 2 people/70 to over 80 years), this social focus and the weaker individual user preferences with regard to pure entertainment can be traced back to the different meaning of images of (successful) aging, which, despite the often relatively young age here, has an effect on digital practices and the taming of media and technologies against the background of religious faith. What could also influence the social focus of participants can be the contrast in values between the generations and the corresponding confrontation of these and its transformation against this background, which for them can be associated with a lack of appreciation and interest, disrespect and loss of religious practice associated with younger family members.

Likewise, meaning is revealed in the deliberate non-use of media content or the non-ownership of technology, for example, one's own smartphone (P6), as is the case in maintaining one's personal religious identity. As with other religious groups, cultural attitudes and religious orientations set limits to the appropriation of media and technology to protect certain collective values (Bell 2006; Lindtner et al. 2012; Zimmerman Umble 1992). In Bangladesh, these are a particular image of ageing and an accompanying pious way of life, which shape the "moral economy of the household" and "modify, cultivate or tame" medial wildness in the form of specific use or non-use (Campbell 2007).

6. Conclusion

We have unfolded an explorative study that shows a corresponding use case in terms of accessibility and use of media and technology, their controlled restriction of media or non-use of certain content, and the willing rejection of ownership by the target group of older adults. Within this framework, we have made reference to both traditional and new media. In doing so, we have taken into account cultural, structural, socio-economic, age-related and individual effects. While exploring the individual lifeworlds of the participants through a qualitative approach, we learned more about the areas of their habits on communication via technologies and media or their avoidance and entertainment, personal values, behavioural patterns, and self-images on (successful) ageing.

So-called disruptions through digital practices in social events and in one's own (mobile) domesticity were found with regard to the 'correct' practice of religious faith and in the field of entertainment. The new media can be seen here as an intruder that disrupt the religious life of the participants, in that they represent a constant temptation to consume certain content that is seen as pleasurable on the one hand, and sinful on the other. The degree of spirituality and its connection to the definition of successful ageing attribute its meaning and importance to the digital medium and its offers.

Following the assumption that media are 'wild' and need to be 'tamed' (Hartmann 2019; Silverstone 2003; Ward 2006), we were able to show that the empirical material supports such an assumption as the regulation of digital practices through reduction or abstinence of media content or ownership of technology were solutions of control for the participants. The domestication concept thus represents an enriching extension for the HCI as well as CSCW community.

Against the background of the small sample and the low diversity within it, the results shown here on domestication processes of older people in Bangladesh cannot be generalized. This also applies to factors favouring or impeding such processes, However, we were able to show that even under these circumstances, a multitude of characteristics, especially social bonding and religious faith, affect these processes and determine the 'taming' of media and technologies. With our results, we sketch out first impressions of the ageing society in Bangladesh and thus expand the research landscape in the field of domestication in Asian regions and their ageing society. However, further qualitative and quantitative research is needed to complete this picture in more detail and to be able to make generalizing statements.

Acknowledgements

This work was funded by the Deutsche Forschungsgemeinschaft (DFG, German Research Foundation) – Project-ID 262513311 – SFB 1187.

References

Ahad, Annie Dayani/Anshari, Muhammed/Razzaq, Abdur (2017): "Domestication of Smartphones Among Ain Brunei Darussalam." In: International Journal of Cyber Behavior, Psychology and Learning, 7/4, pp. 26–39.

Ahmed, Syed I./Haque, Md Romael/Chen, Jay/Dell, Nicola (2017): "Digital Privacy Challenges with Shared Mobile Phone Use in Bangladesh." In: Proceedings of the ACM on Human-Computer Interaction, 1, pp. 1–20.

Amin, Iftekhar (2017): "Perceptions of Successful Aging Among Older Adults in Bangladesh: An Exploratory Study." In: Journal of cross-cultural gerontology, 32/2, pp. 191–207.

Bangladesh Bureau of Statistics/UCEP Banlgadesh/Diakonia Banlgadesh (2017): "Education Scenario in Bangladesh: Gender Perspectives, Jauary 16, 2023 (http://bbs.portal.gov.bd/sites/default/files/files/bbs.portal.gov.bd/page/4c7eb0f0_e780_4685_b546_b4fa0a8889a5/BDcountry%20project_final%20draft_010317.pdf).

Bell, Genevieve (2006): "No More SMS From Jesus: Ubicomp, Religion and Techno-spiritual Practices." In: International Conference on Ubiquitous Computing, pp. 141–158.

Busch, Peter André/Hausvik, Geir Inge/Ropstad, Odd Karsten/Pettersen, Daniel (2021): "Smartphone Usage Among Older Adults." In: Computers in Human Behavior 121, pp. 1–12.

Campbell, Heidi (2007): "'What hath God wrought?' Considering How Religious Communities Culture (or Kosher) the Cell Phone." Continuum, 21/2, pp. 191–203.

Cerna, Katerina,/Müller, Claudia (2021): "Fostering Digital Literacy Through a Mobile Demo-kit Development: Co-designing Didactic Prototypes With Older Adults." In: Adjunct Publication of the 23rd International Conference on Mobile Human-Computer Interaction, pp. 1–6.

Cheong, Kakit,/Mitchell, Alex (2016): Helping the Helpers: Understanding Family Storytelling by Domestic Helpers in Singapore. In: Sun Sun Lim (ed.), Mobile Communication and the Family: Springer, pp. 51–69.

Devine, Joe/Hinks, Timothy/Naveed, Arif (2018): "Happiness in Bangladesh: The Role of Religion and Connectedness." In: Journal of Happiness Studies 20, pp. 351–371.

Flick, Uwe (1995): Handbuch Qualitative Sozialforschung. Weinheim: Beltz.

Foong, P. S. (2016): "The Value of The Life Course Perspective in the Design of Mobile Technologies for Older Adults." In: *Mobile Communication and the Family*, Springer, pp. 165–181.

Hartmann, Maren (2019): "Domestizierung, mobile Medien und anderes (un) häusliches mehr". In: Linke, Christine/Schlote, Isabel (eds.), Soziales Medienhandeln: Springer, pp. 101–116.

Hope, Alexis/Schwaba, Ted/Piper, Anne Marie (2014): "Understanding Digital and Material Social Communications for Older Adults." In: Proceedings of the SIGCHI Conference on Human Factors in Computing Systems, pp. 3903–3912.

Islam, M. Mazharul/Hasan, A. H. M. Saidul (2000): "Mass Media Exposure and its Impact on Family Planning in Bangladesh." In: Journal of biosocial science 32/4, pp. 513–526.

Islam, Md Nazrul/Saidul Islam, Md (2018): "Politics and Islamic Revivalism in Bangladesh: The Role of the State and Non-State/Non-Political Actors." In: Politics, Religion & Ideology 19/3, pp. 326–353.

Kaur, Ravinder/Shruti, Ishita Shruti (2016): "Mobile Technology and "Doing Family" in a Global World: Indian Migrants in Cambodia." In: Sun Sun Lim (ed.), Mobile Communication and the Family: Springer, pp. 73–91.

Lim, Sun Sun (2016): "Asymmetries in Asian Families' Domestication of Mobile Communication." In: Sun Sun Lim (ed.), Mobile Communication and the Family: Springer, pp. 1–9.

Lim, Sun Sun/Rahayu (2016): Balancing Religion, Technology and Parenthood: Indonesian Muslim Mothers' Supervision of Children's Internet Use. In: Sun Sun Lim (ed.), Mobile Communication and the Family: Springer, pp. 33–50.

Lindtner, Silvia/Anderson, Ken/Dourish, Paul (2012): "Cultural Appropriation: Information Technologies as Sites of Transnational Imagination." In: Proceedings of the ACM 2012 conference on computer supported cooperative work, pp. 77–86.

McDonald, Tom (2016): "Desiring Mobiles, Desiring Education: Mobile Phones and Families in a Rural Chinese Town."In: Sun Sun Lim (ed.), Mobile Communication and the Family: Springer, pp. 33–50.

Miller, Daniel/Rabho, Laila Abed/Awondo, Patrick/de Vries, Maya/Duque, Marilia/Garvey, Pauline/Haapio-Kirk, Laura/Hawkins, Charlotte/Otaegui, Alfonso/Walton, Shireen/Wang, Xinyuan (2021): The Global Smartphone: Beyond a Youth Technology, London: UCL Press.

Müller, Claudia/Hornung, Dominik/Hamm, Theodor/Wulf, Volker (2015): "Measures and Tools for Supporting ICT Appropriation by Elderly and Non Tech-Savvy Persons in a Long-Term Perspective." In: Nina Boulus-Rødje, Gunnar Ellingsen, Tone Bratteteig, Margunn Aanestad, & Pernille Bjørn (eds.), ECSCW 2015: Proceedings of the 14th European Conference on Computer Supported Cooperative Work, 19-23 September 2015, Oslo, Norway, Springer, pp. 263–281.

Rabbi, A. M. Fazle (2012): "Mass Media Exposure and Its Impact on Fertility: Current Scenario of Bangladesh." In: Journal of Scientific Research 4/2, pp. 383–383.

Röser, Jutta (2007): "Der Domestizierungsansatz und seine Potenziale zur Analyse alltäglichen Medienhandelns." In: Jutta Röser (ed.), MedienAlltag. Domestizierungsprozesse alter und neuer Medien: Springer, pp. 15–30.

Roy, Rituparna P. (2018): Researching Middle-Class Consumption in Bangladesh: Contextualising Technology and Moral Economy. PhD Thesis, Auckland.

Silverstone, Roger (2003): Television and Everyday Life. London: Routledge.

Silverstone, Roger/Hirsch, Eric/Morley, David (1991): Listening to a Long Conversation: An Ethnographic Approach to the Study of Information and Communication Technologies in the Home. Cultural Studies, 5/2, pp. 204–227.

Sultana, Sharifa/Guimbretière, François/Sengers, Phoebe/Dell, Nicola (2018): "Design Within a Patriarchal Society: Opportunities and Challenges in Designing for Rural Women in Bangladesh." In: Proceedings of the 2018 CHI Conference on Human Factors in Computing Systems – CHI '18, pp. 1–13.

Takashi, Usami/Noriyoshi, Fukuoka (2021): Implications of Bangladesh's Graduation from Least Developed Countries Status on Japanese Companies. In: Journal of Contemporary Research in Social Sciences 3/2, pp. 28–39.

Ward, Katie (2006): The Bald Guy Just Ate an Orange. Domestication, Work and Home. In: Thomas Berker/Maren Hartmann/Yves Punie/Katie J. Ward (eds.), Domestication of Media and Technology: Open University Press, pp. 145–163.

Wikipedia: "Religion in Bangladesh.", January 15, 2023 (https://en.wikipedia.org/wiki/Religion_in_Bangladesh).

Worldbank Data (2023a): "Population, total", January 15, 2023 (https://data.worldbank.org/indicator/SP.POP.TOTL?most_recent_value_desc=true).

Worldbank Data (2023b): "Literacy rate, youth female (% of females ages 15-24) – Bangladesh", January 15, 2023 (https://data.worldbank.org/indicator/SE.ADT.1524.LT.FE.ZS?locations=BD).

Zimmerman Umble, Diane (1992): The Amish and the Telephone: Resistance and Reconstruction. In: Roger Silverstone/Eric Hirsch (eds.), Consuming technologies: Media and information in domestic spaces: Routledge, pp. 103–108.

Conceptual/Theoretical Reflection

Doing Home by Using Digital Assistive Technologies

On the Role of Meaning and Materiality in the Use of Digital Assistive Technologies at Older People's Domesticity

Cordula Endter, Florian Fischer and Tobias Wörle

Abstract

This paper focusses on the material-spatial entanglements of smart home technologies used by older people in their domesticity. Everyday lifeworlds of older people are crucial for the use and appropriation of smart home and assistive technologies. However, they are rarely considered from a materialist and spatially orientated perspective. By contrast, this conceptual paper explicitly focusses on the material-spatial configuration of home in the use of digital assistive technologies by older people.

Fundamental to this perspective are theoretical considerations of the configuration of age(ing), space, body, and knowledge in material-spatial practices. Therefore, we draw on praxeological approaches and the concept of domesticity to understand how "home" as a materialised space of belonging and security is constituted in affective, material, and spatial practices of technology use. In this paper, we discuss these practices by describing critical incidents in the use of digital assistive technologies in the home of older people. We thus aim to provide further theoretical as well as methodological insights into the construction and acquisition of (smart) homes among older people.

Keyword

Digital assistive technologies; media appropriation; age; materiality; space; affect

1. Introduction

Home is a category with fundamental meaning for human beings. A home is associated with protection and security, privacy and meaningful activity, self-efficacy and sociality. All of this leads to or is associated with well-being and quality of life (Kane 2001). It is often understood as an expression of one's own individuality, and quite a few consumer sectors accordingly have focused on the design of people's homes as a safe space and cosy place. Home materialises the feeling of belonging (Lähdesmäki et al. 2016) that seems to be ageless and culturally fundamental (Hurdley 2013). Even though adaptive responses towards various stimuli (from the inside and outside of the home) differ according to cultural identities, the individual handling of the factors impacting on the understanding of "home" leads to how one relates with the home (Kim 2015). But what about the age-specific of home? How does home and its spatial-affective values change in the course of life? And what if home is no longer a familiar safe space?

In this paper, we focus on these questions by discussing how the implementation and use of digital assistive technologies transform older people's spatial, affective and symbolic perception of home and their lifeworlds and, within the scope of this discussion, give special consideration to the key ideas of agency, security and meaning. To this end, we refer to the concept of domestication (Silverstone/Hirsch/Morley 1991; Silverstone/Hirsch 1993; Silverstone 2006) in chapter 2 and present critical incidents based on a literature review in chapter 3. In chapter 4, we discuss the theoretical implications for a better understanding of the critical incidents in the implementation and use of digital assistive technologies in the homes of older people. In chapter 5, we summarise our ideas by recommending theoretical stepstones that seem to be promising to foster the implementation and use of digital assistive technologies in the lifeworlds of older people and thereby strengthen their ability to maintain a self-determined life while ageing in place. Following the guiding question of how material-spatial practices change through the use of smart home technologies, these conceptual ideas should lead to further theoretical as well as methodological insights into the construction and acquisition of (smart) homes among older people.

1.1 Ageing in place – a fundamental need for older people

There is a wealth of evidence that clearly highlights that most people want to stay in their own homes when they get older, even in case of multimorbidity (Cunningham/Cowie/Methven 2022) or need of care (Hajek et al. 2017). Care in the home environment is associated, among other factors, with an independent life in familiar surroundings (Kuhlmey et al. 2010). Thus, regardless of the place and type of care needed, the desire for individuality and autonomy plays an important role (Heuchert/König/Lehnert 2017). The concept of ageing in place,which emphasises the preferences and premises for growing older at home, goes beyond a deficit-oriented view of ageing (Lewis/Buffel 2020). Furthermore, it points to the resources in terms of environmental characteristics at home and in the neighbourhood needed to facilitate an active ageing approach which is associated with well-being and life satisfaction (Oswald et al. 2011).

Within active ageing policies but also in the subjective experience and behaviour of older people, ageing in place is strongly linked to independence and autonomy and to individuality and security (Wiles et al. 2012). It guarantees the ability to maintain the lifestyle led in previous stages of life at the stage of old age, and it offers a space for development. Home becomes the material-spatial expression of independence and autonomy (Haak et al. 2007). The home, however, is not always the material-spatial nucleus of independent living in old age. For example, due to housing barriers and housing cost burdens, it is often a space that makes it difficult to age independently and to successfully overcome age-related challenges such as physical limitations or cognitive impairments (Naumann/Oswald 2020; Nowossadeck/Engstler 2017). Gerontological studies show that it is, above all, steps, staircases, but also hallways that are too narrow or doorsteps within the home that pose risks, such as that of falls or other accidents. The bathroom in particular is a frequent source of accidents, not only for the elderly residents but also for informal caregivers or nursing staff (Meyer/Eberhardt/Thiel 2016).

Since older people particularly in urban areas often live in existing housing, corresponding renovation measures have been scarce up until now and regional housing cooperatives tend to shy away from them (Apfelbaum/Schatz 2013; Verband Sächsischer Wohnungsgenossenschaften 2012). Even beyond structural barriers, the social environment can be a limiting factor for independent living in old age, namely when the loss of a partner or the long distance to children, siblings or family members limits the social network or when people can only rarely leave their homes due to physical limitations and can thus only make limited use of services for the elderly (Böger/Huxhold/Wolff 2017; Ehrlich/Kelle 2019). There is a risk of social isolation and the experience of loneliness (Huxhold/Engstler 2019), as well as a decline in subjective well-being and health (Spuling/Cengia/Wettstein 2019).

Moving beyond individual needs, however, living independently in their own homes for as long as possible is not only of concern to older people themselves but is also in the interest of other actors, especially the state, which is responsible for the care of its older citizens in terms of welfare state services (Denninger et al. 2014). In light of demographic change, the primary focus of social policy lies on individual responsibility and caring communities. This refers particularly to family caregivers and social support actors in the neighbourhood and less so to professional caregivers, in part because the latter are often lacking (BMFSFJ 2016).

1.2 Autonomy enabling technologies in the lifeworld of older people

Technical assistance systems and digital technologies have received much attention since the end of the 2000s. This is due to several reasons: Firstly, a growing number of older people reaches a higher age. Secondly, family care structures increasingly destabilise due to job-related mobility and increasingly diverse family structures Thirdly, capacities of outpatient and inpatient care are limited (Endter 2021). Assistive technologies are therefore intended to enable older people to live independently in their own homes for as long as possible and to carry out their everyday activities with technical support despite physical or cognitive impairments. The idea behind is that it is technically possible to develop technical solutions tailored to the individual support and care needs of older people. It is also assumed that it is possible for older people, family caregivers or professional caregivers to operate these systems competently and appropriately and to use them according to their own needs. Last but not least, it is assumed that the users can afford and are willing to use these technologies, although perceptions of high costs may lead to concerns related to smart home technologies (Tural et al. 2021).

This list illustrates that we are dealing with ideal-typical ideas rather than with real conditions for success. Rather, it becomes clear how multifacetted the use of technical assistance systems and digital technologies is. This is especially true when older users have little technical competence or affinity for technology, or when the structural equipment of their homes makes it difficult to use technology (Kortmann et al. 2021). Of course, the availability and proper functioning of broad-band internet and an adequate technical infrastructure in rural areas also play a role in this regard (Biniok/Selke/Achatz 2019).

Nonetheless, both state-funded and market-based technology development are continuing to produce technical innovations. The main areas addressed are everyday support, mobility, informal home care and health, especially e-health and telemedicine (for an overview of the situation in Germany see e.g. Deutsche Bundesregierung 2020). Not surprisingly, the development and use of technology is not only the subject of technological research, but also of social science research and, with regard to the target group of older people, gerontological research (Endter 2016, 2018; Meurer et al. 2018).

1.3 Opportunities and risks of digital assistive technologies in older people's homes from a gerontological and social science perspective

Despite the preference for and value of home, there are several concerns about ageing in place in gerontology and age-related social sciences. These concerns relate to aspects of mobility (such as getting around at home and in town), social activities (e.g., meeting friends or relatives), as well as safety and housing concerns. Each of these concerns can, however, also entail positive emotional experiences related to (assistive) technology, such as security, independence, and relativeness (Chen 2020; Tural/Lu/Austin Cole 2021). The increasing availability, affordability, and accessibility of technologies within the home have led to both opportunities and challenges. Irrespective of the substantial advances in developing digital technologies within the home, these applications tend to ignore the role of technologies in terms of materiality within home (Carnemolla 2018). To date, technology development for enabling or supporting safe and liveable ageing at home has either been technology-driven or policy-driven. It has been demand-driven and user-orientated to a much lesser extent (Zhang/Li/Wu 2020).

Against this backdrop, we focus on two problem areas that we consider central for the application of digital assistance technologies in the homes of older people:

a) enabling autonomy through agency and b) maintaining the subjective experience of belonging and security in one's own home as a safe place. In order to consider these problem areas sufficiently broadly, we do not limit our analysis to the individual experience. Instead, we extend previous psychological, gerontological, and social science considerations by a relational perspective, which understands the production of autonomy and agency as well as that of belonging and security as the result of affective, material and spatial practices. Accordingly, we are concerned with precisely those affective-material-spatial entanglements in the implementation and use of digital assistance technologies in the domesticity of older people. For this purpose, we refer to praxeological concepts of a relational sociology on the one hand, and to the sociological concept of domestication on the other. While the primary characteristic of the former inclued the decentring of the subjects, the latter is one of the guiding concepts of this special issue.

2. Theoretical approach

2.1 Doing age by doing home – a praxeological constitution of age and home

The theoretical consideration of age as a phenomenon constituted by multiple practices is fundamental to the praxeological perspective (Schroeter 2005; Wanka/Gallistl 2018; Höppner/Wanka/Endter 2022). In this respect, such an understanding follows constructivist theoretical references (Schroeter/Künemund 2010), but applies them in relation to practices. These are not limited to social practices, but also consider non-human actors as agents (Endter 2021; Schillmeier 2008; Urban 2017, 2019). In this regard, relational praxeological approaches go beyond constructivist approaches and make stronger reference to actor-network theory (ANT) and post-humanist approaches. The key difference is not only the denaturalisation of old age as a fixed, unchangeable, and, above all, natural phase of life, but also the bringing forth of this phase of life as a phenomenon through an interplay of both human and non-human actors. This explicitly involves affective, material, and spatial practices that are crucial for the constitution of old age.

The concept of *doing age* may serve as a prominent example for such an approach. It was first developed by (Laz 1998) for the international context and by Schroeter (2005) for German-speaking gerontology with reference to feminist conceptions of a doing age (West/Zimmerman 1987). The assumption behind this concept is that age develops in the form of a social practice. According to this assumption, age is constituted through social interactions and, thus, displayed in performance (Laz 1998; Schroeter 2005). In this article, we extend this conception to the context of domesticity and raise the question to what extent domesticity is also involved in the constitution of age and what role technology plays in this. Thus, we are concerned with the question of how both ageing and domesticity are constituted in the appropriation of technology as a domestic support system. The central idea is the assumption that different human and non-human actors are involved in the construction of domesticity and age (Andrews/Evans/Wiles 2013; López Gómez 2015; Pols 2012; Schillmeier/Domenech 2016).

Regarding older people's doing home by using smart home technologies, it can be stated that smart home technologies need to become 'successfully' integrated into older people's everyday lives through harmonising such technologies with the household-specific entanglements of meaning, materiality, and practice. In doing so, domesticity is to be seen "as a product of interwoven, social and cultural processes in which information and communication technologies [...] play an increasingly important role" (Hartmann 2008b: 404; translation by the authors). Doing home is to be understood as a constant re-constitution (i.e., stabilisation) of household-specific thought and action routines and spatial orders through mental, individual-psychological processing on the one hand and sociocultural practices on the other. Any new technology intervenes both as a material object and as a carrier of meaning in the flow of those otherwise self-evident and taken-for-granted patterns of order of a household and its members.

2.2 Media appropriation in the context of domesticity

New media technologies need to be explored, interpreted and, in doing so, 'tamed' or 'domesticated' by their users through their practices of usage. The domestication[1]-approach conceptualises media appropriation in the domestic context. First, appropriation includes processes of commodification and imagination. Certain narratives and promises of value get ascribed to a technology and 'create' a prospective consumer. Certain patterns of meaning, practice and material characteristics are inscribed into technological objects even from the outset, for instance by its design (Silverstone/Haddon 1996). Second, appropriation refers to processes of incorporation (or objectivation and routinisation): A user's handling of the technology represents socially meaningful practice, by which attitudes towards that technology as both an object as well as a technology as such are being expressed. By way of using them, technical objects are discursively and physically-materially assigned to specific places and meanings of relevance within our lifeworlds. By dealing with the technology, habituation begins, and (potentially new) habits and routines of practices may arise. Third, appropriation comprises social processing (or: conversion) of the use of a technology. People show their usage of a technology,

---

1   On domestication as a concept of media appropriation see the contributions of Berker et al. 2006; Silverstone 2006; Hartmann 2008a, 2008b. For a more detailed overview see even Hartmann 2006, 2013, 2009, 2019; Haddon 2007; Röser 2007; Röser/Peil 2012; Silverstone 1994; Silverstone/Hirsch/Morley 1991; Silverstone/Hirsch 1993; Krotz/Thomas 2007.

discuss their attitudes towards it with others and interpret and speak about its contents collectively in the context of their social environments (Hartmann 2009; Lull 1990). In doing so, users deal with technology in a both practical and discursive way and thereby establish connections between otherwise not necessarily related meanings and things. In cultural studies, this is referred to as double articulation (Hartmann 2009), which finally refers to the constitution of social sense in the everyday interplay between matter, practice and meaning.

2.3 Home as basic security

The state of being or feeling 'at home' respectively refers to a subjective feeling of being at home as a familiar space. This 'feeling at home' may partly remain unconscious. From this perspective, it is characterised by stability in the emotional dimension (feelings), the social dimension (i.e., patterns of meaning or practice) and even the spatial-material dimension (e.g., in the form of experiencing the familiar physical structures of a well-known place such as one's own living room with its familiar furniture). Within the everyday course of life, a volatile equilibrium of familiar convictions and emotions, material surroundings and behavioural routines and even our usual bodily condition is taken for granted (Krotz/Thomas 2007). This gives us fundamental confidence and trust in the stability and order of our everyday lifeworld. These unquestioned convictions of security and controllability are a fundamental part of our social existence and actions. In the domestication literature, therefore, these convictions of security are referred to as 'ontological security'. This refers to our fundamental convictions of 'everything is in order' and 'everything is under control'. In this sense, feeling at 'home' is basically characterized by such a state of ontological security. It represents the fundamental trust in the continuity and consistency of self-identity as well as the continuity, consistency and 'controllability' of the surrounding social and material domestic environment. Such convictions are supposed to be maintained as our fundamental basis for being able to feel safe and secure.

2.4 Why 'taming', why 'wild'?

In domestication theory, even the metaphor of 'taming' a 'wild' technology refers to the fundamentally important convictions of controllability and predictability of the social and material structures of our everyday life. New technologies may be challenging. In particular, this may be the case regarding older people living at home. As a premise, in contrast to other locations of everyday life, home is mainly experienced as a realm of autonomy, agency, belonging and security. Hence, the existence and use of smart home technologies at home may not be autonomously self-selected. It may rather be experienced as 'externally' implied by individual circumstances like a person's diagnosed status of health, for instance, or ascribed needs for assistance. Accordingly, either informal caregivers or professional actors recommend or even insist on the use of supportive technologies to create a feeling of safety. Therefore, when the need for assistive technologies arises, older people may be (or rather get) in a situation of particular vulnerability. This may be very unsettling and include feelings of insecurity, perhaps even alienation within an otherwise familiar place of belonging, autonomy, self-efficacy (agency), security, and control.

In this context, metaphorically speaking, domestication refers to the fundamental socio-cultural tension of civilisation versus wilderness, or, in other words: security versus insecurity. Against this backdrop, the concept refers to the constant need of maintenance and restoration of a fragile equilibrium between household-related and personality-related identity constructions on the one hand, and the impositions and interventions from the outside world (such as other people, the economy, the society or even a new technology) on the other hand. The intrusion of new technologies and, thus, new content it transports, bring about potentially unfamiliar patterns (or even stronger: appeals, imperatives) of thought and practice. Those are being transported by new media technologies but may not be brought in line instantly with familiar mind sets and social routines of behaviour that accompany and characterise one's 'home'. This may be disturbing, causing insecurity. Not only on the personal level but in the social domain as well.

In the process of dealing with influences from outside (this also applies to unfamiliar technologies) attempts are made to align them with their own mental, behavioural and spatial-material order. This process can be more or less active and conscious, and it can be more or less successful. When people engage with new technologies in their domesticity, ontological security is the implicit benchmark for feeling at 'home'. It is reached by constantly (re-)creating consistency between influences from the outside and the internal socio-cultural system of a household and its members. The latter includes identity constructions, behavioural and socio-spatial patterns that those people have in common out of a shared history, including material aspects like significant rooms or objects of furniture (Hartmann 2009).

'Domesticity' is not an island, however. Such an internal culture of a household is interdependent with the broader cultural system of society. It is not restricted to an isolated domestic area but linked to other social networks (Haddon 2003, 2004). It is dynamic and bi-directional in as much as socio-cultural patterns of both the household (and its members) and of the outside world may constantly change. By using new technologies like smart home systems, new practices may emerge, and correlated mind sets may shift when people appropriate new technologies.

Furthermore, appropriation processes may not be limited to domesticity in general (Hartmann 2009). In particular, the use of mobile media does not end at the threshold of one's front door but also takes place within the public sphere. Despite the critique that imaginations of 'the household' among early authors appear quite narrow and a bit outdated (ibid.), in many older people's everyday lives domesticity still represents a significant area of intersection between socio-cultural structures on the micro and macro level. In that sense, 'their' domesticity is of particular importance when it comes to their domestic practices of doing home by using smart home technologies.

3. Critical incidents in the appropriation of smart home technologies in home care settings

3.1 Theoretical shortcomings in the field of gerontechnology

There are several barriers which adversely affect the appropriation of smart home technologies in home care settings among the elderly. Several theoretical frameworks have already tried to synthesise ageing barriers that influence aspects such as mobile health usability for older adults (Wildenbos/Feute/Jaspers 2018) or gerontechnology acceptance by the elderly in general (Chen/Chan 2014). These concepts mainly focus on aspects related to the individual (e.g., cognition, motivation, perception, and physical abilities), privacy and security (Demiris 2016), or cultural factors impacting on individuals' attitudes. These aspects are important for variations in perceptions of home as well as technology acceptance. However, facilitating conditions are not included in detail. These facilitating conditions are to be defined as conditions associated with the (subjective) perception of (objective) factors in the environment – including the home itself or the social, natural and built environment around it – that support the usage of smart home technologies (Venkatesh/Morris/Davis 2003). Within the overarching Unified Theory of Acceptance and Use of Technology (UTAUT), facilitating conditions can be separated into three constructs: 1) perceived behavioural control (adopted from theory of planned behaviour), 2) facilitating conditions (adopted from model of personal computer utilisation), and 3) compatibility (adopted from innovation diffusion theory) (Venkatesh/Morris/Davis 2003).

However, from our point of view, a more nuanced view on barriers to the appropriation of smart home technologies in home care settings should consider agency, security, privacy, and entanglements between affectual, spatial and material aspects in the context of home.

3.2 Technology and agency: contradictions between security and privacy

Older adults' self-reported barriers to ageing in place primarily relate to aspects of home mobility and safety, such as stair safety, lighting, fall hazards, decluttering, front door accessibility and bathroom mobility (Brim/Fromhold/Blaney 2021). Consequently, the built environment at home intersects with ageing in place and the opportunities as well as challenges which smart home technologies may offer (Carnemolla 2018). On the one hand, smart homes offer the possibility to support active agency (Sallinen/Hentonen/Kärki 2015). On the other hand, technology scepticism and privacy concerns are described as significant determinants of attitudes which adversely affect the use of smart home technologies (Tural/Lu/Austin Cole 2021). For example, there is growing concern about privacy and data security in using cameras or sensors, particularly when they can be handled remotely (Gochoo et al. 2021). Cozza et al. (2021) describe the active role of technologies as objects in care for older people. They conceive these objects as 'more-than-human caregivers' and point to aspects of power and domination. For this reason, one may ask "who acts" – taking into consideration that technologies as more-than-human actors may have "a life of their own that is beyond our complete control" (Lupton 2016: 3). This, in turn, relates to the concept of doing age (Höppner/Wanka 2021; Schroeter 2005) and agency, which emerges from the interrelations between heterogeneous (human and non-human) actors (Reckwitz 2012).

Furthermore, people fear that data-driven technologies – as in the case of artificial intelligence – do not explicitly consider (ethical) aspects regarding the social impact of such technologies on stakeholders' or users' relationships with others (Ho 2020). This is reinforced by the fact that risk perceptions or risk tolerance of living more or less autonomously at home may differ between elderly and their informal or professional caregivers (Rolison/Hanoch/Freund 2019). In addition, older people face the challenge that these measures for providing additional security are difficult to customise according to their preferences (Mort/Roberts/Callén 2013). Therefore, older people may perceive smart home technologies more like a restriction or limitation in their privacy than a potential for promoting agency (Kenner 2008). As a result, technology is perceived as "coercion in austerity" rather than as a supportive tool (Mort/Roberts/Callén 2013).

3.3 Affective-material-spatial entanglements

Research on the emotional impact of technology use among the elderly has shown low acceptance of digital applications as daily living aids because of uncertainty or even fears related to these new technologies, which has been phrased as 'technophobia' (Di Giacomo et al. 2019). It has also been shown that digital technologies may exacerbate feelings of being old and alienated from society (Pirhonen et al. 2020). As insights from co-design living labs, for instance, suggest, these affective dimensions hindering the appropriation of smart home technologies are closely linked to the material and spatial environment where these technologies are supposed to be embedded (Angeli et al. 2016; Wanka/Gallistl 2021). Perceptions of the benefits and integrability of technology are highly important, because ensuring older people's habits and familiar environments, which are drivers for the preference of ageing in place, may be adversely affected by installing new technologies. People are used to their living arrangements and are only willing to allow changes if the 'new' either provides an explicitly perceived benefit and/or when it merges with the surroundings they are used to. As ageing is interwoven with human and non-human relationships (Endter/Kienitz 2017), materialities are not only relevant in the ageing process itself. They go far beyond that, as commodity items, spaces, and technologies are entangled with emotions, experiences and perceptions of old people and shape ageing as a relational process which is situated within material and non-material environments (Höppner/Urban 2018).

4. Taming the theory?

In the given context, a holistic view demands capturing all entanglements between aspects in the affective-emotional and spatial-material domain as well as in the domain of social practice. Through the notion of home as a realm of ontological safety, the domestication approach captures the use of technology in the context of doing home as socially structured (and structuring) practice. Furthermore, it considers the aspect of social meaning and knowledge in its relation to the subjective psychological dimension (affect), the intersubjective dimension (interaction and social practice) and even the material dimension (technological objects).

Despite the unquestioned potential of domestication theory, the integration of relational concepts of space appears to be particularly helpful when it comes to conceptualising entanglements between all of the dimensions and aspects mentioned above. In this regard, one may draw upon relational sociology (Löw 2016). It allows conceptualising the above mentioned entanglements as specific allocations of time, matter, (social) practice, knowledge, and social goods. In relational sociology, two basic concepts are being used to describe and explain how such entanglements develop: First, space is structured physically by (physically) arranging people and objects (like buildings, walls, a TV set etc.) to each other. This is referred to as processes of 'spacing'. Second, these spacing processes are accompanied by social "processes of perception, imagination or memory", which includes social interactions and other meaningful elements such as symbols. By such social processes, people and objects get meaningfully interrelated and combined into places (Löw 2016). These social processes of synthesis between people, objects and meaning are referred to as 'placing'.

Integrating this relational perspective allows accurately theorising practices of doing home as domestic practices of spacing and placing in the context of new socio-technological entanglements.[2] Such a perspective even allows to thoroughly integrate contextual aspects. In the given context, for instance, this might apply to interrelations with a person's built environment in the neighbourhood or discur-

---

[2] For a fruitful and illustrative plea to engage with such a relational perspective in gerontology in the context of the elderly's everyday domestic life and affect, see Andrews et al. (2013). With respect to a place's structures of meaning, they refer to "imbedded knowledge [sic!]" (Andrews/Evans/Wiles 2013: 1345).

sive framing through communications among family, caregivers or friends who are involved in those processes of spacing and placing.

As already called for in recent debates, appropriation processes should not be regarded as linear but rather as dynamic, as they may include repeating processes of re-appropriation (Hartmann 2008b). Furthermore, according to Hartmann (2008b), processes of rejection, resistance or "weaning" should be considered. This also seems particularly relevant in the context of older people's use of smart home technologies in their domesticity. This is the case as any introduction and appropriation of smart home technologies may potentially lead to conflicts and difficulties with practices of doing home to which these people were accustomed to. As can be seen above, doing home is much about the reconstitution of feelings of fundamental security within and even beyond one's own domesticity. At the same time, however, media and specific media practices (Röser 2007) may themselves represent an instrument for the production, assurance and maintenance of 'home' in everyday life. Accordingly, without adequate appropriation and implementation in their everyday living environment – their 'homes' in particular – these technologies lose their efficacy.

Therefore, in the context of ageing in place, technologies are associated with challenges and opportunities alike. Accordingly, the 'taming' of technology is to be understood in a double sense, after all: (New) technologies need to be tamed by their elderly users in the context of (re-)gaining convictions and feelings of fundamental security within (and perhaps even beyond) their domesticity. This taming takes place in the context of entanglements among habits, habitualities and material-spatial circumstances which suggest safety. But at the same time, assistive and smart home technologies may enable older people to deal with barriers and challenges within their domestic life. To that end, a technology's agency is intended to serve the desire of the elderly for agency, autonomy, belonging and security.

Considering the co-constitutive, mutually disposing and disposed character of technology and its users, even the question of the distribution of agency becomes relevant. Users and technology interact with each other, which has implications for the investigation of appropriation of technology. In the context of domestication research, Hartmann (2008b) already proposed integrating questions towards the agency of technological artifacts. As it is not yet clear who is actually tamed by whom, "different forms of 'agency' (including the content) in this interplay of forces" are to be considered (ibid.). Without doubt, there is agency inherent to such technologies that makes a difference to the established, well-known and familiar ways to interact, to collect data and to control the domestic surroundings at an older person's home. There are apps supporting new ways to coordinate or to interact with family, friends and other supporters or with healthcare professionals. There are technologies of surveillance and data collection working quite autonomously beyond the influence of the older person who is, yet, being focused by this technology. There are new forms of mediatised, data-driven interactions among human as well as non-human actors. This deeply concerns shifts and diffusions in established distributions of agency and the autonomy of social action. Ethical or legal questions of data sovereignty or privacy at home are quite obvious consequences. Perceptions like that of being publicly exposed by being captured on camera, feeling controlled, and getting 'tamed' by such technologies are among the ordinary consequences, which are less obvious, however.

From a more critical perspective, domestication processes may thus even be understood as older people's struggle with forms of colonisation (Habermas 1981) of their lifeworlds by technologies and technological objects. On the one hand, such technologies (both as technology and as objects) represent a means to make it possible or easier to remain in one's own domesticity, to maintain or regain health and well-being, and to increase the efficacy and impact of health and care services. On the other hand, by bringing in new urges, ideas and orders of a more instrumental, functionalist logic (represented by such technologies and the content and 'scripts' of use inherent in them) may more or less intensely collide with those everyday practices of doing home (Krctz/Thomas 2007). As pointed out by Habermas (1981), the system represents modern societies' sphere of bureaucracy, of economic rationality, and functional differentiation. It is thus quite in contrast with savagery or the more traditional forms of society, where the lifeworld dominated a society's material reproduction. Against this backdrop, at least from the perspective of older people doing home, it appears to be quite the other way round: It is the technical innovations that need taming. Not because of their wildness, actually, but because of the rather instrumental, functionalist logic which is inherent in them, their perfectness, their brave new order that needs taming in order to fit into the elderly's domestic lifeworlds without disturbing or destroying it.

5. Conclusion and recommendations

It has become clear by now, that doing home is a genuine part of technology use or media practices respectively in the everyday domestic life of older people. Older people's everyday lives are characterised by practice-based affective-material-spatial entanglements resulting from the endeavour to maintain their agency as autonomous subjects on the one hand and their home as a familiar place of belonging and security on the other.

Referring to the concept of domestication, we discussed barriers in the implementation and usage of digital assistive technologies in the home of older people. In doing so, we placed a special focus on questions of autonomy, agency and security by analysing affective, material and spatial practices and their interplay in the appropriation of digital assistive technologies in the domestic context.

Against the background of our analysis, we see the following needs in the theoretical-conceptual development of approaches to better understand and further advance the use of digital assistive technologies in the home:

1. The analysis of the doing home of older people by using smart home technologies requires holistic concepts. In this regard, one of the main advantages of the domestication approach is its holistic view on everyday life practices. This approach addresses the use, appropriation and social construction from a context-sensitive perspective as genuine parts of everyday social life, embedded in the entire everyday media ensembles of older people's homes.
2. The domestication approach directly relates domesticity with the use of technology in everyday life. It thus depicts a particularly important place in the living environment of older people, especially those with assistance requirements.
3. The domestication approach is dedicated to the acquisition and appropriation of new media technologies as a process. This fits into how older people deal with newly established smart home technologies in their domesticity during a certain period of time of appropriation (or even rejection and re-appropriation).
4. The approach allows the integration of structures of meaning (i.e. intersubjectively shared, social sense), practice (i.e. social, communicative, discursive action) and materiality (i.e. physical-spatial structures like a door or objects like a fall prevention sensor) in similar ways.
5. Furthermore, there is a high sensitivity to different sorts and levels of context as well as to the fundamental interrelation between social, emotional and material structures. Within practices of doing home, use and utility in and of themselves represent indivisible entanglements of physical-material, practical components and factors of emotion, cognition and perception. The tension between space which is given and which is to be newly constituted is utterly relevant. In the development and design of smart home technologies, material aspects of (doing) home together with its interrelations with social and cognitive-emotional aspects should be considered very carefully to overcome the bias in technology driven development. In this regard, the domestication approach may serve as an integrative conceptual basis, as it already highlights interrelations between facilitating, supporting, and intervening into living conditions and individual factors like cognition, motivation, perception, and physical (dis)abilities. This includes sensitivity for (subjective) perceptions of ('objective') factors of the environment (i.e. the domestic area, the natural or any built environment) such as physical factors aggravating the problem of getting around in the neighbourhood, getting into the bathtub at home (mobility) or factors that have negative implications for safety issues (e.g. fall prevention).

It became obvious that everyday entanglements between affective, material and spatial aspects may represent barriers for the use and implementation of technologies in everyday domestic life. We highlighted that technological objects may interfere with patterns of practice and social meaning even by their design and technical construction. As a consequence, when it comes to co-creation and participatory design of such technologies with older users, such incidents may then even affect practices of participatory design and collaborative development of technologies. Therefore, one needs to pay attention to those entanglements and capture needs and practices of usage from a holistic view, too.

References

Andrews, Gavin J./Evans, Joshua/Wiles, Janine L. (2013): "Re-Spacing and Re-Placing Gerontology: Relationality and Affect." In: Ageing and Society 33, pp. 1339–1373.
Angeli, Antonella de/Cozza, Michela/Jovanovic, Mladjan/Tenolli, Linda/Mushiba, Mark/McNeill, Andrew/Coventry, Lynne (2016): "Understanding Motivations in Designing for Older Adults." In: International Reports on Socio-Informatics 13, pp. 101–107.
Apfelbaum, B./Schatz, T. (2013): Die Wohnungswirtschaft als Netzwerkakteur der kommunalen Demografiestrategie. Altersgerechte Erweiterungen des Angebotsportfolios als Schlüssel zu Mieterbindung und -gewinnung, Ostbevern: Verlag Karla Grimberg.
Berker, Thomas/Hartmann, Maren/Punie, Yves/Ward, Katie (Eds.) (2006): Domestication of Media and Technology, Maidenhead, Berkshire: Open University Press.
Biniok, Peter/Selke, Stefan/Achatz, Johannes (2019): "Soziodigitale Nachbarschaften: Der Wandel von Nachbarschaftsverhältnissen unter dem Einfluss von Digitalisierung." In: Rolf G. Heinze/Sebastian Kurtenbach/Jan Üblacker (eds.), Digitalisierung und Nachbarschaft, Baden-Baden: Nomos Verlagsgesellschaft, pp. 33–60.
BMFSFJ (2016): Sorge und Mitverantwortung in der Kommune – Aufbau und Sicherung zukunftsfähiger Gemeinschaften. Siebter Bericht zur Lage der älteren Generation in der Bundesrepublik Deutschland, Berlin: Bundesministerium für Familie, Senioren, Frauen und Jugend.
Brim, Brianna/Fromhold, Stacy/Blaney, Shannon (2021): "Older Adults' Self-Reported Barriers to Aging in Place." In: Journal of Applied Gerontology 40, pp. 1678–1686.
Carnemolla, Phillippa (2018): "Ageing in Place and the Internet of Things – How Smart Home Technologies, the Built Environment and Caregiving Intersect." In: Visualization in Engineering 6, 7.
Chen, Ke (2020): "Why Do Older People Love and Hate Assistive Technology? An Emotional Experience Perspective." In: Ergonomics 63, pp. 1463–1474.
Chen, Ke/Chan, Alan H. S. (2014): "Gerontechnology Acceptance by Elderly Hong Kong Chinese: A Senior Technology Acceptance Model (STAM).' In: Ergonomics 57, pp. 635–652.

Cozza, Michela/Bruzzone, Silvia/Crevani, Lucia (2021): "Materialities of Care for Older People: Caring Together/Apart in the Political Economy of Caring Apparatus." In: Health Sociology Review 30, pp. 308–322.

Cunningham, Nicola A./Cowie, Julie/Methven, Karen (2022): "Right at Home: Living with Dementia and Multimorbidities." In: Ageing and Society 42, pp. 632–656.

Denninger, Tina/van Dyk, Silke/Lessenich, Stephan et al. (2014): Leben im Ruhestand. Zur Neuverhandlung des Alters in der Aktivgesellschaft (Gesellschaft der Unterschiede, Bd. 12), Bielefeld: transcript Verlag.

Deutsche Bundesregierung (2020): Achter Bericht zur Lage der älteren Generation in der Bundesrepublik Deutschland. Ältere Menschen und Digitalisierung und Stellungnahme der Bundesregierung. Drucksache 19/21650, Berlin: Deutsche Bundesregierung.

Demiris, George (2016): "Consumer Health Informatics: Past, Present, and Future of a Rapidly Evolving Domain." In: IMIA Yearbook of Medical Informatics Suppl. 1, pp. 42–47.

Di Giacomo, Dina/Ranieri, Jessica/D'Amico, Meny et al. (2019): "Psychological Barriers to Digital Living in Older Adults: Computer Anxiety as Predictive Mechanism for Technophobia." In: Behavioral Sciences 9, 96.

Ehrlich, Ulrike/Kelle, Nadiya (2019): "Pflegende Angehörige in Deutschland: Wer pflegt, wo, für wen und wie?" In: Zeitschrift für Sozialreform 65, pp. 175–203.

Endter, Cordula (2016): "Skripting Age – The Negotiation of Age and Aging in Ambient Assisted Living." In: Emma Domínguez-Rué/Linda Nierling (eds.), Ageing and Technology, Bielefeld: transcript Verlag, pp. 121–140.

Endter, Cordula (2018): "How older people matter – Nutzer- und Nutzerinnenbeteiligung in AAL-Projekten." In: Harald Künemund/Uwe Fachinger (Eds.), Alter und Technik, Wiesbaden: Springer Fachmedien, pp. 207–225.

Endter, Cordula (2021): Assistiert Altern. Die Entwicklung digitaler Technologien für und mit älteren Menschen, Wiesbaden: Springer VS.

Endter, Cordula/Kienitz, Sabine (2017): Alter(n) als soziale und kulturelle Praxis, Bielefeld: transcript Verlag.

Gochoo, Munkhjargal/Alnajjar, Fady/Tan, Tan-Hsu et al. (2021): "Towards Privacy-Preserved Aging in Place: A Systematic Review." In: Sensors 21, 3082.

Haak, Maria/Fänge, Agneta/Iwarsson, Susanne et al. (2007): "Home as a Signification of Independence and Autonomy: Xxperiences Among Very Old Swedish People." In: Scandinavian Journal of Occupational Therapy 14, pp. 16–24.

Habermas, Jürgen (1981): Theorie des kommunikativen Handelns, Frankfurt am Main: Suhrkamp.

Haddon, Leslie (2003): "Domestication and Mobile Telephony." In: James E. Katz (ed.), Machines That Become Us. The Social Context of Personal Communication Technology, London: Taylor and Francis, pp. 43–55.

Haddon, Leslie (2004): Information and Communication Technologies in Everyday Life, Oxford: Berg.

Haddon, Leslie (2007): "Roger Silverstone's Legacies: Domestication." In: New Media & Society 9, pp. 25–32.

Hajek, André/Lehnert, Thomas/Wegener, Annemarie et al. (2017): "Who Should Take Care of Me? Preferences of Old Age Individuals for Characteristics of Professional Long-term Caregivers: An Observational Cross-sectional Study." In: BMC Research Notes 10, 382.

Hartmann, Maren (2006): "The Triple Articulation of ICTs: Media as Technological Objects, Symbolic Environments and Individual Texts." In: Thomas Berker/ Maren Hartmann/Yves Punie/Katie Ward (eds.), Domestication of Media and Technology, New York: McGraw-Hill, pp. 80–102.

Hartmann, Maren (2008a): "Domestication of Technology." In: Wolfgang Donsbach (ed.), The International Encyclopedia of Communication, Chichester, UK: John Wiley & Sons Ltd. pp. 1–3.

Hartmann, Maren (2008b): "Domestizierung 2.0: Grenzen und Chancen eines Medienaneignungskonzeptes." In: Carsten Winter/Andreas Hepp/Friedrich Krotz (eds.), Theorien der Kommunikations- und Medienwissenschaft, Wiesbaden: VS Verlag für Sozialwissenschaften, pp. 401–416.

Hartmann, Maren (2009): "Roger Silverstone: Medienobjekte und Domestizierung." In: Andreas Hepp/Friedrich Krotz/Tanja Thomas (eds.), Schlüsselwerke der Cultural Studies, Wiesbaden: VS Verlag für Sozialwissenschaften, pp. 304–315.

Hartmann, Maren (2013): Domestizierung, Baden-Baden: Nomos-Verlag.

Hartmann, Maren (2019): "Domestizierung, mobile Medien und anderes (un)häusliches mehr." In: Christine Linke/Isabel Schlote (eds.), Soziales Medienhandeln, Wiesbaden: Springer Fachmedien, pp. 101–116.

Heuchert, M./König, H-H/Lehnert, T. (2017): "Die Rolle von Präferenzen für Langzeitpflege in der sozialen Pflegeversicherung – Ergebnisse von Experteninterviews." In: Gesundheitswesen 79, pp. 1052–1057.

Ho, Anita (2020): "Are we ready for artificial intelligence health monitoring in elder care?" In: BMC Geriatrics 20, 358.

Höppner, Grit/Urban, Monika (2018): "Where and How Do Aging Processes Take Place in Everyday Life? Answers From a New Materialist Perspective." In: Frontiers in Sociology 3, 7.

Höppner, Grit/Wanka, Anna (2021): "un/doing age Multiperspektivität als Potential einer intersektionalen Betrachtung von Differenz- und Ungleichheitsverhältnissen." In: Zeitschrift für Soziologie 50, pp. 42–57.

Höppner, Grit/Wanka, Anna/Endter, Cordula (2022): "Linking Ages – Un/doing Age and Family in the Covid-19 pandemic." In: Journal of Family Research 34, pp. 563–581.

Hurdley, Rachel (2013): Home, Materiality, Memory and Belonging. Keeping Culture, New York: Palgrave Macmillan.

Huxhold, Oliver/Engstler, Heribert (2019): "Soziale Isolation und Einsamkeit bei Frauen und Männern im Verlauf der zweiten Lebenshälfte." In: Claudia

Vogel/Markus Wettstein/Clemens Tesch-Römer (eds.), Frauen und Männer in der zweiten Lebenshälfte, Wiesbaden: Springer, pp. 71–89.

Kane, R. A. (2001): "Long-term Care and a Good Quality of Life: Bringing Them Closer Together." In: The Gerontologist 41, pp. 293-304.

Kenner, Alison M. (2008): "Securing the Elderly Body: Dementia, Surveillance, and the Politics of "Aging in Place"." In: Surveillance & Society 5, pp. 252–269.

Kim, Young Yun (2015): "Finding a "Home" Beyond Culture: The Emergence of Intercultural Personhood in the Globalizing World." In: International Journal of Intercultural Relations 46, pp. 3–12.

Kortmann, Lisa/Hagen, Christine/Endter, Cordula et al. (2021): "Internetnutzung von Menschen in der zweiten Lebenshälfte während der Corona-Pandemie: Soziale Ungleichheiten bleiben bestehen." In: DZA Aktuell, pp. 3–21.

Krotz, Friedrich/Thomas, Tanja (2007): "Domestizierung, Alltag, Mediatisierung: Ein Ansatz zu einer theoriegerichteten Verständigung." In: Jutta Röser (ed.), MedienAlltag, Wiesbaden: Springer VS, pp. 31–42.

Kuhlmey, A./Dräger, D./Winter, M. et al. (2010): "COMPASS – Versichertenbefragung zu Erwartungen und Wünschen an eine qualitativ gute Pflege." In: DZA-Informationsdienst Altersfragen 37, pp. 4–11.

Lähdesmäki, Tuuli/Saresma, Tuija/Hiltunen, Kaisa et al. (2016): "Fluidity and flexibility of "belonging"." In: Acta Sociologica 59, pp. 233–247.

Laz, Cheryl (1998): "Act Your Age." In: Sociological Forum 13, pp. 85–113.

Lewis, Camilla/Buffel, Tine (2020): "Aging in Place and the Places of Aging: A Longitudinal Study." In: Journal of Aging Studies 54, 100870.

López Gómez, Daniel (2015): "Little Arrangements That Matter. Rethinking Autonomy-Enabling Innovations for Later Life." In: Technological Forecasting and Social Change 93, pp. 91–101.

Löw, Martina (2016): The Sociology of Space. Materiality, Social Structures, and Action, New York: Palgrave Macmillan.

Lull, James (1990): Inside Family Viewing. Ethnographic Research on Television's Audiences, London: Routledge.

Lupton, Deborah (2016): "Digital Companion Species and Eating Data: Implications for Theorising Digital Data–Human Assemblages." In: Big Data & Society 3, 2053951715561994.

Mahne, Katharina/Wolff, Julia K./Simonson, Julia/Tesch-Römer, Clemens (eds.) (2017): Altern im Wandel: zwei Jahrzehnte Deutscher Alterssurvey (DEAS), Wiesbaden: Springer VS.

Meurer, Johanna/Müller, Claudia/Simone, Carla et al. (2018): "Designing for Sustainability: Key Issues of ICT Projects for Ageing at Home." In: Computer Supported Cooperative Work (CSCW) 27, pp. 495–537.

Meyer, S./Eberhardt, B./Thiel, M. (2016): Smarte Bäder der Zukunft. Eine Trendstudie, Berlin.

Mort, Maggie/Roberts, Celia/Callén, Blanca (2013): "Ageing with Telecare: Care or Coercion in Austerity?" In: Sociology of Health & Illness 35, pp. 799–812.

Naumann, Dörte/Oswald, Frank (2020): "Wohnen im Alter." In: Kirsten Aner/ Ute Karl (eds.), Handbuch Soziale Arbeit und Alter, Wiesbaden: Springer, pp. 369–377.

Nowossadeck, Sonja/Engstler, Heribert (2017): "Wohnung und Wohnkosten im Alter." In: Katharina Mahne/Julia K. Wolff/Julia Simonson/Clemens Tesch-Römer (eds.), Altern im Wandel: zwei Jahrzehnte Deutscher Alterssurvey (DEAS), Wiesbaden: Springer, pp. 287–300.

Oswald, Frank/Jopp, Daniela/Rott, Christoph et al. (2011): "Is Aging in Place a Resource for or Risk to Life Satisfaction?" In: The Gerontologist 51, pp. 238–250.

Pirhonen, Jari/Lolich, Luciana/Tuominen, Katariina et al. (2020): ""These Devices Have Not Been Made for Older People's Needs" – Older Adults' Perceptions of Digital Technologies in Finland and Ireland." In: Technology in Society 62, 101287.

Pols, Jeannette (2012): Care at a Distance On the Closeness of Technology, Amsterdam: Amsterdam University Press.

Reckwitz, Andreas (2012): "Affective Spaces: A Praxeological Outlook." In: Rethinking History 16, pp. 241–258.

Rolison, Jonathan J./Hanoch, Yaniv/Freund, Alexandra M. (2019): "Perception of Risk for Older Adults: Differences in Evaluations for Self versus Others and across Risk Domains." In: Gerontology 65, pp. 547 559.

Röser, Jutta (2007): "Der Domestizierungsansatz und seine Potenziale zur Analyse alltäglichen Medienhandelns." In: Jutta Röser (ed.), MedienAlltag. Domestizierungsprozesse alter und neuer Medien, Wiesbaden: VS Verlag für Sozialwissenschaften, pp. 15–30.

Röser, Jutta/Peil, Corinna (2012): "Das Zuhause als mediatisierte Welt im Wandel. Fallstudien und Befunde zur Domestizierung des Internets als Mediatisierungsprozess. " In: Friedrich Krotz/Andreas Hepp (eds.), Mediatisierte Welten, Wiesbaden: VS Verlag für Sozialwissenschaften, pp. 137–163.

Sallinen, Merja/Hentonen, Outi/Kärki, Anne (2015): "Technology and Active Agency of Older Adults Lin Service House Environment." In: Disability and Rehabilitation. Assistive Technology 10, pp. 27–31.

Schillmeier, Michael (2008): "Actor-Networks of Dementia." In: The Sociological Review 56, pp. 141–158.

Schillmeier, Michael W. J./Domenech, Miquel (eds.) (2015): New Technologies and Emerging Spaces of Care, London: Routledge.

Schroeter, K. R. (2005): "Doing Age, Korporales Kapital und Erfolgreiches Altern." In: SPIEL 24, pp. 147–162.

Schroeter, Klaus R./Künemund, Harald (2010): "„Alter" als Soziale Konstruktion – eine soziologische Einführung." In: Kirsten Aner/Ute Karl (eds.), Handbuch Soziale Arbeit und Alter, Wiesbaden: VS Verlag für Sozialwissenschaften, pp. 393–401.

Silverstone, Roger (1994): Television and Everyday Life, London: Routledge.

Silverstone, Roger (2006): "Domesticating Domestication. Reflections on the Life of a Concept." In: Thomas Berker/Maren Hartmann/Yves Punie/Katie Ward (eds.), Domestication of Media and Technology, Maidenhead, Berkshire: Open University Press, pp. 229–248.

Silverstone, Roger/Haddon, Lesslie (1996): "Design and the Domestication of Information and Communication Technologies: Technical Change and Everyday Life." In: Robin Mansell (ed.), Communication by Design. The Politics of Information and Communication Technologies, Oxford: Oxford University Press, pp. 44–74.

Silverstone, Roger/Hirsch, Eric (eds.) (1993): Consuming Technologies. Media and Information in Domestic Spaces, London: Routledge.

Silverstone, Roger/Hirsch, Eric/Morley, David (1991): "Listening to a Long Conversation: An Ethnographic Approach to the Study of Information and Communication Technologies in the Home." In: Cultural Studies 5, pp. 204–227.

Spuling, Svenja M./Cengia, Anja/Wettstein, Markus (2019): "Funktionale und subjektive Gesundheit bei Frauen und Männern im Verlauf der zweiten Lebenshälfte." In: Claudia Vogel/Markus Wettstein/Clemens Tesch-Römer (eds.), Frauen und Männer in der zweiten Lebenshälfte. Älterwerden im sozialen Wandel, Wiesbaden: Springer VS, pp. 35–52.

Tural, Elif/Lu, Danni/Austin Cole, D. (2021): "Safely and Actively Aging in Place: Older Adults' Attitudes and Intentions Toward Smart Home Technologies." In: Gerontology & Geriatric Medicine 7.

Urban, Monika (2017): "'This Really Takes It Out of You!' the Senses and Emotions in Digital Health Practices of the Elderly." In: Digital Health 3.

Urban, Monika (2019): ",Erfolgreiches' Altern in digitalen Zeiten. Zum Zusammenhang von digitalen Gesundheitspraktiken, Alter(n)sbildern und Ungleichheiten." In: Holger Angenent/Birte Heidkamp/David Kergel (eds.), Digital Diversity, Wiesbaden: Springer, pp. 215–238.

Venkatesh/Morris/Davis (2003): "User Acceptance of Information Technology: Toward a Unified View." In: MIS Quarterly 27, pp. 425–478.

Verband Sächsischer Wohnungsgenossenschaften (2012): AlterLeben – die „Mitalternde Wohnung": Sicher & selbstbestimmt wohnen; Sicherheit, Gesundheit, Komfort, Freizeit. (https://alter-leben.vswg.de/konzept/)

Vogel, Claudia/Wettstein, Markus/Tesch-Römer, Clemens (eds.) (2019): Frauen und Männer in der zweiten Lebenshälfte. Älterwerden im sozialen Wandel, Wiesbaden: Springer VS.

Wanka, Anna/Gallistl, Vera (2018): "Doing Age in a Digitized World – A Material Praxeology of Aging With Technology." In: Frontiers in Sociology 3/6.

Wanka, Anna/Gallistl, Vera (2021): "Socio-Gerontechnology – ein Forschungsprogramm zu Technik und Alter(n) an der Schnittstelle von Gerontologie und Science-and-Technology Studies." In: Zeitschrift für Gerontologie und Geriatrie 54, pp. 384–389.

West, Candace/Zimmerman, Don H. (1987): "Doing Gender." In: Gender and Society 1, pp. 125–151.
Wildenbos, G. A./Peute, Linda/Jaspers, Monique (2018): 'Aging Barriers Influencing Mobile Health Usability for Older Adults: A literature based framework (MOLD-US)." In: International Journal of Medical Informatics 114, pp. 66–75.
Wiles, Janine L./Leibing, Annette/Guberman, Nancy/Reeve, Jeanne, Allen, Ruth E. S. (2012): "The Meaning of "Aging in Place" to Older People." In: The Gerontologist 52, pp. 357–366.
Zhang, Quan/Li, Meiyu/Wu, Yijin (2020): "Smart Home for Elderly Care: Development and Challenges in China." In: BMC Geriatrics 20, 318.

Entering the Field

Domestication of Smart Speakers by Older Users
Preliminary Findings From an Exploratory Qualitative Study

Alexander B. Kucharski and Sebastian Merkel

Abstract

This paper examines the domestication of commercially available smart speakers like Amazon's Echo by older users and presents preliminary results of an ongoing qualitative study. So far, seven empirical cases have been analyzed with the aim of reconstructing older users' perspectives of and understanding how older users negotiate the appropriation, meaning and (non) use of smart speakers. The analysis of interviews shows that smart speakers can have multiple effects in lifeworlds of older adults, i.e. change/create new daily routines, values, and self-perceptions. Warm experts like family members play a crucial role in the appropriation processes.

Keywords

gerontechnology, smart speaker, voice assistants, aging, older persons.

Introduction

Due to their increasing diffusion in private households, commercial intelligent/voice-controlled personal assistants – generally called smart speakers – such as Amazon Echo or Google Home have recently attracted increasing attention across multiple scientific disciplines. In the field of aging and technology – or gerontechnology – the devices have recently received attention and their benefits are (critically) discussed in multiple scenarios. This includes, for instance, the aim to reduce loneliness and isolation among older users (cf. Merkel/Kucharski 2022). Moreover, studies have investigated different aspects such as technology acceptance of smart speakers (cf. Koon et al. 2020), reasons for (non) use (cf. Trajkova/Martin-Hammond 2020), ontological perceptions (cf. Pradhan et al. 2019), or privacy concerns (Bonilla/Martin-Hammond 2020). Most of these studies report results of technology deployment projects with instructed use and, with rare exceptions such as a paper by Nimrod and Edan (2021), lack a perspective on the domestication of smart speakers in old age. Such a perspective, however, helps to better understand the increasing diffusion of the devices among older people and focuses on practices of technology use rather than simply trying to explain their (non) use (cf. Gallistl et al. 2021).

In this vein, we apply the Co-constitution of Aging and Technology (CAT) model that is repeatedly used in studies in the field of technology and aging. The model conceptualizes aging and technology as co-constituted, and its overall aim is to provide a framework for the analysis of networks of aging-technology relations (Peine/Neven 2020). The model describes four arenas: (1) design worlds; (2) technological artifacts; (3) lifeworlds of older people; (4) images of aging (Peine/Neven 2020: 6). The starting point of the analysis can be chosen arbitrarily and allows to examine each of the arenas individually or the development and use of a technology in several or all of arenas together (Peine/Neven 2020: 5). The basic mechanism of the model is based on the concept of scripts (cf. Akrich 1997; cf. Sørensen 2004). A simplified and exemplary description of the co-constitution of aging and technology, which sets the starting point of the process in the "design world", can read as follows (Peine/Neven 2020): Images of aging, which can arise on the basis of various sources (e.g. ethnographic studies or just simplified assumptions of developers about older people and their lifeworld), are interpreted by relevant actors, e.g. designers and/or companies, within "design worlds". From these specific interpretations, "user representations" are formulated, which are "inscribed" into a technology as a "script" in the development process. This results in technological artifacts that carry the "scripts" into the lifeworlds of older people. Once there, the artifacts, because of their "script" can enable certain practices of use and restrict others. At the same time, older people are not understood as "passive recipients", but as active users who deal with the technologies and incorporate them in their own way into their lifeworld, i.e. they use them (partly), adapt them, or reject them altogether. When artifacts are used, practices, relationships, and meanings within the lifeworlds are rearranged. As a result, the way in which aging is realized and the role that the respective technology plays in this process only emerges within a specific constellation. Finally, this can lead to new images of aging and provoke a new cyclical co-constitution of aging and technology.

Applying these theoretical concepts, we chose to study the relations between aging and smart speakers within the lifeworlds of older smart speaker users by systematically reconstructing their domestication experiences and relevant contexts (see below for themes of the interview guide). We argue that this perspective is needed to understand how older users engage with these technologies, to analyze patterns of use, and ultimately to see whether the devices meet the expectations of their users but also their developers. Since commercial smart speakers are age-unspecific devices, the always-on microphone and the control of various applications and interactions with the intelligent assistant via voice commands was understood as the general user script. If and how certain images of aging and/or age scripts (e.g., those of certain applications for older users) asserted agency within the individual aging-smart-speaker-relations of older people was left open to be explored.

Method

The qualitative research tradition of the domestication approach usually conducts research in an ethnographic and methodologically pluralistic manner (Hartmann 2013: 53). Although interviews are now among the most common methods used in domestication studies and are primarily intended to capture the perspectives of those being studied (cf. Haddon 2017), they are often accompanied by other methods such as diaries. Against the background of the pandemic and older people being considered as a high-risk group, we chose to conduct interviews exclusively. Following a theoretical sampling approach, we selected participants aged 60+ who have used one or more commercial smart speakers for at least four months. We did not make any restrictions considering the level of digital skills of the participants, as we assumed that older people using a smart speaker for a longer period, four months in our case, have a level of digital literacy and skills sufficient to use digital technology and navigate in the digital world. Following this approach, it should be noted that we face the "common" sampling bias in studies with older technology users to mainly include participants with a high level of education and/or income, who are tech savvy (cf. Merkel/Kucharski 2019). Participants were recruited through member organizations of a digital initiative *(Digital-Kompass)* of the German National Association of Senior Citizens' Organizations (BAGSO) and signed informed consent to participate. As there is no typical method to gather interview data in domestication studies (Hartmann 2013: 53), we chose to conduct semi-structured interviews, which allow participants to provide answers to multiple aspects as well as specific questions by the interviewers. The interview guide was developed drawing on theoretical assumptions provided by domestication theory and the CAT model and covered four themes: (1) lifeworlds and everyday life, (2) technologies and household, (3) smart speakers in everyday life, and (4) summarizing and outlook. The interviews were audio-recorded and transcribed verbatim. Data was analyzed via content analysis, using an inductive-deductive coding approach (cf. Schreier 2014).

So far, seven semi-structured interviews were conducted, two via telephone and five via online video conferencing software. The sample consisted of three elderly women, one with visual impairments, and four elderly men. All of the participants live in different parts of Germany. The youngest interview partner was 60 years old and the oldest was 76 years old at the time of the interview. Four of the seven interview partners were using at least two smart speakers within their households (the maximum number was four).

Interview	Age	Gender	Household Composition	Number and type of smart speakers in household	Interview mode
I1	69	Male	2 persons	4 (All Amazon Echo Dot)	Phone
I2	65	Female	1 person	2 (All Amazon Echo Dot)	Phone
I3	60	Female	1 person	1 (Amazon Echo)	Video-Call
I4	66	Male	1 person	2 (Amazon Echo and Amazon Echo Show)	Video-Call
I5	76	Female	1 person	1 (Google Home)	Video-Call
I6	70	Male	1 person	3 (1x Amazon Echo, 1x Google Home, 1x T-Online)	Video-Call
I7	69	Male	2 persons	1 (Amazon Echo)	Video-Call

Table 1: Sample Overview

Preliminary results and discussion

General usage practices

Overall, usage practices in our sample range from utilizing smart speakers for entertainment (primarily music) or information (e.g. planning out trips or complementing desk work), using applications to operate other devices (e.g. lighting, including for security purposes while away from home), to compensate physical and memory limitations (e.g. creating shopping lists or organizing appointments – reported by a visually impaired user) or improve one's well-being (e.g. overcoming the beginning of depressive episodes or feelings of isolation by interacting with the digital assistant), to organizing care or communication with elderly parents (e.g. proactively finding a way to realize video calls with an older family member with limited technological competencies living in assisted housing – during the lockdown and ban of visits). Thus, the results show that the devices were used for more efficient daily planning or work, regaining or maintaining autonomy, fulfilling entertainment/social needs, and realizing an enhanced sense of communication and care or home security. Additionally, in some cases smart-speaker use (and technology use overall) was reported as a means to train or keep up cognitive/mental capacities, as a necessity for social participation, or as possibility to feel distinguished in one's own ability to use technology. All people interviewed reported daily and repeatedly use and the integration into daily routines (e.g., starting the day with smart speaker services, having a fixed schedule for video calls to be together/organize care through smart speaker calls or integrating it into cooking/evening entertainment routines), but no use of any age specific or third-party skills (except music streaming services) was mentioned. However, the interviewees reported different developments of their usage routines.

The overall assessment of smart speakers shows a wide range: perceiving it as a toy or source of comfortable entertainment, viewing smart speakers as an assistive technology or as a tool to organize informal care, to make life easier and allowing social participation; using it as a pleasant addition within the smart home.

Personalization and experimentation

While most of the participants only addressed certain needs with specific applications and stuck to them over the entire course of their ownership, others reported the willingness to experiment or overcome initial fears of interacting with the voice assistant, "Yes, at first, as I said, there was a lot of experimentation with it, a lot of asking, in a lot of different genres, to see how far does it engage in discussions" (I6). Another interviewee reported, "There are certain barriers and fears, who knows who's going to join in and listen in and so on, and then you slowly progress. And then maybe, step by step, you reach higher and higher levels and then at some point, you start to get cheeky and try to test the device." (I7). Other ways of learning about how the devices can be personalized by downloading additional applications, e.g., reading online about skills or asking the voice assistant, were mostly rejected by other interviewees. However, some interviewees expressed the willingness to (re-) consider certain applications, based on one's own health status or critical incidents. "I was home alone, I thought, 'what are you going to do now if you faint?' I would imagine a function especially for older people as useful here, as an addition." (I3). Besides (changes in) the health status, privacy concerns, and interactions with family members or "non-human actors" (see below) were important leading to further explore the possibilities of the devices. However, as mentioned above, all interviewees tended to stick to the use of standard built-in applications. Thus, the results are in line with other studies observing smart speaker use by older people over longer periods (cf. Pradhan et al. 2019; Kim 2021).

Overall, a variety of perceptions and adaptations of the general user script was reported: While some perceived the "always-on-microphone" as a threat to privacy/data autonomy and changed everyday practices (e.g. disconnecting their smart speaker from the power supply in case of visits or private conversations), others trust the available means to secure privacy provided by the device (e.g. muting the microphone or deleting recorded speech inputs) or do not engage with the "always-on-microphone" at all (e.g. out of comfort, because of having no "fears" or no knowledge of the functioning of smart speakers). Fears included being the subject of long-term analysis by smart speaker companies and thus being controlled or manipulated with respect to consumption decisions or received information. Negotiations during the domestication of smart speakers mainly showed the influence of media representations of the "online giants" (e.g., "almighty

Amazon", weakening local economies), institutions (e.g., laws on data privacy), general attitudes towards the internet (e.g., having no data autonomy anyway) and aging-technology-discourses (e.g., smart speakers for improving quality of life vs. smart speakers for surveillance of loved ones). We found no negotiations with other users within the households.

The role of warm experts

Six of seven users reported being made aware of smart speaker and their capabilities through their social network (e.g., friends, children, grandchildren), or what is referred to as "warm experts" (Bakardjieva 2005: 98; Olsson/Viscovi 2018). Warm experts are nonprofessionals and usually closely related people who are involved in nearly all stages of technology domestication but specifically in the appropriation and incorporation phase (Olsson/Viscovi 2018: 326). The cases underline the results of Olsson and Viscovi (2018: 338): Warm experts for older technology users are their friends and family members, particularly (grand-) children who identify the needs for technology and/or are involved in the set-up of the device including the installation and teaching of how to use them – even those users with prior experience. Hence, warm experts link two dimensions of the CAT model, the lifeworlds and the technical artefacts. Based on their images of aging, warm experts have identified smart speakers as a technology that is well suited for the needs of older persons. However, while smart speakers are easy to use, this, does not hold true for the installation and customization of the devices. Unsurprisingly, warm experts in our sample were mostly involved in the initial stages of the appropriation. In two cases, interviewees were introduced to smart speaker by visiting friends, who were already using the device. Both interviewees reported that observing the casual use and ease of usage practices (of certain applications, e.g., listening to music without finding a CD) prompted the interest in smart speaker. In two cases, the oldest interviewee and the visually impaired interviewee, it was the interviewees' children who initiated the domestication process by giving a smart speaker to their elderly parent. The reasons for device purchase differed: In case of the visual impairment, the potential of smart speaker as an "easy to use" assistant prompted the device purchase. However, there was no discussion about specific usage scenarios. In case of the oldest interviewee (I5), the device purchase was prompted by prior discussions between the older interviewee and her daughter about the use of smart speaker in the social network. Similarly, no specific usage scenarios were discussed as useful. The interviewee reported instead, "she must have thought that this is something for me" (I5). In both cases, device set-up and learning how to use applications required help from the gifting children. In the case of I5, her daughter assisted with important information to ensure successful use: "And that's why I've got this wording directly, I've got, we've searched that once on the Internet, with what I can ask the, what I can ask specifically and then also the right answer comes." (I5).

On the other hand, older people can also function as "warm experts" themselves and/or family members can be the trigger for looking into smart speaker Thus, one interviewee (I6) reported proactively taking on his grandchildren's desire of having a smart speaker and consequently researched smart speakers and gave a device to his grandchild, setting it up as well as teaching safe usage practices. This in turn prompted the interviewee to purchase a device for himself to further explore its capabilities: "Then I thought, 'well, if you gave him this, I might as well finish what I've started'. So, I wanted to know, 'what are these voice assistants about?'" (I6). Likewise, another interviewee reported being made aware of smart speaker by his grandchild, who was already using a smart speaker and wanted "grandma and grandpa to join in" (I7). Only one interviewee (I4) reported learning about smart speaker because of an advertisement that made him/her curious and finally purchasing a device. "Yes, so it was this big thing here with this Alexa at that time, I have to say quite simply that was really curiosity. 'What can this do?' I read about it, but (…) could hardly imagine how it might work." (I4). This interviewee reported the use of a smart speaker with his older mother, who lives in assisted living apartment and can thus be considered a warm expert himself.

In this sense, the social dynamics within households (and/or families) play a crucial role (cf. Murdock/Hartmann/Grey, 1992). Our findings suggest that warm experts are part of the larger social network, but in most cases do not belong to the household, as most of the interviewees live alone (see table 1). The household composition seems to influence domestication processes and particular on the appropriation, as shown by the example of I5. In case of I5, a widow who lost her husband, it also affected the objectification (see e.g., Bille 2022) as she placed the smart speaker into the office of her deceased husband. All other interviewees placed their smart speakers strategically according to applications primarily used (as mentioned above e.g., listening to music in certain rooms or having video calls at the coffee table).

Smart speaker and aging

The CAT model helps to analyze the relationship of older users and smart speakers. Although smart speakers have not been designed exclusively for older persons, our results reveal that the devices can influence practices of aging. Due to their versatility, smart speakers are not only used in one context or use case but offer the possibility to be integrated in various settings. Hence, the data shows vastly different usage scenarios of elderly smart speaker users, which can lead to potential implications for aging processes. This includes smart speaker use stimulating cognitive capacities and improving quality of life, losing independence/privacy due to smart speaker applications, and providing the ability to enhance remote care taking of even older parents. As there was no use of age specific applications, none of the interviewees reported engagement with "age scripts".

However, images of aging and individual perspectives on aging were discussed. One interviewee mentioned the importance of being active and self-sufficient for as long as possible and thus not using certain applications provided by the smart assistant (e.g. organizing shopping lists or memorizing appointments). The same interviewee reported the use of an emergency call smart speaker application instead of a common "emergency button", which was perceived as a service for much older people. It can thus be argued that the use of smart speaker applications depends on but also challenges perceptions of devices as well as perceptions of the self. While one interviewee reported the successful use and allowing an enhanced participation and quality of life for his mother living in assisted facility, one elderly interviewee challenged this idea as being an unethical care taking practice because of being able to "listen in" on relatives.

Conclusion and outlook

This paper presents the preliminary findings of an ongoing research project and analyzes domestication processes of seven elderly smart speaker users. To specifically investigate networks of aging-technology relations, we draw on the CAT model. We find that smart speakers have become an important part of the living arrangements of our interviewees. The analysis of the first seven interviews shows that smart speakers can reconfigure/challenge meanings and practices, e.g., sense of privacy at home, self-perceptions or daily care taking routines. Overall, warm experts such as (grand-) children play an important role in the appropriation phase. Smart speakers are not specifically designed for elderly users, but their user interface allows using them without the need of getting accustomed to visual interfaces. Here, the results indicate that smart speakers are seen as an ideal technology for elderly users. This could lead to more age specific smart speaker applications which are based on negative images of aging. As pointed out, our sampling strategy has several limitations. For future course of this research, we will address this and try to sample users with different experience levels with digital technology. Another limitation of our research is the fact that we only gathered data at a single point of time. Here, longitudinal studies (e.g., Pradhan et al. 2019; Sunyoung/Choudhury 2021) can help to analyze usage patterns in more depth.

References

Akrich, Madeleine (1997): "The Description of Technical Objects". In: Wiebe E. Bijker/John Law (eds.), Shaping Technologies/ Building Society. Studies in Sociotechnical Change, Cambridge/London: The MIT Press, pp. 205–224.
Bakardjieva, Maria (2005): Internet Society: The Internet in Everyday Life, London: Sage.

Bille, Mikkel (2022): "Material Culture Studies: Objectification, Agency, and Intangibility." In: Maja Hojer Bruun/Ayo Wahlberg/Rachel Douglas-Jones/ Cathrine Hasse/Klaus Hoeyer/Dorthe Brogård Kristensen/Brit Ross Winthereik (eds.), The Palgrave Handbook of the Anthropology of Technology, Singapore: Springer Singapore; Imprint: Palgrave Macmillan, pp. 85–103.

Gallistl, Vera/ Rohner, Rebecca/ Hengl, Lisa/ Kolland, Franz (2021): „Doing digital exclusion – Internet practices of older internet non-users." In: Journal of Aging Studies 59, pp. 1-8.

Kim, Sunyoung (2021): "Exploring How Older Adults Use a Smart Speaker-Based Voice Assistant in Their First Interactions: Qualitative Study." In: JMIR mHealth and uHealth 9/1, pp. 1-12.

Koon, Lyndsie M./ McGlynn, Sean A./ Blocker, Kenneth A./ Rogers Wendy A. (2020): "Perceptions of Digital Assistants From Early Adopters Aged 55+." In: Ergonomics in Design 28/1, pp. 16–23.

Merkel, Sebastian/Kucharski, Alexander B. (2019): Participatory Design in Gerontechnology: A Systematic Literature Review. In: The Gerontologist, 59/1, pp. e16–e25.

Merkel Sebastian/ Kucharski, Alexander (2022): „Echo, HomePod und Co. für ältere Menschen · Digitale Assistenten als Gewinner der Pandemie?" In: Dennis Krämer/ Joschka Haltaufderheide / Jochen Vollmann (eds.), Technologien der Krise. Die Covid-19-Pandemie als Katalysator neuer Formen der Vernetzung, Bielefeld: transcript-verlag, pp. 155-174.

Murdock, Graham/Hartmann, Paul/Grey, Peggy (1992): "Contextualizing Home Computing: Resources and Practices." In: Roger Silverstone/Erich Hirsch (eds.), Consuming Technologies: Media and Information in Domestic Spaces, London: Routledge, pp. 146–160.

Nimrod, Galit/Edan, Yael (2022): "Technology Domestication in Later Life." In: International Journal of Human–Computer Interaction 38/4, pp. 339–350.

Olsson, Tobias/Viscovi, Dino (2018): "Warm Experts for Elderly Users: Who are They and What Do They Do?" In: Human Technology, 14/3, pp. 324–342.

Peine, Alexander/Neven, Louis (2021): "The Co-Constitution of Aging and Technology – a Model and Agenda." In: Aging and Society, 41/12, pp. 2845–2866.

Pradhan, Alisha/Findlater, Leah/Lazar, Amanda (2019): "'Phantom Friend' or 'Just a Box with Information'". In: Proc. ACM Hum -Comput. Interact. 3/ CSCW, pp. 1–21.

Sørensen, Knut H. (2004): Domestication: The Social Enactment of Technology. STS-working paper. 08/04. Trondheim: Norwegian University of Science and Technology – Department of interdisciplinary studies of culture – Centre for Technology and Society.

Trajkova, Milka/Martin-Hammond, Aqueasha (2020): "'Alexa is a Toy': Exploring Older Adults' Reasons for Using, Limiting, and Abandoning Echo." In: Regina Bernhaupt/Florian 'Floyd' Mueller/ David Verweij/ Josh Andres/ Joanna McGrenere/ Andy Cockburn et al. (eds.), Proceedings of the 2020 CHI

Conference on Human Factors in Computing Systems. CHI '20: CHI Conference on Human Factors in Computing Systems, New York: Association for Computing Machinery, pp. 1–13.

Crafting Home with E-Textiles: Accessing Concepts of the Home in a Socially and Culturally Diverse Setting

Anne Weibert, Konstantin Aal, Sarah Rüller, Marcus Rohde and Volker Wulf

Abstract

The concept of crafting is multifaceted; it is described as a skill for manipulating materials into physical objects (Strohmayer 2021; Bardzell et al. 2012; Bean/Rosner 2012; Rosner/Ryokai 2009; Torrey et al. 2009) and is recognized to be a process that combines design and manufacture (Löwgren 2006: 200) and results in a functional and tangible artifact. Research in digital media studies, socio-informatics, and Human Computer Interaction (HCI) have recognized how digital and physical aspects can be linked in and with crafting, and individual and joint, collaborative perspectives be expressed. Our work discusses the crafting of an interactive e-textile tapestry as a creative mode of expressing and accessing concepts of the home in a socially and culturally diverse setting. By using a participatory action research (PAR) approach with ethnographic methods and working very closely with the target group, we explore the building and maintaining of home as practice through crafting. Designed and collaboratively sewn and programmed, the tapestry was made to express experiences and viewpoints on family life across borders and cultures and to visualize and discuss digital practices in homes 'on the move'. Simultaneously, digital crafting practices formed the expression of these joint explorations. Our findings indicate that the textile crafting of symbolic objects and their combination with digital, audio elements are a means to enable bi-directional perspectives on the home and digital and non-digital practices therein. Members of the receiving and of migrant communities form a community of practice (Wenger 1998) around and with their textile work and can share and discuss their views through the crafting.

Keywords

Crafting, E-Textiles, Home, Migration, Participatory Action Research

1. Introduction

How does one build community? This question is of enduring relevance, as migration and flight continue to shape societies across the globe and people are facing the necessity to adjust to a new place figuring out how to shape it as their home, and/or position themselves in, with and between their local communities and neighbourhoods (Bhabha 2012; Fortier 2000; hooks 2009; Jones 2007).

Technological development has had profound effects in this realm in that it has rendered time and space relations almost invisible at times, digitally supporting 'finding home' by fostering the building and maintenance of identities and relations across borders (Adamson 2003; Al-Ali/Koser 2003, Krüger et al. 2021; Maitland 2018; Ponzanesi/Leurs 2014; Weibert et al. 2019). But it is also enabling the manifestation of exclusionary, repulsive structures, designed to signal not-belonging, and bound to put people in a perpetual state of non-arrival (Rosas 2016; Vieira 2016).

Simultaneously, technological development has enabled new ways to approach, understand and position the material and immaterial elements which constitute home. Research in HCI and related disciplines has explored this from different angles. Thus, there is a focus on identity and social relations, explored and expressed e.g., through storytelling (Lenette et al. 2019, Chisholm/Trent 2013; Alexandra 2008). Furthermore, scientific discourse in this realm has focused on traditions, materials, things, and practices, explored and expressed through crafting and making where physical manufacture and digital design are combined (Meissner et al. 2018; Searle/Kafai 2015; Strohmayer 2021). Salih (2013) has studied, among Moroccan migrant women in Italy, how the material and immaterial parts of 'home' are managed across borders in order to establish and maintain a sense of belonging that can span both countries. While the above works have a strong focus on the individual perception of the home, our study explores how crafting can be a means to bring multiple concepts of the home into discourse. Combining a participatory action research approach and ethnographic methods, our study seeks to understand how the building and strengthening of community in a neighbourhood that is socially and culturally diverse can be fostered through such collaborative craft practice around the topic of building and maintaining home.

1.1 Related Works

Our work approaches conceptualizations of the home in the specific context of migration. In this context the home was previously recognized as a space whose constituent parts get reconsidered and repositioned (e.g., Al-Ali/Koser 2003; Hill 2011) – a re-view of the process of "bringing things home" that domestication describes (Silverstone 2006: 233). Constituent parts of the home are material points of connection to a person's place of origin as well as to the place where one is about to become 'at home' (hooks 2009; Salih 2013). Such a process of reconsideration and repositioning is inherently socio-cultural (Kinefuchi 2010). It happens in constant interaction with others negotiating daily the use of material things and the practice-based enactment of customs and traditions (e.g., Ahmed et al. 2020; Pipher 2002; Salih 2013). According to Berger, such a concept of the home is plurilocal, not merely inscribed in a building or territory, but instead manifest in "words, jokes, opinions, gestures, actions, even the way one wears a hat" (Berger 1984: 64). Silverstone posits that such domestication bridges "the macro social and the micro social: the continuous affordances of the wild and the environmentally abundant out there, with the mobilization of material resources, skills, cultural values and social competences and capabilities in here" (Silverstone 2006: 233), involving dimensions of *commodification* and *imagination, appropriation*, and *conversion* (Hartmann 2008: 405). Morley has discussed how changes in (mediated) communication and physical mobilities have demanded for reconsideration of what it means to find home, and to build and maintain sociality and community in relation to this (Morley 2000, 2021).

Such reconfigurations of home and belonging and related materialities and practices have demanded for creative exploration and expression, and here, crafting has been researched to foster learning in close relation to identity and individual reflection (Strohmayer 2021). It is recognized as a skill for manipulating materials into physical objects (Bardzell et al. 2012; Bean, Rosner 2012; Rosner/Ryokai 2009; Torrey et al. 2009). It is described as a process combining design and manufacture (Löwgren 2006: 200) and resulting in a functional, tangible artifact. Research in digital media studies, socio-informatics and HCI recognized how digital and physical aspects can be linked through crafting, and individual and joint perspectives be expressed. Building on these works and contributing to the still underrepresented conceptualization of home for people who are or have been migrating, our study explores experiences and viewpoints on home and family life across borders through crafting, enabling the visualization and discussion of (digital) practices in homes 'on the move'.

1.2 Methods

This work deploys crafting in combination with electronics and programming to bring various identities and conceptualizations of the home into discourse. Engaging as tutors in a computer club setting, an informal exploration space that allows low-threshold interaction with various kinds of technology, we have combined participatory action research with ethnographic methods (Kemmis et al. 2014) in this work.

2. Setting

The activity took place at a community centre in a socially and culturally diverse neighbourhood of a mid-sized town in Germany. It is a diverse neighbourhood with many families living there, but perspectives are difficult for many. Unemployment is high; access to higher education is often difficult. Migration has shaped the neighbourhood in subsequent phases, with migrants arriving as 'guest workers' mainly from Turkey, Greece, and Spain in the 1960s and 70s, people arriving from Eastern European countries like Bulgaria and Romania in large numbers around 2010, and recently refugees coming to the city from countries such as Syria, Afghanistan, Iraq and Iran. Interestingly, every third newcomer to this city has their first address in this neighbourhood. The community centre is one among the many structures of help and support that have formed in the neighbourhood, to provide aid with the (bureaucratic) process of arrival, as well as to foster community answers to the diversification of neighbourhood and support mutual engagement and respect. Within, a computer club functions as an open and low-threshold space (Weibert et al. 2017) for collaborative, creative engagement with computers and digital media.

3. Project and Data Collection

Following a participatory action research approach, the project took the various perspectives, ideas, questions, and problems around 'finding home' that people bring with them to the community centre as its starting point. Inviting adults and adolescents from the neighbourhood to jointly craft a tapestry from felt and fabric on the topic of home, it also made connection with sewing and stitching traditions and skills present in several of the local communities. The tapestry was equipped with a programmable touch board[1] and sewn-in circuits to enable interactivity by turning any conductive artefact into a sensor which then can be deployed to trigger a sound. The board contains twelve capacitive electrodes. It is Arduino-based and can be programmed to either make use of the on-board MP3 decoder and MIDI synthesizer or be used as a USB Serial, MIDI interface, mouse, and keyboard.

Participation in the workshop resembled the diversity of the surrounding neighbourhood, with adults and adolescents from Morocco, Romania, Poland, Syria, and Turkey taking part. The crafting activity unfolded in subsequent steps and the young and adult participants collaborated as a community of practice (Wenger 1998). First, the group worked with visuals as prompts to enable brainstorming of ideas about the home and its constituent parts. Following this activity, common elements of 'home' were identified, and teams were formed according to interest to

---

1   https://www.bareconductive.com/products/touch-board

Crafting Home with E-Textiles   217

work on those specific aspects to design and craft something that could eventually become a part of a large joint tapestry. In a last step, audio recordings were made to enrich the different parts of the tapestry with explanations, stories, and sound.

Fig. 1: Perceptions of the home and its constituent parts were first brainstormed by the group and then crafted and sewn together in one joint tapestry.

Two of the authors who were involved in the workshop as tutors documented the activity in jottings that were then fleshed out to full field notes. Thematic analysis (Clarke/Brown 2014) of the materials yielded *practices and habits and their relation to things, (changing) relationships* and *aesthetics* as key themes.

4. Findings and Discussion

The group initially approached the home in a very straightforward manner focusing on its material constituent parts such as kitchen and living room, and space for leisure and play. Through the task of crafting, however, discourse quickly emerged that centred on the emotional, immaterial meaning(s) of material things in the home. That way, the group engaged in what Silverstone has called the "negotiation of personality and domesticity, both in their location and their dislocation" (Silverstone 2006: 233), then translating this engagement into crafted expression.

As the young and adult participants in the workshop teamed up to detail one topical part of the home they were most interested in, lively discussions unfolded reflecting *practices and habits and their relation to things*. As the workshop took place around Christmas time, one team decided there should be a Christmas tree in the tapestry. It was discussed how the tree could be sewn in a way that it could incorporate experiences of Christmas in Germany, as well as experiences from Romania, where members of that workshop team had family roots. A present was cut from red and yellow felt and equipped with conductive fabric to serve as the touchable element that would start audio files containing the conversation about Christmas and its meanings. Another example is the gaming controller which was designed by a team of teenagers. They engaged in discussions about leisure time practices and play and how they enjoyed these in the home and beyond, also reflecting on changes across a distance, in Germany and in their family's countries of origin. A couch with cushions was designed and put next to the gaming controller to express the importance of relaxing and cosiness in the home.

A group of women immediately said that the kitchen was 'their place', once teams were formed. Here, they felt they could contribute most, and really had things to say about cultural practices, traditions, habits – many of which could be told in relation to food and its preparation. As the women combined migration experiences from Morocco and Spain in their group, they decided to create an audio file to go along with their kitchen design in multiple languages (Arabic, French, Spanish), so everyone in the group was comfortable talking. Perceived *changing relations* were an important aspect in the discussions in this workshop team, as the women reflected on differences they noticed in their practices around cooking, preparing for religious holidays, keeping contact with family in their respective home countries at long-distance, and figuring out their (new) position in the neighbourhood they now lived in. Through crafting, they jointly realized the home (and the kitchen within) as an entity that spans places and countries – resonating with Morley's notion of the home as "symbolic habitat, a performative way of life and of doing things in which one makes one's home while in movement" (Morley 2000: 47).

The design space that the crafting provided enabled reflections outside of the communicative realm that words provide. A man from Syria argued that an image from the mosque of his hometown needed to be in the tapestry. Triggered by the discussions around the Christmas tree in the other team, he said that religion is an important element of 'being at home' for him – but thinking about it made him realize how the familiar space for that is now not only rendered inaccessible to him (because it is far away in Syria) but irreversibly lost (because the mosque was completely destroyed in the war). This situation opened up space for future activities where, through crafting, the shared or diverging understandings of things can be assessed, and their reconfiguration (or dismissal) be further explored and understood.

Aesthetics was an important driver for design choices made by the teams. This was concerned with material e.g., when a teenage girl in one team hesitated to move from a paper sketch to cutting and sewing the elements in fabric. It would not be as pretty as what she had drawn on paper, so she assumed and insisted that her drawing would be included in paper form. All teams explored how interaction with the 'home' would be possible in the tapestry: what serves as the trigger? What is triggered in the first place? How to transport 'the message'? Some interactions were enabled with conductive fabric that was sewn onto lose artefacts (such as an apple in the kitchen, a cushion on the sofa) that could otherwise be connected by means of velcro tape to the fabric of the tapestry. Other interactions were enabled by direct touch of the circuit that was sewn onto the tapestry. The crafting of the interactions objectifies the discussion giving it a shape, form, and place in the joint carpet, thus resonating with domestication's perspective on the home and the role of technology within and beyond (Hartmann 2008; Morley 2021; Silverstone 2006).

The crafting in the workshop found a continuation in subsequent meetings where more detail was added, and the existing elements were further refined. When a large city-wide event came to town, the tapestry became part of an exhibition, and some of the workshop participants who crafted it took part in the exhibition to provide explanations on its making to visitors. Our project has captured one specific moment in time. A path for future works could explore such joint crafting works as a material means to accompany evolving and potentially changing perceptions of the home over time.

Conclusion

Our project has shown how the textile crafting of symbolic objects and their combination with digital audio elements can be a means to enable bi-directional perspectives on the home and analog and digital practices therein, as well as reflection of their migration-led recombination and reconfiguration. We have seen the young and adult participants in our workshop collaborate as a community of practice (Wenger 1998), understanding and appropriating (changing) perceptions of the home through and with their textile work. Sharing their perspectives on the home and creatively translating and conversing them into fabric and felt elements, they formed a community through the crafting learning about similarities as well as differences.

Acknowledgements

Gefördert durch die Deutsche Forschungsgemeinschaft (DFG) – Projektnummer 262513311 – SFB 1187. Funded by the Deutsche Forschungsgemeinschaft (DFG, German Research Foundation) – Project-ID 262513311 – SFB 1187.

References

Ahmed, Sara/Castañeda, Claudia/Fortier, Anne-Marie/Sheller, Mimi (Eds.) (2020): Uprootings/Regroundings. Questions of Home and Migration. London: Taylor & Francis.

Alexandra, Darcy (2008): "Digital Storytelling as Transformative Practice: Critical Analysis and Creative Expression in the Representation of Migration in Ireland". In: Journal of Media Practice 9/2 (2008), 101–112.

Al-Ali, Nadje/Koser, Khalid (2003): New Approaches to Migration?: Transnational Communities and the Transformation of Home. New York: Routledge.

Bardzell, Shaowen/Rosner, Daniela K./Bardzell, Jeffrey (2012): "Crafting Quality in Design: Integrity, Creativity, and Public Sensibility." In: Proceedings of the 2012 ACM Conference on Designing Interactive Systems, pp. 11–20, ACM.

Bean, Jonathan/Rosner, Daniela (2012): "Old Hat: Craft Versus Design?". In: Interactions, 19(1), pp. 86–88, ACM.

Berger, John (1984): And Our Faces, My Heart, Brief as Photos, London: Writers and Readers Press.

Bhabha, Homi K. (2012): The Location of Culture. London: Routledge.

Chisholm, James S./Trent, Brandie (2013): "Digital Storytelling in a Place-based Composition Course". In: Journal of Adolescent & Adult Literacy 57/4 (2013), pp. 307–318.

Clarke, Victoria/Braun, Virginia (2014): "Thematic Analysis". In: Encyclopedia of critical psychology New York: Springer, pp. 1947-1952.

Desjardins, Audrey/Wakkary, Ron/Odom, William (2016): "Behind the Lens: A Visual Exploration of Epistemological Commitments in HCI Research on the Home". In: Proceedings of the ACM Conference on Designing Interactive Systems, pp. 360-376, ACM.

Fortier, Anne-Marie (2000): Migrant Belongings. Memory, Space, Identity. London: Routledge.

Hartmann, Maren (2008): „Domestizierung 2.0: Grenzen und Chancen eines Medienaneignungskonzeptes". In: Theorien der Kommunikations-und Medienwissenschaft. Wiesbaden VS Verlag für Sozialwissenschaften, pp. 401-416.

Hill, Anita (2011): Reimagining Equality: Stories of Gender, Race, and Finding Home. Boston, MA: Beacon Press.

hooks, bell (2009): Belonging: A Culture of Place. Routledge: New York.

Jones, Elizabeth H. (2007): Spaces of Belonging: Home, Culture and Identity in 20th-Century French Autobiography. Amsterdam: Brill

Kemmis, Stephen/McTaggart, Robin/Nixon, Rhonda (2014): The Action Research Planner: Doing Critical Participatory Action Research. Singapore: Springer.

Kinefuchi, Etsuko (2010): "Finding Home in Migration: Montagnard Refugees and Post-Migration Identity". In: Journal of International and Intercultural communication 3/3 (2010), pp. 228–248.

Krüger, Max/Weibert, Anne/de Castro Leal, Débora/Randall, Dave/Wulf, Volker (2021): "It Takes More Than One Hand to Clap: On the Role of 'Care' in Maintaining Design Results". In CHI Conference on Human Factors in Computing Systems, ACM.

Lenette, Caroline/Brough, Mark/Schweitzer, Robert D./Correa-Velez, Ignacio/Murray, Kate/Vromans, Lyn (2019): 'Better than a Pill': Digital Storytelling as a Narrative Process for Refugee Women. Media Practice and Education 20, 1 (2019), pp. 67–86.

Löwgren, Jonas (2008): "Interaction Design Considered as Craft." In: Erickson, T., MacDonald, D. (Eds.), HCI Remixed: Reflections on Works that have Influenced the HCI Community. Cambridge: MIT Press, pp. 199–203.

Maitland, Carleen (Ed.). (2018): Digital Lifeline?: ICTs for Refugees and Displaced Persons. Cambridge: MIT Press.

Meissner, Janis L./Strohmayer, Angelika/Wright, Peter/Fitzpatrick, Geraldine (2018): "A Schnittmuster for Crafting Context-Sensitive Toolkits". In: Proceedings of the 2018 CHI Conference on Human Factors in Computing Systems, pp. 1–13, ACM.

Morley, David (2000): Home Territories. Media, Mobility and Identity. London: Routledge.

Morley, David (2021): "Mobile Socialities: Communities, Mobilities, and Boundaries". In: Annette Hill/Maren Hartmann/Magnus, Andersson (Eds.) The Routledge Handbook of Mobile Socialities. New York: Routledge.

Pipher, Mary Bray (2002): The Middle of Everywhere: The World's Refugees Come to Our Town. Houghton Mifflin Harcourt, Orlando, FL.

Ponzanesi, Sandra/Leurs, Koen (2014): "On Digital Crossings in Europe". In: Crossings: Journal of Migration & Culture, 5/1, 3-22.

Rosas, Gilberto (2016): "The Thickening Borderlands: Bastard Mestiz@s,"Illegal" Possibilities, and Globalizing Migrant Life". In Critical Ethnic Studies. Duke University Press, pp. 344–359.

Rosner, Daniela K./Ryokai, Kimiko (2009): "Reflections on Craft: Probing the Creative Process of Everyday Knitters". In: Proceedings of the 7th ACM conference on Creativity and Cognition, pp. 195–204, ACM.

Salih, Ruba (2013): Gender in Transnationalism: Home, Longing and Belonging among Moroccan Migrant Women. Routledge: London.

Searle, Kristin A./Kafai, Yasmin B. (2015): "Culturally responsive making with American Indian girls: Bridging the identity gap in crafting and computing with electronic textiles". In: Proceedings of the 3rd conference on genderIT, pp. 9-16, ACM.

Silverstone, Roger (2006): "Domesticating Domestication. Reflections on the Life of a Concept". In: Berker, Thomas/ Hartmann, Maren/ Punie, Yves/Ward, Katie. Domestication of media and technology. London: Open University Press, pp. 229-248.

Strohmayer, Angelika (2021): Digitally Augmenting Traditional Craft Practices for Social Justice: The Partnership Quilt. Singapore: Springer Nature.

Torrey, Cristen/Churchill, Elisabeth F./McDonald, David W. (2009): "Learning How: the Search for Craft Knowledge on the Internet". In: Proceedings of the SIGCHI Conference on Human Factors in Computing Systems, pp. 1371–1380, ACM.

Wenger, Etienne (1998): Communities of Practice: Learning, Meaning, and Identity. Cambridge: Cambridge University Press.

Weibert, Anne/Krüger, Max/Aal, Konstantin/Salehee, Setareh S./Khatib, Renad/ Randall, Dave/Wulf, Volker (2019): "Finding Language Classes: Designing a Digital Language Wizard with Refugees and Migrants". In: Proceedings of the ACM on Human-Computer Interaction, 3 (CSCW), pp. 1–23, ACM.

Weibert, Anne/Randall, Dave/Wulf, Volker (2017): "Extending Value Sensitive Design to Off-the-Shelf Technology: Lessons Learned From a Local Intercultural Computer Club". In: Interacting with Computers, 29/5, 715–736.

In Conversation with

The Questions Are Still Good
Domestication Theory and Digital Media Today

Leslie Haddon in Conversation with Niklas Strüver and David Waldecker

Leslie Haddon is currently a visiting lecturer in the Department of Media and Communications at the London School of Economics and Political Science (LSE). He was an early collaborator of Roger Silverstone and involved in the establishment of domestication theory. In his early work, he dealt with home automation, something known as smart home today, and he later worked on a number of projects that focused on mobile media and children's media use. There, he collaborated with Sonia Livingstone on a comparative study of children's Internet use in a number of European countries. He is the co-editor of The Routledge Companion to Children and Digital Media (2020), and Smartphone Cultures (2018).

David Waldecker (DW): Thank you very much for granting us this interview. I'll start with the beginning of the whole domestication approach. I wonder how did you personally come in touch with the topic of domestication? You write a lot about the history of the concept in your publications, I wonder if you could go into more detail and tell us what the academic landscape was at that time and how domestication research came into being – how was it conceived and how did it respond to the intellectual situation at that time?

Leslie Haddon (LH): I think you have to go back to the 1980s and although there were different intellectual strands within media studies, semiotics was most influential. So, you're looking at what processes are happening in texts. And then you get some people who take a different perspective. The first one being David Morley, in *The Nationwide Audience* (1980), who looked at how audiences are decoding what they see, even if that word 'decoding' didn't exist at the time. It was interesting, he was actually, for the first time, asking about how people from different backgrounds make sense of watching television programmes. And that's the first time that you're asking about real agency in this process. And then Dorothy Hobson (1980) asked how television fits into the lives of housewives and how it changes what they do. So, to use an example from my own life, I often sit and have lunch at one o'clock and watch the news simultaneously because I have no appointments on that day. That means that the media schedule affects the timing of when I eat. This fitting television into their lives also included housewives turning the television on and wandering back and forth listening to the sound for its companionship. A few years later you have David Morley with *Family Television* (1982) asking even more questions about what we are actively doing when television is taking place. How do we manage television? Are you flicking or is it pre-planned? Are you talking about the programmes while the television is on? Are you multitasking or does television have your full attention? Who's got their hand on the remote control? Are some people experiencing enforced viewing? I thought this was marvellous actually because this raised even more questions about the nature of agency when watching television. James Lull (1990) wrote a literature review about the social uses of television ten years later detailing, for example, how we focus on television when we don't want to talk to people, or how we draw on it when we want to raise a sensitive issue that's being talked about on television – we use that as the way into that discussion. He outlined over 20 such social uses.

All this was happening before domestication research took off. And I think that this thinking was a big input into Roger Silverstone's work. At the same time, other studies of technologies beyond the media were being published, for example, early studies of satellite television (Brundson 1991), I was involved in the early studies of home computers (Haddon 1988), there were studies of the video recorder (Gray 1992), studies of the telephone (Rakow 1988; Moyal 1989). This is why that early domestication work moved away from the stance that domestication is focusing on media in order to focus on ICTs more broadly. Obviously, Roger Silverstone was particularly interested in the new discipline of consumption studies and how it was influenced by anthropology, in asking questions such as: How do we arrange furniture in our homes? Or, how do we make choices about clothes? The single most striking point relates to the question: What do the artefacts we consume symbolise to us and to others? To give an example from satellite television or big TV sets, a family might say: "We wouldn't have that because all the neighbours will think we're the type of people that watch TV all day." So, having a satellite dish or having a big TV in itself would give a message to other people.

So how did I get involved? Well, the domestication researchers at Brunel University had the funds to develop this theoretical framework, carry out empirical studies and develop a methodology. And they had the idea that they would launch their idea within a more wide-ranging book, which became *Consuming Technologies* (Silverstone/Hirsch 1992) – which is an interesting choice of word anyway because until then you didn't usually use the word "consume" with TV or any other technology. Using the word signifies you're doing something different. In preparation for the book there was a workshop at Brunel University and I was invited to attend. There were about eight to ten guests, and the academics at Brunel university gave their presentations on domestication and we all had to give our feedback. They invited us all to write chapters for the book, which I did. Then, Roger Silverstone got another three years' money to develop the concept further, looking beyond nuclear families. However, by that time everyone in the team had left. I got a telephone call one day saying, "Would you like three years' worth of work because you know the subject and we need someone who hits the road running, and if you say 'yes', can you start tomorrow?" So, obviously, no pressure! That's how I got into it. And then straight after the three years a company came to us asking us to conduct a domestication analysis and after that another company approached us. So that's why I was heavily involved at that point in time.

DW: What I find striking reading those texts today is the focus on the household. For me, the household is a concept that relates to demographics. It is a rather dull, technical term that just describes people living in one unit together. Here it became a focal point of interest and I just wonder why it was chosen and not "families" or the "home," because, as you said, the early research actually dealt with nuclear families?

LH: I can answer this question at two levels, one my personal one and one relating to the introduction to the 1992 volume on *Consuming Technologies* (Silverstone/Hirsch 1992). I never asked Roger why he emphasised the household in that text. In fact, if you read it carefully, it sometimes says "the household/family," sometimes he says "the family system" – you'll find the use of the word "home" in that article, but I would agree with you that the major term used is "household". I don't know why that choice had been made. My experience later on is, I'd been carrying out research for a few years and I was reporting that first body of paid work. I was invited to go to what was essentially a feminist conference with all the big names at that time. It wasn't my best presentation; I had made the mistake of a junior researcher, only thinking about my presentation when I was on the train on the way to the conference. At one point I happened to mention the word "family" in my presentation. That that was bitterly criticised as I was reminded of all the critiques of the family. And I was scolded, with one person arguing that I did not know anything about feminism. That experience, especially since my PhD dealt with gender themes, was rather embarrassing. So, I never used the word "family" again. I was looking for a very dull word and "household" really suited me.

Niklas Strüver (NSt): That makes a pretty great reason for that dull word! (laughter)

LH: It's strange, because now, 20 years later on, my colleagues are asking me why I didn't use the word "family?" So obviously things have moved on in those discussions.

NSt: Yes, obviously! After your early research, you also moved on from the household and researched more mobile devices and touch screens. We were wondering how you applied the domestication framework to those new contexts. As you point out in "Domestication Analysis and the Smartphone" (2020), there are a lot of different things that go into choosing the way in which you apply the domestication framework to any given subject. We wanted to know how you address this development of technologies that are becoming more generalistic and ubiquitous, as with smartphones and tablets in general?

LH: So, what you are asking is, "How much do you make changes to the theory because of something that happens in the technological landscape?" I am a bit sceptical about doing that with theory – one of the major reasons being, at any particular point in time there are a number of new technologies that could qualify as making a significant difference to everyday life. I wonder if this justifies changing the theory, because in 10 or in 20 years' time, there will be another set of technologies to adapt to. It just makes me a bit wary of simply saying we must make a change to the theory because of a difference in the technology that is available now. Having said that, the prime example you pick is mobile phones. Here, I had thought that this really forces us to look outside the home, because unless you see how people are interacting with mobile phones outside the home, you don't fully understand the experience of the mobile phone. I was arguing that before anyway. When I attended that workshop where they launched the domestication paradigm, one of my arguments in my own PhD research was that you understand a certain amount about what people do with computers by looking at interactions within the home, but that you have to look outside, too. For instance, I was particularly interested in my PhD in the gender patterns of gaming. I was trying to make sense of the difference experience of gaming. It wasn't that girls were not playing games. They were. But, when you asked boys and girls, "Do you discuss games at school?", the boys would say, "Yes, it's one of our major topics of conversation." And the girls would say that it isn't. "And what about discussing how to play the game?" The boys said they did the girls said "No." "Well, what about actually exchanging the games?" The boys say they did, girls did not. "And what about discussing computer magazines and what you're reading?" The boys say they did, the girls say "No." Anyway, you had to understand what was happening in their leisure time outside of the home – e.g., in schools – to understand this different orientation to games. So, I've certainly been arguing that before mobile phones appeared and other people, like Mackay (1997), were also saying you should be willing to look outside the home.

NSt: You said that you would not change the theory just because technologies are changing. When you said that I wondered about the current developments that are shifting towards a dominant discourse about platforms, data and algorithms. This development certainly will be dominant in the next coming years. The consequence of this is that media are no longer a one-way street, basically, because the users shape the system through the analysis of their usage data and through algorithms that adapt to their behaviour. I was wondering how people are domesticated in that sense by these new technologies and if there is any way to account for this bi-directionality in domestication theories?

LH: So, what you are suggesting is that the data you produce is used to influence the choices that you're offered, for example. Basically, you said to some extent this is beyond your control. To some extent you cannot even see it at a day-to-day level even if you may know about it. But I would say, while that's true, that was true before the discussion of algorithms, of data mining and of what Facebook is doing. On the one hand, you are trying to control media in the household. That is the essence of all this discussion in domestication theory, of how people fit technologies into their life, of how individuals try to limit their effects, etc. But, even in the case of older technologies, there were always things that were beyond their control.

People nowadays are warned to be careful when putting personal information on social media, especially if they're young, because when they apply for a job later on those interviewing them might find this information even though it wasn't intended for this audience. Or, if you post a picture, other people can take that picture and circulate it. And in these senses maybe you're more aware now that you put things out there on the internet and you can lose control of them. And that's in these discussions of danah boyd (2014) where she suggests that these technologies can amplify negative aspects like gossiping and bullying. It is easier to spread this information because it's in electronic form. However, that's not only true of social media. It was true of e-mail beforehand. It was true if people forwarded your e-mails to audiences for whom they were not intended. In principle, this was even true of other media. Letters could be passed on, pictures could be passed on. But I think it was made easier once you're doing all these things electronically. So, I would agree, in the sense, that you lose more control. There's suddenly some part of the internet trying to sell you things. Some parts of the online world have become more unruly and beyond your control. But to an extent this was true beforehand, it was true before the algorithms discussion.

How does domestication theory fit in when it comes to the bidirectionality of data flows? Take the word "domestication". It originally emphasises what we do to animals. In "taming" them we change them, we fit them into the organisation of our life. But, of course, this changes the lifestyle of the domesticator as well. When you domesticate the cow, then you have to go out and milk the cow, so it has changed your behaviour. When you domesticate other animals, you have to build buildings for them for the winter. Domestication changes the person doing the domesticating. But in the original use of the word, that is understressed. It's a bit of an afterthought. The main stress is what we do to the animals. And, to be quite honest, I think that is what's happened to a large extent in the discussion of domestication with regards to media and technology – and I am also guilty of that as well. When I have to summarise what is the most important idea in domestication research, it tends to be what we do to technologies to fit them in our lives. That's the opening statement. But look what happens in actual studies. As I was studying young people's use of technology and their social media use, they were complaining, "The problem is, I feel obliged to keep checking what everyone's saying, otherwise when I go to school the next day, I won't know what they're talking about. But this is a problem because it is taking up too much of my time, really. I am not even doing my hobbies now because I find myself doing this all the time to stay social." It is quite clear that these young individuals realise that the technology use is changing their life for the worse. It is domesticating them, to use your phrase. There's a recent article on WeChat in China about using the idea of re-domestication (Huang/Miao 2020). The authors argue that the chief problem with WeChat is that it is disrupting users' lives because they are being contacted all the time and they can't get on with the rest of their work. It is actually disruptive. So, these users try to find ways of controlling WeChat, for example, by only checking it sometimes, by doing things like moving the WeChat icon further down the screen on the phone's menu so it's less obvious, etc. – ways to make you less inclined to use it. But what's going on here is re-domestication. It comes with a realisation that: "I've adopted a technology and it's changing my life for the worse, and I've got to do something about it." Or take another example, an early text by Bakardijeva (2006), where she suggests that one of the things researchers don't do enough is look at empowerment. In examining how media use empowers us, she is essentially examining the consequences of media use. While I would say that the theme of "what the consequences are for us" has been there, it doesn't get emphasised in the major statements about domestication, it is only implied in actual studies. I remember reading an article of by Blank and Dutton (2005) that says domestication is inherently conservative because it's always asking what we do to technologies rather than what technologies do to us. I thought that's a little bit unfair. But I can understand why they are making those statements given that if you look at the start of most domestication articles the emphasis is on what you're doing to tame things.

DW: It is interesting that you say that, that if you read the actual studies, there is this influence of technology on people in their daily lives – as in how people organised their schedules around TV and people not calling each other at 8 o'clock because that's the time that, in Germany at least, the main news channel has its news programme. You also mentioned social media, so how people deal with controlling their image on social media is one thing, but what we are interested in is how there is also this more technical feedback through data that you didn't have with analogue TV or radio, for example.

There's this discussion on how targeted advertising online adds a certain new level of control over users to the platforms and service providers. Shoshana Zuboff calls this process *surveillance capitalism* (2019), or Couldry and Mejias (2019) call it *digital colonialism*. This is a critical stance towards the phenomenon and I just wonder how you would discuss this with the domestication framework in mind – with respect to processes that are happening behind the users' backs, so to speak. They don't know what's happening with servers or the algorithms, so it's a lot harder to control it, isn't it?

LH: Yes, it is. I agree and the difference compared to my examples is that the process is less visible to them. However, I have a suspicion that there's actually more awareness that these things are happening, even if people feel they can't do anything about it. Some of my students looked into this as part of their thesis for example. Users might think: "Because you are making it free, I'll go along with you and give you my labour and you can do what you want with it. And I know that's happening and that's life!"

I just have to ask myself, well, because of this new dimension, should domestication theory somehow adapt to or engage with this? But then, I wonder if this new development changes anything about the questions I ask. Some people look at domestication theory as a checklist of questions. I actually think it's a bit more than that. But, you know, those original questions were good, I still ask them. Given what may be happening nowadays, the answers have just got more complicated. But the questions are still good.

DW: Yes, I guess, what domestication research would do is to look at how users actually deal with data even if you can't control them the way that you can control a TV by turning it on and off. As you say, it's a fact of life and you've got to deal with it.

LH: I think it's an interesting research question, to actually have a project which tries to delve into that, by asking question such as: "If you know about this, does it make any difference at all to what you do? Do you sometimes actually put false information out there to try and defeat the system?" I think some people do, most people probably don't. It's just another interesting topic to say: How do you cope with this development?

DW: Well, then we got this one right. That's what we're doing actually, asking users about these things.

We do this with a focus on practices. We try to relate domestication research to the ongoing debate about practices in social theory and social research and we wonder about their relationship. In some way, domestication research has a strong focus on media consumption as a practical problem because the theory stresses that media are not only content or, as you said, text that has to be decoded semiotically, but that they are related to objects that have to be placed in the household that need be turned on, that need to be handled by somebody. So, I think there's an inherent practical dimension to that research and I just wonder what you would say about this whole practice theory connection.

LH: Well, I can answer that in terms of my own situation and a general observation. One is I don't tend to read that literature on practices so it's very hard for me to comment on it. It may be there, but it's beyond what I choose to look at. The second comment is, I too haven't seen any articles which ask how domestication should engage with discussion of practices. I haven't seen anyone writing about that – and I collect everything I can in this field of domestication. That's a short answer but it's very honest.

DW: Okay, that's interesting to us because that's what we're trying to do with that special issue too, to see how handling media is a practical affair and also handling data is a practical affair. So, it's good for us to know that we're on to something new here to a certain extent.

NSt: Let's come back to another subject that you mentioned already. You referred to the connection between taming and domestication; these are two different words or terms to describe similar practices. There are, however, important differences between the two. In a workshop we had with Maren Hartmann in February 2022, she talked about the history of the word taming and domesticity as well. In making the connection to modern media, she pointed out that things are unruly, as we said earlier, and they are becoming increasingly unruly. That means that people are less in control and this is where she made a distinction between domestication and taming. While the common term is the "domestication" of media, it might be more reasonable to speak of "taming" of modern media because there's always some degree of resistance or even danger in handling those devices. The same is true of animals because an animal that has been tamed can still bite back even though it has been tamed. So, we were wondering what you make of this distinction?

LH: Well, I think taming is the worse one to use because, as I said before, you are emphasising what we do to technology. Domestication, if you think it through, the original word, allows you to see both sides, to see how we change because of the domestication process. So out of the two words I would prefer to use domestication, and just go out of my way to say the danger is if we use taming instead, many people may use it in one direction only. That could be very misleading.

I mean, I am still happy with domestication as a metaphor. Because labelling things through metaphors is a way to make them more accessible. With this metaphor, you're talking about the subject by moving away from it, in this case by talking about our relationship to animals, for example. You're asking people to stand back basically. And you know it's a simplification. I compare this with, for instance, the discussions of social exclusion. There's an expression, "the digital divide." It is prominently used in the literature and it has caused such a backlash. It is misleading, because "the divide" implies that there is a single binary divide and that's not really the case. It has been a real point of contention in that field. And even so, some proponents say, at the end of the day, using that word as a simplification got it onto a lot of people's agenda, especially in the policy area. If you would've gone along with the academics and tried to use something more complicated because it was more accurate it may have never gotten off the ground. So, in comparison to the digital divide, I think domestication might be a little misleading but good enough.

And, in preparation for this interview, I thought that when I have to do yet another update of domestication I might re-word my introduction to stress the two-way nature of it, just to compensate for how that has been misleading in the past.

NSt: We're making an impact here. (laughter) Okay, coming back to the relation of domestication theory and current developments, we were wondering what do you think of conceptual extensions and adaptions of the theory. For example, if I think about a text that has been talked about at our workshop by Saba Brause and Grant Blank (2020) where they propose *externalisation* as a new dimension of domestication.

LH: I can really comment about it in general first. I mark PhDs on the subject. And as you can imagine, it's almost inevitable in the theory section at the end that they have to say how domestication theory could be improved. It's almost obligatory because it's a PhD. And there are constant suggestions coming from their particular research questions and the particular people they are researching, about adding a certain concept or term or making a new subheading. I've seen that again and again, also in journal papers. And some of these new additions are taken up by other researchers and become more successful. Re-domestication is an example, coming originally from Norwegian research, not from what was happening the UK. I have also encountered "dis-domestication" and "reverse domestication". You can understand why people are making such suggestions. But I also know from experience researchers have made a lot of suggestions in the past that haven't gone anywhere. No one has used these proposed terms. Now I thought actually that Brause and Blank did a good job in that article on the domestication of voice assistants. They managed to do the analysis using all the existing tools of the trade, then they suggested an additional term. I thought, well you've already managed to do everything with the existing terms, what's the added value of adding the new one? It is true, there is a change in the ways devices are connected and the domestication of one item has an impact on the domestication of another item. I can see the argument, but, you know, if things are changing, you could simply provide more complex descriptions.

NSt: That is, more complex descriptions with the existing theoretical tools?

LH: Yes, I think, well, I know they went through the standard headings objectification, incorporation, etc. You see this in many articles. Here, they are using exactly these concepts to explain how they apply to voice assistants. So, yes, they were literally asking the same questions as in the classic texts.

NSt: Yes, they were. But, I still I see their point because it is hard to answer these questions with the already existing tools without the externalisation concept.

LH: Okay, so my answer then is go ahead, and I'm quite willing to incorporate it, if it proves to be a success and other people make use of it. I'll keep an open mind.

DW: The thing is – if you look at it empirically – that we talked about this idea at the workshop extensively and three or four people mentioned that concept in their papers, it is the first time maybe that it is of a certain relevance.

LH: Yes, if I were to see that happening, where a new dimension to domestication has been repeatedly mentioned in different articles, then I'd say it has found its way onto this field of discussion. It's viable. You've made the argument and obviously it is a believable argument and so people have taken it up. Fine!

DW: There is another concept that is central to the early conceptualisation of domestication – the "moral economy of the household" (Silverstone/Hirsch/Morley 1992) – and I think it has a salience that connects to current debates on the sociology of valuation and evaluation (Lamont 2012) and new economic sociologies that examine how economic values and evaluations are interrelated (e.g., Boltanski/Chiapello 2005). I find this idea of the moral economy actually relates to this field in that people connect economic and personal values in their media usage; simultaneously, the household is a moral as well as an economic unit. It relates to what you said earlier, that people have sort of an economy of personal time they can allocate to things which becomes obvious when, as you said, people complain that they have to spend too much time on social media and that this interferes with other things. However, this concept of the moral economy has been criticised as being somewhat conservative in its understanding of the household (Bakardjieva 2006). This is a bit surprising because it was originally used by the somewhat radical social historian E.P. Thompson in his *The Making of the English Working Class* (1966; cf. 1971). I wonder if you could comment on that.

LH: Right. You may find – go through my work carefully – that I very rarely use the words "moral economy". I talk about the other concepts like conversion; but you might have noticed it's a gap. I sometimes mention it in passing when I'm referring to the belief systems in families where parents might for instance agree about what they think their children should be doing or shouldn't be doing. But, as soon as I started actually interviewing people in the household units, I kept coming across disagreements about values. This discussion of the moral economy as a system implies a consensus that everyone has signed up to – but this is often only partially true. In virtually every household I came across there were different opinions about something. It could be about things like the domestic divisions of labour in the home, where there are disagreements. You're most likely to get this agreement about children, but even then, the mother and father will sometimes complain about each other because one parent thinks the children should be allowed to do this and the other parent thinks they shouldn't. Right from the start I found empirical problems with this idea and so I simply avoided using it.

DW: I think in some way you've rephrased that criticism. It relates to the critique of the use of the word "family" you encountered yourself – to see the household as a unit when it actually isn't. But I think the other strength of the domestication approach is the focus on the household and that the household members, even though they come from different generations, use media differently, as you highlighted with the gendered use to gaming. The fact is that with all their different and sometimes conflicting media practices, they still live in that same household. And as such they have to come to terms with each other in some way.

LH: My immediate thought is, have you read divorce figures recently? I remember interviewing one particular couple. I first interviewed them separately, and it was clear that they didn't agree about anything. Between the first and second interview they split up and filed for divorce. So, you say they have to learn to live with different views, but sometimes they don't. Instead, they seek other arrangements with new partners, still with the aspiration of "we'll believe the same thing and have the same values". Certainly, the aspiration might be there, but again, I think any consensus is often only partial. And if you go back to even Roger Silverstone's original use of word, in the same article where he discusses the moral economy, he also refers to the "politics of the household" (Silverstone/Hirsch/Morley 1992: 16), which is an acknowledgement of inevitable conflicts and tensions.

DW: Yes, that's a good point. While examining the tensions within the household, we still focus on the household. What struck me about the domestication approach is the focus on the household as one important part of everyday life. It still is important and it has become even more so with the pandemic, where people were locked inside their homes.

LH: I just want to mention one point that you haven't made yet. With respect to the household, what are the alternative paradigms to analysing media and technology use? One prominent one I keep coming across is the uses and gratification approach (e.g., Ruggiero 2000). I would say it is even more prominent in media and technology research than the domestication approach. And I think that one of the major differences is that it is very individualistic; it is interested in why individuals want to use certain services or make the decisions to use them. And I think this is one of the benefits of domestication research, whether this was inside the home or outside the home, is that you have to see people interacting, negotiating, developing rules, developing etiquette. All these aspects are the context in which people are making decisions about technology, and I thought that was an improvement on uses and gratification.

DW: Yes, I think this is also an answer in a certain way to the continuing relevance of the household.

NSt: I think what makes the domestication approach better is that it looks outside of the individual plane. Also, if you look towards Norway, their strand of theory includes the household but the macro level, too. And I realised that critiques of the approach have taken the terms too much at face value. If you are not reading the fine print strongly enough, it is very easy to misunderstand it. I remember reading a critique of domestication research by Andrew Feenberg (1999: 107). I was not sure if he was right and, to be honest, after our conversation, I do not think he is.

LH: To come back to the point about reading the small print, I raise the question with my students about what counts as a domestication study. A lot of writers will automatically go back to that first 1992 article (Silverstone/Hirsch/Morley 1992) and use the particular words from that text. Or they might consider additions from a few years later – as with re-domestication – and use those concepts. I suggest to students that they should understand domestication research as the whole body of studies that have been conducted using that concept since it was first introduced. So, you know, apart from looking at the small print is important to read broadly when deciding whether a particular piece of research counts as a domestication study.

NSt: Yes, I agree. That makes the concept very adaptable as well.

LH: It does. And I've said this before, if you just stay with the classic concepts, you can argue that you need to adapt domestication to today's changing technological circumstances. But if you look at what people have actually done over a thirty-year period, domestication has already proved to be very adaptable.

NSt: Right, then I might just add a last concluding sort of question. If you maybe reflect on the type of questions that we asked and with what interest we're going into this domestication idea, is there anything that you want to add about our approach or ideas?

LH: There's nothing I particularly wish to ask, because I've already conveyed the idea that I will be sceptical. Because – as I said right at the start of the interview – I'm wary of saying that we have to do something new with the theory because of the changing nature of the technology. So, I'll await with interest to see what you actually do write, given you know you're going to have audiences like me.

NSt: I am looking forward to that discussion then. (laughter)

DW: Is there anything else?

LH: Obviously, I can say a lot about domestication. Part of the reason is, once Roger Silverstone died, a lot of people would ask me to write updates about how the field was developing and make comments about subsequent domestication studies, whereas if Roger had still been alive, I think they'd have asked him. Although even he, in his later works, was losing interest in domestication. I still use domestication as a framework for the questions I ask, but in addition it's like the external academic world keeps dragging me back to this topic because they want me to make a comment on it all the time. So, developments in domestication are interesting to me, but rather than being one of my burning interests which I'm trying to fight for, it's really because of the external pressures on me to keep making comments that I am still very immersed in this topic.

DW: Yes, but I think this relates to the fact that people still find the approach interesting. And, as you said, it still produces interesting results if you continue to stick to the original questions, and I think one of them is this focus on the household. But I think, as you said, it looks at the fact that people don't use media individually or as part of a cohort, but as part of a concrete set of interactions with other people, be it in the school yard, be it at home, be it at work. Our task is to work out how these concrete interactions are shaped by furniture, by other media that are present, other members of the family, pets, etc.

LH: Yes, and going up a level, also how it is shaped discursively, how the discourses in wider society themselves influence negotiations within the home. So, when parents refer to some debate about children being addicted to games, that broader discussion influences their ideas and interactions with their children – we have that level to think about as well.

DW: Yes, that is of course something that we noticed too, in our study on voice assistants, that people refer to the discussions about data breaches and the negative image of Facebook when they talk about data practices.

LH: Yes, and that's the important part of the whole process being aware of being influenced.

References

Blank, Grant/Dutton, William H. (2015): "Next Generation Users: Changing Access to the Internet." In: Anja Beckman/Stine Lomborg (eds.), The Ubiquitous Internet: User and Industry Perspectives, London: Routledge, pp.11-34.

Bakardjieva, Maria (2006): "Domestication Running Wild. From the Moral Economy of the Household to the Mores of Culture." In: Thomas Berker/Maren Hartmann/Yves Punie/Kathie J. Ward (eds.), Domestication of Media and Technologies, Maidenhead: Open University Press, pp.62-79.

Boltanksi, Luc/Chiapello, Ève (2005): The New Spirit of Capitalism, London: Verso.

Brause, Saba Rebecca/Blank, Grant (2020): "Externalized Domestication. Smart Speaker Assistants, Networks and Domestication Theory." In: Information, Communication & Society 23/5, pp. 751-763.

Brundson, Charlotte (1991): "Satellite Dishes and the Landscapes of Taste." In: New Formations No. 15, 23-42.

boyd, danah (2014): It's Complicated. The Social Life of Networked Teens, New Haven, CT: Yale University Press.

Couldy, Nick/Mejias, Ulises A. (2019): The Costs of Connection. How Data Is Colonizing Human Life and Appropriating It for Capitalism, Stanford: Stanford University Press.

Feenberg, Andrew (1999): Questioning Technology, London: Routledge.

Gray, Ann (1987): "Behind Closed Doors. Women and Video Recorders in the Home." In: Helen Baer/Gilian Dyer (eds.), Boxed In: Women and Television, New York: Pandora, pp.38-52.

Haddon, Leslie (1988): "The Home Computer: The Making of a Consumer Electronic." In: Science as Culture 1/2, pp. 7-51.

Haddon, Leslie (2020): "Domestication Analysis and the Smartphone." In: Rich Ling/Leopoldina Fortunati/Gerald Goggin/Lim Sun Sun/Li Yuling (eds.), The Oxford Handbook of Mobile Communication and Society, Oxford: Oxford University Press, pp. 14–28.

Hobson, Dorothy (1980): "Housewives and the Mass Media." In: Stuart Hall (ed.), Culture, Media, Language. Working Papers in Cultural Studies, 1972–79, London: Routledge, pp. 93-102.

Huang, Ying/Miao, Weishan (2020): "Re-domesticating Social Media when It Becomes Disruptive: Evidence from China's 'Super App' WeChat." In Mobile Media & Communications 0/0, pp. 1-18.

Lamont, Michèle (2012): "Toward a Comparative Sociology of Valuation and Evaluation." In: Annual Review of Sociology 38, pp. 201-221.

Lull, James (1990): Inside Family Viewing. Ethnographic Research on Television's Audience, London: Routledge.

Mackay, Hugh (1997): "Consuming Communication Technologies at Home." In: Hugh Mackay (ed.), Consumption and Everyday Life, London: Sage, pp. 259-308.

Morley, David (1980): The Nationwide Audience, London: British Film Institute.

Morley, David (1982): Family Television. Cultural Power and Domestic Leisure, London: Comedia.

Moyal, Ann (1989): "The Feminine Culture of the Telephone. People, Patterns and Policy." In: Prometheus, 7/1, pp. 5-31.

Rakow, Lana F. (1988): "Women and the Telephone: The Gendering of a Communications Technology." In: Cheris Kramarae (ed.), Technology and Women's Voices: Keeping in Touch, London: Routledge and Kegan Paul, pp. 207-228.

Ruggiero, Thomas E. (2000): "Uses and Gratifications Theory in the 21st Century." In: Mass Communication and Society 3/1, pp. 3-37.

Silverstone, Roger/Hirsch, Eric (eds.) (1992): Consuming Technologies. Media and Information in Domestic Spaces, London: Routledge.

Silverstone, Roger/Hirsch, Eric/Morley, David (1992): "Information and Communication Technologies and the Moral Economy of the Household." In: Roger Silverstone/Eric Hirsch (eds.), Consuming Technologies. Media and Information in Domestic Spaces, London: Routledge, pp. 13-28.

Thompson, E.P. (1966): The Making of the English Working Class, New York: Vintage.

Thompson, E.P. (1971): "The Moral Economy of the English Crowd in the Eighteenth Century." In: Past & Present No. 50, pp. 76-136.

Zuboff, Shoshana (2019): The Age of Surveillance Capitalism. The Fight for a Human Future at the New Frontier of Power, London: Profile.

Biographical Notes

Konstantin Aal is a research associate at the Institute for Business Informatics and New Media, University of Siegen.

Tanja Aal is a PhD candidate and research assistant at the Collaborative Research Center 1187 "Media of Cooperation", University of Siegen.

Hendrik Bender is a PhD candidate in media studies and researcher at the Collaborative Research Center 1187 "Media of Cooperation", University of Siegen.

Marcus Burkhardt is a lecturer in media studies at University of Siegen and principal investigator at the Collaborative Research Center 1187 "Media of Cooperation", University of Siegen.

Cordula Endter is professor for social work in the digitalized society at Catholic University of Applied Sciences Berlin.

Florian Fischer heads the division on public health at the Bavarian Research Center for Digital Health and Social Care at Kempten University of Applied Sciences.

Katharina Graf is a postdoctoral research fellow at the Institute of Cultural Anthropology and European Ethnology at Goethe University Frankfurt, where she leads the DFG-funded ethnographic research project "Cyborg Cook".

Leslie Haddon is a visiting lecturer in the Department of Media and Communications at the London School of Economics and Political Science (LSE).

Maren Hartmann is professor for communication and media sociology at Berlin University of the Arts (UdK) with a focus on mobilities and domestication.

Md. Rashidul Hasan is a master's student of Human-Computer Interaction at the University of Siegen.

Tim Moritz Hector works as a research assistant at the Collaborative Research Center 1187 "Media of Cooperation", University of Siegen, and is a PhD-candidate in applied linguistics.

Max Kanderske is a PhD candidate at the chair of Science, Technology & Media Studies at the University of Siegen and a research associate at the Collaborative Research Center 1187 "Media of Cooperation".

Dennis Kirschsieper is a research assistant at the Collaborative Research Center 1187 "Media of Cooperation", University of Siegen.

Vera Klocke is a research assistant at the Berlin University of the Arts who wrote her dissertation on television in households.

Alexander Bajwa Kucharski is a Researcher at the research department "Health-industries & Quality of Life" at the Institute for Work and Technology (IAT) of the Westphalian University of Applied Sciences.

Sebastian Merkel is Junioprofessor at the faculty of social science at the Ruhr-University Bochum.

Claudia Müller is professor (substitute) for Information Systems, esp. IT for the Aging Society, at the University of Siegen.

Markus Rohde studied psychology and sociology at the University of Bonn and is one of the founders of the International Institute for Socio-Informatics (IISI).

Sarah Rüller is a research associate at the Collaborative Research Center 1187 "Media of Cooperation", University of Siegen.

Niklas Strüver is a PhD student in sociology at the Collaborative Research Center 1187 "Media of Cooperation", University of Siegen.

David Waldecker is a sociologist and post-doctoral researcher at the Collaborative Research Center 1187 "Media of Cooperation", University of Siegen.

Anne Weibert is a research associate at the Institute for Information Systems and New Media, University of Siegen.

Tobias Wörle is a postdoc researcher at the Bavarian Research Center for Digital Health and Social Care. He is head of the research unit "Communication and Coordination in Mixed Homecare".

Volker Wulf is a professor for Information Systems and New Media at the University of Siegen.

Cultural Studies

Gabriele Klein
Pina Bausch's Dance Theater
Company, Artistic Practices and Reception

2020, 440 p., pb., col. ill.
29,99 € (DE), 978-3-8376-5055-6
E-Book:
PDF: 29,99 € (DE), ISBN 978-3-8394-5055-0

Markus Gabriel, Christoph Horn, Anna Katsman, Wilhelm Krull, Anna Luisa Lippold, Corine Pelluchon, Ingo Venzke
**Towards a New Enlightenment –
The Case for Future-Oriented Humanities**

October 2022, 80 p., pb.
18,00 € (DE), 978-3-8376-6570-3
E-Book: available as free open access publication
PDF: ISBN 978-3-8394-6570-7
ISBN 978-3-7328-6570-3

Sven Quadflieg, Klaus Neuburg, Simon Nestler (eds.)
(Dis)Obedience in Digital Societies
Perspectives on the Power of Algorithms and Data

March 2022, 380 p., pb., ill.
29,00 € (DE), 978-3-8376-5763-0
E-Book: available as free open access publication
PDF: ISBN 978-3-8394-5763-4
ISBN 978-3-7328-5763-0

**All print, e-book and open access versions of the titles in our list
are available in our online shop www.transcript-publishing.com**

Cultural Studies

Ingrid Hoelzl, Rémi Marie
Common Image
Towards a Larger Than Human Communism

2021, 156 p., pb., ill.
29,50 € (DE), 978-3-8376-5939-9
E-Book:
PDF: 26,99 € (DE), ISBN 978-3-8394-5939-3

Anna Maria Loffredo, Rainer Wenrich,
Charlotte Axelsson, Wanja Kröger (eds.)
Changing Time – Shaping World
Changemakers in Arts & Education

September 2022, 310 p., pb., col. ill.
45,00 € (DE), 978-3-8376-6135-4
E-Book: available as free open access publication
PDF: ISBN 978-3-8394-6135-8

Olga Moskatova, Anna Polze, Ramón Reichert (eds.)
Digital Culture & Society (DCS)
Vol. 7, Issue 2/2021 –
Networked Images in Surveillance Capitalism

August 2022, 336 p., pb., col. ill.
29,99 € (DE), 978-3-8376-5388-5
E-Book:
PDF: 27,99 € (DE), ISBN 978-3-8394-5388-9

**All print, e-book and open access versions of the titles in our list
are available in our online shop www.transcript-publishing.com**